RUDOLF STEINER

The Karma of Untruthfulness
Volume Two

Twelve Lectures given in Dornach
1 to 30 January 1917

Translated by Johanna Collis

RUDOLF STEINER PRESS

Translation based on *Das Karma der Unwahrhaftigkeit, Zweiter Teil*, published by
Rudolf Steiner Verlag, Dornach, Switzerland, 1983

Bibliography No 174 in the complete German Edition of the works of Rudolf Steiner

Edited by Joan M. Thompson

ISBN cloth 1 85584 180 0
     paper 1 85584 185 1

Typeset by EMSET, London NW10
Printed and bound in Great Britain by
WBC Limited, Bridgend, Mid Glamorgan

CONTENTS

characteristics: envy, jealousy, avarice. Psychiatry will have to learn to distinguish between the abnormalities caused by the freeing of the different components. The earth works on man through the solid element, the angeloi through the fluid element, the archangeloi through the airy element, the folk spirits through the system of ganglia. The working of the folk spirits is removed from consciousness and therefore demonic. This is utilized by secret brotherhoods who pursue the egoistic aims of their groups.

INTRODUCTION

The first volume of these lectures was published in an English translation in 1988. In *Anthroposophy Today* No.8 I wrote a short article
in which I said that they needed a careful introduction and extended
notes if they were not to baffle the English-speaking reader. Recently
I was asked to write such an introduction for the second volume. It
became clear to me that I was insufficiently prepared for this task.
I am not a professional historian nor have I access to any large library.
The circumstances of my life make it impossible for me to supply
the factual notes which I should have liked to provide. I also doubted
whether the introduction I could write would really be helpful. My
hesitation disappeared when I read in Lecture Eleven:

> 'One who possesses the sense for truth is one who unremittingly
> strives to find the truth of the matter, one who never ceases
> to seek the truth and who takes responsibility for himself even
> when he says something untrue out of ignorance.'[1]

I have occupied myself with these lectures for the last thirty years
and have discussed them with friends. I have read fairly widely some
relevant literature and often changed my mind in the light of new facts
and with, I hope, more mature judgement.

The English-speaking reader might be disturbed by three particular
aspects of these lectures. They present a description of the causes of
the War of 1914-18 which differs fundamentally from what had been
learned at school; they seem to reveal a pro-German bias; and they
repeatedly portray Rudolf Steiner in an emotional mood to which we
are not accustomed. It is these points which to some extent I hope
to clarify. This will involve a brief study of the lecturer himself and
also the question as to what extent subsequent historical events have
borne out Steiner's main contentions.

There are two underlying contentions: the existence and aims of
certain occult societies; and what is called the Karma of Untruth —
in contemporary language the conscious manipulation of the media
by power elites which may or may not be influenced by these societies.
Today, the second contention can hardly be disputed by any thinking
woman or man. Some of us still remember the late Dr Goebbels. All
of us can ask ourselves what information we were fed day by day

during the Gulf War and what we were allowed to know about Iraq
in those days when it was at war with Iran. Steiner could understand
the Briton who wanted to defend the Empire which his ancestors had
built up over four centuries. But why the cant and why the smears?
So we come to the first of Steiner's main points: the existence of
secret societies. A reader who is not prepared to consider the
possibility of such groupings is advised not to read any further —
neither this Introduction nor the lectures themselves. Rudolf Steiner
spoke about these societies mainly during three periods. In the autumn
of 1915 he lectured about *The Occult Movement in the Nineteenth
Century*,[2] dealing particularly with the history of Helena Petrovna
Blavatsky. Then came the lectures under consideration here, while
a number of subsequent lectures, mainly on social themes, find secret
societies responsible for the establishing of Communism in Russia.

But it is particularly the present lectures which make us appreciate
Steiner's position: He is involved in an occult, that is, a secret battle.
Steiner and his adversaries agree on certain facts. They agree that
ours is the age of the 'consciousness soul' in Steiner's terminology
— the age of alienated man and woman, divorced from the Divinity,
nature and their fellow men, but endowed with clear, dispassionate
thinking. These characteristics blossomed particularly among the
English-speaking peoples who became the pioneers of science,
industrialization, commerce and banking; of capitalism and
imperialism. But here the paths divide. Steiner is concerned with the
next stage — the greening of the globe, the establishment of a new
social culture and of a new awareness of the mysteries of the human
being and its connections to the universe. These insights were to be
conveyed to anybody ready to listen regardless of rank, sex or colour.
The other side — according to Steiner — were anxious to keep this
knowledge to themselves and thereby create power elites which could
manipulate their fellow citizens and dominate the world.

One passage in these lectures seems to be particularly important in
this context. Does it not show that Steiner knew *in advance* of the ambi-
tions of secret societies? The very least it shows is that he had an amaz-
ing understanding of the course history was to take. In Lecture Six,
using those 'terms which are customary within these secret
brotherhoods', Steiner speaks of a Russian Government that 'is to be
swept away', and of the task 'of carrying out certain quite definite
economic experiments, that is, of instituting a certain form of economic
society of a socialist nature...'[3] These statements were made months
before Kerensky's revolution, let alone Lenin's, had started.

The modern reader is not only struck by Steiner's prescience of the Russian revolution, but also by a number of aspects which testify to his clarity of observation and his modern attitude. I can mention but a few. The last lecture contains an alternative explanation of the origins of the War, an explanation with which most modern scholars would agree. We are living, Steiner tells us, in a 'totally wrong social structure'.[4] In another passage he refers to a 'carcinoma' which he had spoken about in Vienna three months before the outbreak of war. The main fault in our social structure, he had said, lies in the unlimited production of goods. The implication is that individual firms and, behind them, their governments must constantly be looking for new markets — a topic to which further reference will be made. The rapid rise in German industrial potential was perceived by Britain as a threat to the Empire, while Germans could not see why they, the late industrial developers, had not an equal claim to the world markets as the British who for generations had been enjoying a dominant position.

While all Europe believed in the virtue of nationalism, following the Romantic tradition of the nineteenth century, Steiner pointed to its utterly destructive tendency. The strongest statement is near the end of Lecture Nineteen. Nationalism lies in our unconscious depths and has a demonic character. It was — and still is — being manipulated by power elites for their own group interests.

To Steiner it seemed ludicrous to speak of the freedom of nations, one of the professed war aims of the Allies. A human being can be free. A nation is 'free' if it is independent, but what does it profit a free man if the dictator who imprisons and tortures him happens to speak the same language? At the time of writing this introduction the Baltic States, Yugoslavia, Romania are some examples of unresolved nationalistic tensions. To a large extent these countries are a result of the War. In Lecture Seventeen Steiner expresses his wish to preserve Austria-Hungary, the country where federalism had made greater strides than anywhere else in Europe. As a comparison we might take the position of Ireland or Wales in 1914 or remember that not so long ago inhabitants of Friuli protested against their Italian government and bureaucracy by demonstrating under the flags of the old Monarchy. Before 1918, in a multi-lingual country, they had had more regional freedom than in the centralized Italy of the 1970s. Steiner would have liked the federalistic tendencies in Austria-Hungary to be extended and deepened, and this principle to be applied to the whole of Europe. This intuition forms one of the most important points in his subsequent attempts at social renewal. The fallacy of the 'free nation', the demonic character of nationalism, the wrong social structure that made war inevitable — which contemporary of Steiner showed so much foresight and clarity of vision?

Lectures Two, Three and Four give a coherent and persuasive account of Steiner's view that the machinations of secret societies caused — or at least largely contributed to the origin of — the war. Yet is is doubtful whether his account persuaded many readers who were not already aware of his unusual insights. But Steiner never wanted to be believed. He wanted to be taken seriously and be critically evaluated. The writer of this Introduction will attempt to do so.

We said above that there are three reasons why readers of these lectures might feel reservations concerning some of the statements Steiner made. Firstly, many people experience a natural reluctance to accept conspiracy theories — reds under all the beds! Secondly, Steiner seems at times clearly partisan, emotional, exaggerating — a point to which we will return later. But the most important point in readers' reluctance to accept a conspiracy theory is the fact that a convincing case can be made for the origin of the War without reference to secret societies. This applies to the causes of the War as well as to some of the details which Steiner mentions. We can look at a few examples only.

There are three passages in which reference is made to King Edward VII. The king was certainly no friend of Germany. But why? Steiner does not tell us the reason. Was the king's attitude a consequence of his belonging to a secret society? Can it be explained by reference to his biography? His rejection of his father who had tried to educate him in a strict and narrow manner and who, too often for the boy's liking, enumerated the high moral qualities of the Germans? His marriage to a Danish princess whose country was attacked and defeated by Prussia? His enjoyment of the non-puritanical delights of Paris?

A scene which Steiner frequently refers to is Sir Edward Grey's interview with Lichnowsky, the German ambassador. 'Will Britain remain neutral if Germany respects Belgium's neutrality?' Sir Edward fudges. Manipulation by the lodges or logical outcome of a normal process?

After the shock of the Boer War Britain created for the first time a military and naval planning group, the Committee of Imperial Defence. This body was at first primarily concerned with naval and colonial matters. But the military men got their chance when in 1905

France and Britain resolved their difficulties. In conversations with the French General Staff practical propositions were discussed as to how France might be supported in the event of a German invasion. 'Political leaders in London were repeatedly to declare that these were merely contingency plans which did not commit the country to fight for France', but 'their very existence...created a *moral* bond from which it would be difficult to escape'.[5]

The book from which this quotation is taken was published in 1980. It describes a number of causes for the outbreak of hostilities. The most important, however, was commercial rivalry. As we have seen, Steiner did not disagree with this view. He himself quoted figures to show how in the course of less than two generations Germany had turned the tables on Britain, which consequently felt deeply threatened in its commercial dominance of the world.

Now we turn to Steiner himself. In these twenty-five lectures we find discrepancies and, occasionally, factual mistakes. Nor can it be said that the lecturer treats all nations and individuals he mentions with equal understanding and respect. A case in point is his treatment of Sir Edward Grey. Furthermore, Steiner's defence of Germany's innocence is hardly credible today when most official documents of the time are known. We can only quote one example. In 1900 Szögyeny, Austria-Hungary's ambassador in Berlin, a man who had no interest in slandering Germany, wrote in his official dispatches:

'The leading German statesmen, and above all Kaiser Wilhelm, have looked into the distant future and are striving to make Germany's already swiftly-growing position as a world power into a dominating one, reckoning hereby upon becoming the genial successor to England in this respect. People in Berlin are, however, well aware that Germany would not be in the position today or for a long time to assume this succession, and for this reason a speedy collapse of English world power is not desired since it is fully recognized that Germany's far-reaching plans are at present only castles in the air. Notwithstanding this, Germany is already preparing with speed and vigour for her self-appointed future mission. In this connection I may permit myself to refer to the constant concern for the growth of the German naval forces...England is now regarded as the most dangerous enemy which, at least as long as Germany is not sufficiently armed at sea, must be treated with consideration in all

ways...but because of the universal anglophobia it is not easy
[to convince public opinion of this].'[6]

This document precedes by five years the Anglo-French rapprochement.
To understand such weaknesses in Steiner's position we must look
at him more closely. Repeatedly he made it clear that not everything
he says stems from clairvoyant investigations. He was, of course, also
a product of his age. Much comes from the education he received,
the books and newspapers he read. It is unlikely — to take one example
— that he would have spoken about Sir Edward Grey in the way that
he did if he had been able to study the karma of this tragic personality.
A question which might tentatively be asked is this: In Lecture Four
Steiner expresses his conviction that karma grants him the right books
at the right time; in other places he tells us how often and how inten-
sively he had read the sources which he quotes. But could it not be
that in a small number of cases he had not had the time to investigate
clairvoyantly the being of the author quoted, and so trusted him more
than might have been warranted? Where Steiner could not make
special spiritual investigations, he could only know what his age knew.
Had Sir Edward been able to assure Lichnowsky that Britain would
remain neutral provided Germany respected Belgian neutrality, the
German General Staff would have had to inform their government
that this promise did not help the situation at all. They only had one
plan and this one plan could not be slowed down, altered or put into
reverse. But this fact only emerged years after the end of the War.

In the magazine *Anthroposophy Today* No.2 there appeared an
article *In Search of Rudolf Steiner*. In it the present writer gave
examples of the intimate contact which Steiner had with his audience.
In Vienna Steiner described how the emotions of his audience affected
him and that he took care to avoid two particular issues because he
found it difficult to deal with the waves of emotion which arose in
his audience on such occasions. One of these issues was human sexuality. But Steiner put nationalism, a drive in our subconscious, on
the same level as sexuality. We, living at the end of the twentieth
century, have often no idea of the crude, primitive, thoughtless
nationalism of Europeans — British, French, Germans, Italians —
at the beginning of this century. In dealing with burning contemporary
issues Steiner had to expose himself to the nationalistic emotions of
his audience. Is it then surprising that occasionally he was affected
by them?

Nor should it surprise us that a man in search of objective spiritual insights is in some respects like any other human being. Occasionally even prejudices become manifest. Steiner was in an exceptionally burdened situation. A study of his 'prophetic' utterances shows that he was surprisingly aware of the inner and outer history of the remainder of our century. In 1916-17 he stood utterly alone, experiencing the tragedy and the horror which were to overtake Europe in the next two generations if the offer of peace was 'shouted down'. Cassandra-like, he could look into the future, but like Cassandra he could not convince. He would not have been human if in this situation he could have remained calm and collected throughout.

But against this we have to set his desperate cry in Lecture Eighteen:

'Those who believe that I say these things from any kind of nationalistic feeling, simply do not understand me.'[7]

Time and again we find passages and whole lectures in which he spoke with the utmost objectivity. Lecture Seven contains a deeply moving passage about the suffering and heroism of the Serbs.

We can now approach the central question: Why did Rudolf Steiner care so passionately that Germany's international reputation should not be besmirched? We turn to Lecture Twenty:

'And what we now hope for in Central Europe is the development of the element of spiritual science.'[8]

What he called *Mitteleuropa* is a spiritual impulse which fired people living around 1800. Some of their names — Goethe, Novalis, Carus, Schelling — are familiar to students of Steiner's work. In many ways he looked at his own task as a continuation and enhancement of their achievements. But in his lectures in November and December 1918, *The Challenge of the Times*,[9] he clearly distances himself from the Wilhelminian Reich. Repeatedly he quotes Nietzsche's statement that the foundation of this Reich meant the murder (extirpation) of the German spirit. By their endeavour to make all things German despicable, Steiner's occult enemies hoped to deal a mortal blow to Steiner's work, and in particular to his social intentions, the very antithesis of imperialism, capitalism and manipulation.

We might ask: Why should the United States have wanted in 1917 to humiliate Germany? The same United States which from the late 1940s on found not the slightest difficulty in establishing a close relationship with Germany politically and economically? Was it perhaps that apart from Anthroposophy precious little was left of *Mitteleuropa*? And why should we have heard recently such howls of triumph about the death of socialism when what we witnessed was the end of a totalitarian system built on the theories of Lenin and the practice of Stalin?

Lecture Twenty-Five is a farewell to his Dornach audience. Steiner is to speak in Germany and does not know whether the Swiss authorities will permit his return. He sums up the whole series by referring to this occult battle in an amazingly restrained way, far beyond any nationalism:

> 'Today's tragic destiny of mankind is that in striving upwards today, human beings are endeavouring to do so not under the sign of spirituality but under the sign of materialism. This in the first instance is what brought them into conflict with those brotherhoods who want to develop the impulses of the mercantile, commerce and industry, in a materialistic way on a grand scale. This is today's main conflict. All other things are side issues, often terrible side issues. This shows us how terrible maya can be. But it is possible to strive for things in different ways. If others had been in power instead of the agents of those brotherhoods, then we would, today, be busy with peace negotiations, and the Christmas call for peace would not have been shouted down.'[10]

A short postscript concerning an issue which Steiner developed subsequently. He indicated that spiritual powers were at work during the critical days of August 1914 and that a haze descended on the various European chancelleries. (In more general terms this situation is described in Lecture Seventeen). Today this statement can be documented. The panic in the German government when they found that the General Staff had robbed them of any room for diplomatic manoeuvre because the inexorable logic of the Schlieffen plan had already taken over was paralleled by a lack of unanimity and by confusion in the British cabinet. Churchill was ready to go to war — I follow here Kennedy whom I quoted above; Morley and Burns were resolved to avoid a British entanglement on the side of France and resigned when the large majority of waverers inclined more and more to Churchill's side, particularly after the invasion of Belgium.

Two events need special mention: the assassination of Jean Jaurès, a man of great authority and one who had striven for peace; and, even

more dramatic, the murder of the Archduke Franz Ferdinand. He had
been on an official visit to Sarajevo. In the morning a tour of the city
was on the programme. The archduke and his wife travelled in an
open motor car. Suddenly shots were fired, the car accelerated out
of danger. Three young men were arrested. The archduke's party pro-
ceeded to the town hall where there was an official reception and ban-
quet. It was decided to continue the drive in the afternoon, but for
security reasons a few details were altered.

Through the city flows a narrow river — the Miljacka. It is flanked
by promenades, and a number of bridges connect the two banks.
Approaching one of the bridges the driver forgot the change of route.
An adjutant shouted to him, pointing out the mistake. So he reversed
— in those days a rather cumbersome manoeuvre.

But a fourth assassin, Gavrilo Princip, had been overlooked by the
police. He was sitting in an open-air cafe when to his surprise the
archducal cavalcade passed just in front of him. It came to a halt,
reversed; he shot. Princip was arrested and sentenced to death, but
owing to his youth was not executed. After the War he returned to
Serbia and became a schoolmaster. Such were the dramatic and con-
voluted events by which karma became manifested.

Rudi Lissau, August 1991.

References:

1. Rudolf Steiner *The Karma of Untruthfulness* Vol 1, Rudolf Steiner Press, London 1988, p.240.
2. Rudolf Steiner *The Occult Movement in the Nineteenth Century* Rudolf Steiner Press, London 1973.
3. Rudolf Steiner *The Karma of Untruthfulness* Vol 1, p.126-7.
4. Rudolf Steiner *The Karma of Untruthfulness* Vol 2, Rudolf Steiner Press, London 1992, p.212.
5. Paul Kennedy *The Rise of the Anglo-German Antagonism*, Allen & Unwin, London 1980, p.280.
6. The original document can be found in the Staatsarchiv, Vienna.
7. Rudolf Steiner *The Karma of Untruthfulness* Vol 2, p.78.
8. Rudolf Steiner *The Karma of Untruthfulness* Vol 2, p.130.
9. Rudolf Steiner *The Challenge of the Times*, Anthroposophic Press, New York, no date.
10. Rudolf Steiner *The Karma of Untruthfulness* Vol 2, p.222-3.

LECTURE FOURTEEN
Dornach, 1 January 1917

What was said yesterday[1] about so-called poisonous substances indicated strongly how all the impulses of life are graded in relation to one another. For instance, some substance is said to be poisonous, and yet the higher nature of the human being is intimately related to this poison; indeed, the higher nature of man cannot exist without the effects of poisons. We are touching here on a most important area of knowledge, one with many ramifications and without which it is impossible to understand a good many secrets of life and existence.

Looking at the human physical body, we have to admit that if it were not filled with those higher components of existence, the etheric body, the astral body and the ego, it could not be the physical body as we know it. The moment man steps through the portal of death, leaving behind his physical body — that is, the moment the higher components withdraw from the physical body — it begins to obey laws other than those which governed it while those components were present there. The physical body disintegrates; after death it obeys the physical and chemical forces and laws of the earth.

The physical body of man as we know it cannot be constructed in accordance with earthly laws, for it is these very laws which destroy it. The body can only be what it is because there work within it those parts of man that are not of the earth: his higher components of soul and spirit. There is nothing in the whole realm of physical and chemical laws which could justify the presence of such a thing as the human physical body on the earth.

Measured by the physical laws of the earth, the human body is an impossible creation. It is prevented from disintegrating by the higher components of man's being. It follows, therefore, that the moment these higher components — the ego, the astral body and the etheric body — desert the human body, it becomes a corpse.

You know from many earlier lectures that the diagram of the human being we have often given is quite correct as such, but that in reality it is not as simple as some would like. To begin with, we divide the human being into physical body, etheric body, astral body and ego. I have pointed out on other occasions that this in itself implies a further complication. The physical body, of course, is what it is — the physical body. But the etheric body, as such, is something supersensible, invisible, something that cannot be perceived by the senses. It lives in the human being as something that cannot be perceived by the senses. But it has, in a sense, its physical counterpart because it imprints itself on the physical body. The physical body contains not only the physical body itself, but also an imprint of the etheric body. The etheric body projects itself onto the physical body; so we can speak of an etheric projection onto the physical body.

It is the same in the case of the astral body. We can speak of the astral projection onto the physical body. You know some of the details already. You know that the ego projection onto the physical body may be sought in certain features of the blood circulation, where the ego projects itself onto the blood. In a similar way the other higher components project themselves onto the physical body. So the physical body in its physical aspect is in itself a complicated system, for it is fourfold. And just as the most important aspect cannot exist in the physical body if the ego and the astral body are not in it — for it then becomes a corpse — so is it also in the case of these projections, for they are all present in the physical substance. Without the ego there can be no human blood, without the astral body there can be no human nervous system as a whole. These things exist in us as a counterpart of man's higher components.

When the ego has been, shall we say, 'lifted out' of the physical body, when it has passed through the portal of death, the physical body has no real life any longer, but becomes a corpse. In a similar way, under certain conditions, these projections cannot live in a proper way either.

			Ego
		Astral Body	
	Etheric Body		
Physical Body	etheric	astral	ego
	projections onto the physical body		

For instance the ego projection — that is, a certain quality of the blood — cannot be present in a proper way in the human organism if the ego is not properly fostered. To turn the physical body into a corpse it is, of course, necessary for the ego to depart entirely from the physical body. But the blood can go a quarter of the way towards becoming a corpse if you prevent it from being permeated with what ought to live in the ego, so that it can work in the right manner of soul and spirit on the blood. You will gather from this that is possible to bring disorder into man's soul in such a way that the right influences cannot be brought to bear on the blood nature, the blood substance. That is then the point when the blood can change into a poisonous substance — not entirely, for in that case the person would die, but in part. The human physical body is abandoned to destruction if the ego departs from it, and in a similar way the blood is brought into a state of ill health — even if this is not necessarily noticeable — if the ego is not fostered and interwoven with the right care.

So when is the ego not fostered and interwoven with the right care? This is the case under certain quite definite circumstances. Let us look for the moment at the post-Atlantean period. We see that as human evolution proceeds, certain definite capacities, certain definite impulses are developed in each succeeding cultural epoch. It is impossible to imagine people living in the ancient Indian period having a condition of soul development similar to ours. From epoch to epoch, as human beings pass through succeeding incarnations on earth, different impulses are needed for the human soul.

Let me draw you a diagram. Imagine this to be the main, the actual physical body, the one that has to be filled with all the higher components of human nature in order to be a physical body at all.

Of all these higher components, I shall deal solely with the ego, though I could deal with all three. The shading here indicates that the physical body is permeated by the ego. So, in a certain way, the other projections also have to be permeated. Here let me indicate the projection of the etheric body, which is for the most part anchored in the human being's glandular system; for this, too, has to be permeated and interwoven. Thirdly, let me indicate what is anchored chiefly in the nervous system. This, again, in a certain way, must be interwoven with the workings of the ego. And the ego body itself — this, too, has to be interwoven in the proper way.

As I said just now, as man passes through succeeding periods of evolution he has to step into different developmental impulses with each period. He has to absorb whatever the contemporary age requires him to take in. In the first post-Atlantean period, ancient India, impulses of soul and spirit had to be absorbed which enabled the etheric body to be developed; in the next period, ancient Persia, the astral body was developed; in the period of Egypt and Chaldea it was the turn of the sentient soul; in the Greco-Latin period, the intellectual or mind soul; and today, the consciousness soul.

Whether the human being absorbs in the right way whatever is suitable for the age in which he is living will depend on whether he has properly entered into all these bodily principles — just as the physical body is permeated by the higher components of his being — so that they absorb what the age requires. Suppose an individual during the fifth post-Atlantean period were to resist absorbing anything of what ought to be absorbed during this period; suppose he were to reject everything which could cultivate his soul in the manner required by the fifth post-Atlantean period. What would be the consequence?

His bodily nature cannot revert to an earlier state if he belongs to that part of mankind which is called upon at present to absorb the impulses of the fifth post-Atlantean period. Not everyone is called upon at the same time, but at present all the white races are called upon to absorb the culture of the fifth post-Atlantean period. Now suppose an individual were to resist this. A certain member of his bodily nature — above all, the blood — would remain void of all that could be taken in, were he not to put up this resistance. This member of his bodily nature would then lack what ought to permeate its substance and its forces. This substance and the forces living in it — though not to a degree comparable to bodily death brought about by the departure of the ego — would then become sick in its life forces, which become degraded so that man bears them as a poison within him. Thus to remain behind in evolution means that man impregnates his being with a kind of formative phantom which is poisonous. On the other hand, if he were to absorb what his cultural impulses require him to absorb, the state of his soul would be such that he could dissolve this poisonous phantom he bears within him. By failing to do so, he allows this phantom to coagulate and become a part of his body.

This is the source of all the sicknesses of civilization, the cultural decadence, all the emptiness of soul, the states of hypochondria, the eccentricities, the dissatisfactions, the crankinesses and so on, and also of all those instincts which attack culture, which are aggressive and antagonistic towards cultural impulses. Either the individual accepts the culture of his age, and fits in with it, or he develops the corresponding poison which deposits itself within him and can only be dissolved if he does accept the culture. But if the poison is allowed to become deposited, it leads to the development of instincts which are opposed to the culture of the age. The working of a poison is also always an aggressive instinct. In the languages of Central Europe this can be felt quite clearly: many dialects do not say that a person is angry but that he is poisonous. This expresses a deep sense for something that is indeed the case. Someone who is irrascible is described in Austria, for instance, as '*gachgiftig*' which means that he is quick to grow poisonous, quick to anger. Human beings acquire poison, sometimes in a very concentrated form, if they refuse to accept what could dissolve such poison. Nowadays, untold people refuse to accept spiritual life in the form fitting for today, which we have been endeavouring to describe for such a long time, more recently even in public.

In such people, the lotus flower here [on the forehead] reveals very clearly what occurs in these cases, for the effects reach right into the realm of warmth, and such people leap up like flames against anything in the world around them which happens to reveal something that could bring healing to our times. Certainly, Mephistopheles — that is, the devil — is abroad amongst us; but the development of even a small beginning — tiny flames stirring — starts when we refuse to accept something that is fitting for our time, so that we do not dissolve the poison but make it into a partial corpse and allow it to coagulate in our organism as a phantom of formative forces.

If you think this through properly, you will discover the cause of many dissatisfactions in life. For those who bear such a poisonous

phantom within them are unhappy indeed. We would call these people
nervous, or neurasthenic; but it can also make them cruel, quarrel-
some, monists, materialists, for these characteristics are the result,
more often than we might think, of physiological causes brought about
by the poison being deposited in the human organism instead of being
assimilated.

You will see from all this that there belongs to the overall balance
of the world in which we are embedded a kind of unstable equilibrium
between what is good and right on the one hand, and its opposite,
the effects of poisons, on the other. If it is to be possible for what
is good and right to come about, then it must also be possible to err
from what is right, for poisons to have their effect.

If we now apply this to the wider situation, we see that it must be
possible today for people to attain to some degree of spiritual life,
to develop within themselves impulses for a free, inner spiritual life.
To make it possible for the individual to attain to a life of the spirit,
the opposite must also exist, namely a corresponding possibility to
err along the path of grey or black magic. Without the one, the other
is not possible. Just as you, as a human being, cannot maintain yourself
without the firm foundation of the earth beneath your feet, so it is
not possible for the illumination of spiritual life to be pursued without
the resistance which must be permitted to exist and which is inevitable
for the higher realms of life.

We have already mentioned the highly contradictory and yet no less
important fact that the question: To whom do we owe the Mystery
of Golgotha? could elicit the reply: To Judas. For it could be argued
that if Judas had not betrayed Christ Jesus, the Mystery of Golgotha
would not have taken place, so therefore we ought to be grateful to
Judas, since Christianity — that is, the Mystery of Golgotha — stems
from him. However, to be grateful to Judas and perhaps recognize
him as the founder of Christianity is going too far! Wherever we strive
to enter higher realms we have to reckon with living, not dead truth,
and the living truth bears within it its own counter-image, just as in
physical existence life bears death within it.

This is something I wanted to place in your soul today, for on this
basis much can be understood. There has to exist the possibility for
what is spiritual, but also for the deposition of the poison which is
its polar opposite. And if it can be deposited then it can also be used
— it can be utilized in every realm.

Many questions could be asked about this, but today we shall deal with only one: How can we find our way through the maze? Is there not a very great danger that anything we approach in the world might contain the polar opposite, namely the poison, or at least that somebody or other might seek to make something poisonous out of it? Of course there is always this possibility. Everything that is potentially very good can also be perverted and become the opposite. This must be the case in order that human evolution can take its course in freedom in accordance with the present cultural age. Indeed, the very best evolutionary impulses in our age are those most likely to be turned into their opposite.

This is valid for social life as well as for the human organism. In lectures given here[2] last year, we saw that in the present age, to start with only germinally, the capacity is beginning to develop which will enable us to create a life of Imaginations — to develop thoughts which rise up freely — though so far this possibility is denied by materialists. However, it lies in the very nature of our present age that a life of Imagination must develop little by little. What is the counter-image of a life of Imagination? The counter-image of Imaginative life is fabrication, the creation of fabrications about reality and a corresponding thoughtlessness in alleging this or that. I have often described it in these lectures as an inattentiveness to truth, to what is actual and real. The most wonderful thing with which mankind is presented in the fifth post-Atlantean period is the gradual ascent from mere one-sided intellectual life into Imaginative life, which is the first step into the spiritual world. This can err and become untruthfulness, the fabrication of untruths in relation to reality. I am not, of course, referring to poetry, which is entirely justified, but to fabrication with regard to what is real.[3]

Another element which must come into being during the present age — we have discussed this here, too — is a form of thinking that is particularly conscientious and aware of its responsibility. When you see what anthroposophical spiritual science has to offer, you cannot but admit that, to understand what is said, sharply delineated thoughts are needed, thoughts which are imbued with the will to pursue reality in an objective way. Clear thinking is certainly necessary if our teachings — if I may call them that — are to be understood. Above all, what is needed are not fleeting thoughts, but a certain quietness of thought. We must work towards achieving this kind of thinking. We must strive unremittingly to force ourselves to think thoughts with clear contours and not wallow in sympathies and antipathies when alleging something to ourselves and others. We must seek for the foundation, the basis, of what we maintain — otherwise we shall never penetrate in the right way into the realm of spiritual science. We must demand this of ourselves. We shall fulfil our task if we demand this of ourselves. If we are asked what we can do in these difficult times, our answer must be based on what I have just said. We must be fully aware of the fact that at the present time every human being who longs for the evolution of the earth to proceed in a healthy way must seek conscientiously and honestly for objectivity of thinking, in the manner described. This is the task of the human soul today.

It is just because this is so that the corresponding poison can develop, which is a state of being utterly devoid of clarity of thought, devoid of thought that unites with reality and fabricates nothing, but seeks to depict solely what is. During the course of the nineteenth century the yearning for objectivity deserted us increasingly. And the absence of conscience in what we have been describing here as the truth has reached a certain climax in the twentieth century in comparison to all that went before. The effect is at its worst when people entirely fail to notice it; yet, in this very aspect, it is characteristic of our time.

Let me give you a few examples to show you what I mean. Let me place these examples before you sine ira — without sympathies or antipathies. Here is a man whom I know very well, someone who could be called a truly kind and nice person. He holds a position in public life and would certainly not allow himself to stray, even minutely, from the upright attitudes expected of those in public positions. Yet a short time ago this man found it possible to say something quite typical. At the end of an essay he wrote: 'Finally we cannot avoid at least a brief discussion of . . .' [*Gap in report*][4]

It is understandable that such things should be said today, and I have quoted it precisely because the person who said it was such a serious man with truly upright attitudes. Yet when you look more closely, you discover that it is as utterly dishonest as anything can possibly be; for how can you say anything more dishonest than: 'I shall join in singing "Now thank we all our God" and "A safe stronghold our God is still" ' and so on, in a mood that makes these hymns into prayers, if you hold opinions such as those expressed by this man. Frankly, he is eulogizing untruthfulness. You may find such eulogies to untruthfulness wherever you look these days, yet they are given, I am bound to say, in good faith. They are the poison that corresponds to what must develop as a spiritual life of Imagination. The best among us, especially, are prone, more or less unconsciously, to harbouring the effects of this poison. Of course, once you realize that something of this kind pulsating through society is no different from a drop of poison administered to the human organism, then you are in a position to judge all these things correctly. And once you do realize it, you cannot but feel bound to strive for something in life which I have now described a number of times. You will feel bound to be alert to the facts, you will want your observation of life to be sound, for without this there is no way forward today. The karma that is being fulfilled at the moment, the karma about which I have spoken before, is not the karma of a single nation; it is the karma of the whole of European and American humanity in the nineteenth century; it is the karma of untruthfulness, the insidious poison of untruthfulness.

This untruthfulness may be experienced particularly strongly in movements of a more elevated variety. During the course of my life I have come across a great deal of untruthfulness, but I must say I have never met lies as grandiose as those promulgated among certain people who proclaim the principle: There is no religion higher than Truth.[5] I could say that such intense mendacity is only found where there is at the same time a profound consciousness of striving for only the truth and nothing but the truth! The greatest watchfulness is needed when striving for the ultimate. For we must realize that, while in earlier cultural epochs the possibilities of erring were different, today the greatest danger is an aberration into untruthfulness brought about by a failure to take reality into account in a living way — a failure to take reality into account! The man I mentioned, who wrote such lies, would rather have his tongue cut out than consciously speak an untruth. Yet it is through such upright people that these things work, seeping into the social organism and turning into social poison. Obviously, since they must needs exist amongst us, they can also err in the opposite direction. Other human beings can take them into their awareness and use them for all kinds of mischief — to put it mildly.

Some of you might remember how strange it seemed to people when I first made some fairly radical statements about these things a few years ago, in a public lecture in Munich.[6] I said at that time: During the course of human evolution, impulses for both good and evil develop on the physical plane. What causes these impulses to develop? They come into being when certain forces, which actually belong to the higher, spiritual world, are misused down here in the physical world. If thieves were to use their thieving instincts, and murderers their murderous instincts, and liars their lying instincts to develop higher forces, instead of enjoying them here on the physical plane, they would develop quite considerable higher forces. Their mistake is only that they develop their powers on the wrong plane. Evil, I said, is good that has been transposed down from another plane. Of course, if we know this it does not make a thief or a murderer or a liar any better. But we must understand these things, otherwise we cannot fathom what is going on, falling unconscious victim to these dangers.

It is not surprising that many people today simply do not realize that it is becoming mankind's task to be concerned with spiritual matters. Therefore they fail to take up this task, abandoning themselves instead to materialistic instincts. In doing so, they develop within themselves those poisons which ought to be dissolved by the spiritual element. What is the consequence? In those who deny the spirit, the poisons develop into forces which cause them to become veritable liars; whether conscious or unconscious is merely a question of degree. Yet these very forces could be used to achieve a reasonable comprehension of spiritual knowledge.

Consider how important it is for us to understand this and how, in understanding it, we can come to comprehend one of the central aspects of the karma of our time, if we add to it what I said yesterday: that a single instance cannot be detached from mankind as a whole, for mankind is a totality. As a counter-image of spiritual endeavour it is essential for a violent evil to exist. And one of man's tasks today is to recognize the true nature of this evil, in order to be able properly to recognize and oppose it when he comes upon it in life.

In speaking about these things we come to realize the relationship between the greater aspects of the karma of our time and something that is living in our time which is everywhere in the world bringing about very, very much that is terrible. Superficially, we see how falsehood throbs through the world in mighty waves which devour much more than one might think. For falsehood is monstrously vigorous. But as we have seen today, falsehood is nothing other than the corresponding counter-image for spiritual endeavour which ought to exist but does not. The divine, spiritual wisdom of the universe has given to the human being the possibility of spiritual endeavour. We have within us the poison which we can dissolve. Indeed, we must dissolve it, for otherwise it will become a kind of partial corpse within us.

Let me give you examples of such things from daily life. These will at the same time serve the pursuit of our aim to better understand certain things which meet us at every turn today and which are connected with life and with all the evil and suffering of the present time. For one of the things we are striving for in these talks, in so far as we have been permitted to give them, is an understanding of the painful events of today. I bring these things forward in order to show you in a structured way how these impulses work. The examples I give are intended to characterize the facts, not any particular person or persons.

Hanging around here in Switzerland is a man who many years ago was a lawyer in Berlin, a pettifogger who was forced to seek his fortune abroad because of all the mischief he had concocted. He has been hanging around abroad for years, and now that war has broken out has written a book, *J'accuse*, which has caused a furore throughout the countries of the periphery. This whole *J'accuse* affair[7] can be said to be one of the saddest symptoms of our time, because it is so very characteristic. *J'accuse* is a fat book, and certain people who ought to know maintain that there is not a log cabin in distant Norway that does not house a copy. It is, in other words, one of the most widely disseminated books. In Berlin last spring I read an article about it written by quite a well-known person. He says *J'accuse* was recommended to him by someone whom he greatly admires. From the way he describes his friend, we gather who he must mean, namely, someone who counts for a good deal in Holland. Yet this person was quite unable to assess even the gutter-press style of the book. It is possible to be thought a great man and yet be incompetent to form a judgement in such matters.

Now quite recently the author — known, and yet unknown — of *J'accuse* has gone into print once more in *L'Humanité* with the following thoughts. As I have said, I am not concerned with the person himself, but want to characterize something that is typical of our time:

In the Reichstag in Berlin a social democrat gives a speech in which he unfolds his views about various happenings in the period leading up to the outbreak of war. It does not matter whether we agree with him or not; what I am concerned with is the form such things take. In his speech, this member of the Reichstag refers to a remark made by Sir Edward Grey on 30 July 1914 to the effect that if the Austrians would content themselves with marching as far as Belgrade, occupying the city and awaiting the outcome of a possible European congress on the relationship between Austria and Serbia, then it might still be possible to preserve peace. This remark by Sir Edward Grey is well-documented, for he made it to the German ambassador and also wrote it to the English ambassador in St Petersburg. The matter is so well-documented that there can be no doubt that Sir Edward Grey did make this remark. Nevertheless, by bringing it up again in the Reichstag, this member has aroused the anger of the author of *J'accuse*. So what does the author of *J'accuse* do? He writes an utterly slanderous article in *L'Humanité* in which he accuses the member of the Reichstag of mendaciousness, false citation, and so on. Yet the matter is very well-documented, and the member of the Reichstag did not say anything which is not vouched for in books, or in the letter sent by Sir Edward Grey to the English ambassador in St Petersburg. So how can the author of *J'accuse* make the claim of mendaciousness? He did it by saying: What the member of the Reichstag was saying cannot refer to a remark made by Sir Edward Grey on 30 July; it must refer to one made by Sasonov on 31 December. But Sasonov's remark, not Grey's, was as I shall now quote. In other words, the member of the Reichstag quoted Sasonov wrongly, for Sasonov's remark went as follows, and in addition he claims that Sasonov's remark was made by Sir Edward Grey.

The fact is that the member of the Reichstag refers to a remark by Grey. The author of *J'accuse* wants to counter him and says: What he is saying refers not to a remark by Grey but to one by Sasonov, which he misquotes; Sasonov said the following . . .; in other words what he said in the Reichstag in Berlin is doubly false, for firstly the quotation is false, and secondly he claims that the remark was made in London, when in fact it was made in St Petersburg. Ergo, the member of the Reichstag is a liar.

The whole of *J'accuse* is of this calibre; all the argumentation is like this. You see how narrow, how confused and how unscrupulous must be the thinking of a person who is capable of writing such things. And what does he achieve? The countless people who read *L'Humanité* and what the author — known, and yet unknown — of *J'accuse* has to say, will, of course, not check the facts for themselves. They believe what they see before their eyes. So by this means he proves not only that the member of the Reichstag has lied, but also — and the author of *J'accuse* is indeed capable of allowing this to be seen as proof — that the Central Powers never replied to the proposals made by the periphery. The author of *J'accuse* states that the member of the

Reichstag is saying that the Central Powers did react to the proposals made by the periphery. And yet, he says, look what Sasonov said, for it is Sasonov whom he is quoting! The Central Powers never replied, so you see how they managed the affair; they did not even reply to these important proposals.

Now what the member of the Reichstag said did indeed refer to a proposal made by Grey and telegraphed by him to his ambassador, who then passed it on to Sasonov. Sasonov turned Grey's whole proposal, which was not at all bad, upside down. The author of *J'accuse* demands that this proposal, turned into its opposite by Sasonov, should have been taken into account, even though Sasanov did not take it into account. However, it can be proved that Grey sent a telegram to his ambassador in St Petersburg and that this was presented to Sasonov, who took no account of it. At the same time Grey sent his proposal to Berlin and from Berlin it was sent on to Vienna. It can indeed be proved that negotiations were carried on between Vienna and Berlin in order to persuade Austria to make a halt in Belgrade and await European negotiations. This is documented in a letter telegraphed by the King of England to Prince Heinrich. In other words, the Central Powers did indeed consider Grey's proposals. But Sasonov did not consider them! Even so, the author of *J'accuse* concludes that the Central Powers did not reply and have thus made themselves guilty of these terrible events.

This whole matter is not insignificant, for in yesterday's lamentable document the same sentence may be seen. Here we have an extraordinary — let me say — kinship, family relationship, between a terrible document of world history and an individual who has been hanging around for years because his own homeland became too hot to hold him and who now writes all kinds of rubbish under the bombastic title *J'accuse. By a German* — rubbish that is protected by such further excesses as the latest achievement of *L'Humanité*.

It is not surprising if people then defend themselves in the way the German member of the Reichstag has done, having been accused by the author of *J'accuse* of being a slanderer, a hypocrite and a liar. He drew the following comparison: You send your maid on an errand to Mr Miller at Number 35, Long Lane. When she returns after having taken much longer than the expected two hours she says: I couldn't find Mr Miller. I went to No 85, Short Street. Mr Miller the carpenter doesn't live there, but Mrs Smith the washerwoman does. This, said the member of the Reichstag, is just about the level of connection between what the author of *J'accuse* says and what really happened. The author of *J'accuse* is, of course, a particularly nasty example. It is this manner of treating reality which is today the obverse, the corresponding counter-image of spiritual endeavour, flowing as it does through the veins of society in place of what we should all be striving for: spiritual knowledge, spiritual knowledge with which to fill our being. We can find such things everywhere, in manifold variations. I have given you just one example — dishonesty, as it appears in an individual whom I know very well. Everywhere we shall see how such things appear as the counter-image of what is necessary in our time. Spiritual knowing is necessary for those who want to recognize anything worthwhile today; all other knowing lags behind what should be evolving. Therefore, if an attitude of mind disposed towards peace is to come about among the nations of Europe, feelings about these nations will have to develop which are imbued with the spirit, feelings which can come into being if nations are seen in the way they are shown in the lecture cycle about the folk spirits[8] which I gave long before the war in Christiania. We must resolve to approach the spirit of a nation in this way. Only then can our human spirit become active in a manner which will enable us to form a valid judgement which encompasses a whole group, such as a nation. Just think how judgements could be formed about nations if sufficient spiritual preparation had been undertaken first of all! Yet all that we have seen going astray so drastically in one direction or another lives not only in the worst; it also lives in the best of us. In describing this it is not my intention to apportion blame. I am simply describing a lack which exists because there is no will to create the spiritual foundation on which judgements could be formed about the interrelationships of nations. Judgements are formed on the basis of sympathies and antipathies rather than true insights.

A typical example of this may be found in a famous novel[9] written quite recently. A perfectly honest attempt is made in this context to describe a certain nation — in this case the German nation — through the various characters who represent it. Yet the way it is done is defective because a lack of spirituality prevents the author from achieving a judgement based on reality. There would be no reason for me to mention a genuine novel here, for in a true work of art such a question would not arise. But a novel that is tendentious in its descriptions can certainly be quoted in this connection. Let me clarify further what I mean: In a really good novel you will never hear the voice of the author himself, for the characters will express what is typical for their nation, their standing, their class and so on. Thus if John Smith or Adrian Swallowtail says something about the Germans, or the French, or the English, there is no cause to object. But this is not the case in the novel in question. Here, the author keeps stepping out in front of the curtain and giving his opinion, so that when he describes a person he gives his own opinion about the Germans, or whatever. You can see this straightaway in the description of a relative of the hero:

'He was a fine talker, well, though a little heavily, built, and was of the type which passes in Germany for classic beauty; he had a large brow that expressed nothing, large regular features, and a curled beard — a Jupiter of the banks of the Rhine.'

You will agree that this is not likely to lead to an objective judgement, even if it could be true in isolated cases. A German chamber orchestra is described as follows:

'They played neither very accurately nor in good time, but they never went off the rails, and followed faithfully the marked changes of tone. They had that musical facility which is easily satisfied, that mediocre perfection which is so plentiful in the race which is said to be the most musical in the world.'

Now the hero's uncle is described:

'He was a partner in a great commercial house which did business in Africa and the Far East. He was the exact type of one of those Germans of the new style, whose affectation it is scoffingly to repudiate the old idealism of the race, and, intoxicated by conquest, to maintain a cult of strength and success which shows that they are not accustomed to seeing them on their side. But it is as difficult at once to change the age-old nature of a people, the despised idealism springs up again in him at every turn in language, manners, and moral habits, and the quotations from Goethe to fit the smallest incidents of domestic life, and he was a singular compound of conscience and self-interest. There was in him a curious effort to reconcile

the honest principles of the old German *bourgeoisie* with the
cynicism of these new commercial *condottieri* — a compound
which for ever gave out a repulsive flavour of hypocrisy, for
ever striving to make of German strength, avarice, and self-
interest the symbols of all right, justice and truth.'

Of the hero it is said:

'. . . he lacked that easy Germanic idealism, which does not
wish to see, and does not see, what would be displeasing to
its sight, for fear of disturbing the very proper tranquility of
its judgment and the pleasantness of its existence.'

Here is another example of the author peeping out through the curtains
and giving his own opinion:

'Especially since the German victories they had been striving
to make a compromise, a revolting intrigue between their new
power and their old principles. The old idealism had not been
renounced. There should have been a new effort of freedom
of which they were incapable. They were content with a forgery,
with making it subservient to German interests. Like the serene
and subtle Schwabian, Hegel, who had waited until after Leipzig
and Waterloo to assimilate the cause of his philosophy with the
Prussian State . . .'

This gentleman has a strange view of the history of philosophy. Those
of us with a real understanding of what went on know that the principles of Hegel's philosophy on the phenomenology of consciousness
were written down in Jena in 1806 to the thundering of canon as
Napoleon approached. Yet in the novel it is said with a certain 'sense
for the truth' that Hegel waited for the Battle of Leipzig in order to
adapt to the Prussian State.

'. . . their interests having changed, their principles had
changed, too. When they were defeated, they said that Germany's ideal was humanity. Now that they had defeated others,
they said that Germany was the ideal of humanity.'

What a fine sentence!

'When other countries were more powerful, they said, with Lessing, that "*patriotism is a heroic weakness which it is well to be without,*" and they called themselves "*citizens of the world*". Now that they were in the ascendant, they could not enough despise the Utopias "*à la Francaise*". Universal peace, fraternity, pacific progress, the rights of man, natural equality: they said that the strongest people had absolute rights against the others, and that the others, being weaker, had no rights against themselves.'

As you can see, once the war had started, these sentences could have formed the basis for many a leading article in the countries of the periphery. Yet they were written long before the war.

'It was the living God and the Incarnate Idea, the progress of which is accomplished by war, violence, and oppression. Force had become holy now that it was on their side. Force had become the only idealism and the only intelligence.'

Now there is a sentence missing in my notes. You know it is not easy to bring things across the border just now, and I have the book in Berlin.

Let me quote a few more passages in which the author peeps through the curtains:

'The Germans are very mildly indulgent to physical imperfections: they cannot see them; they are even able to embellish them, by virtue of an easy imagination which finds unexpected qualities in the face of their desire to make them like the most illustrious examples of human beauty. Old Euler would not have needed much urging to make him declare that his granddaughter had the nose of the Ludovisi Juno.'

It should be added that this nose and face are described as being especially ugly.
    About Schumann it is said:

'But that was just it: his example made Christopher understand that the worst falsity in German art came into it not when the artists tried to express something which they had not felt, but rather when they tried to express the feelings which they did in fact feel — *feelings which were false.*'

Then we are reminded with a certain amount of pleasure of something said by Madame de Staël:

' "They have submitted doughtily. They find philosophic reasons for explaining the least philosophic theory in the world: respect for power and the chastening emotion of fear which changes that respect into admiration." '

The author of the novel adds that his hero 'found that feeling', namely that they have submitted doughtily, that they have respect and fear:

'. . . everywhere in Germany, from the highest to the lowest — from the William Tell of Schiller, that limited little bourgeois with muscles like a porter, who, as the free Jew Börne says, "to reconcile honour and fear passes before the pillar of dear Herr Gessler, with his eyes down, so as to be able to say that he did not see the hat; did not disobey" — to the aged and respectable Professor Weisse, a man of seventy, and one of the most honoured men of learning in the town, who, when he saw a *Herr Lieutenant* coming, would make haste to give him the path, and would step down into the road. Christopher's blood boiled whenever he saw one of these small acts of daily servility. They hurt him as much as though he had demeaned himself. The arrogant manners of the officers whom he met in the street, their haughty insolence, made him speechless with anger. He never would make way for them. Whenever he passed them he returned their arrogant stare. More than once he was very near causing a scene. He seemed to be looking for trouble. However, he was the first to understand the futility of such bravado; but he had moments of aberration; the perpetual constraint which he imposed on himself, and the accumulation of force in him that had no outlet, made him furious. Then he was ready to go any length, and he had a feeling that if he stayed a year longer in the place he would be lost. He loathed the brutal militarism which he felt weighing down upon him, the sabres clanking on the pavement, the piles of arms, the guns placed

outside the barracks, their muzzles gaping down on the town,
ready to fire.'

All this is interesting for a number of reasons. You know that I am
not mentioning these things for personal reasons or in order to
characterize somebody. Once the novel had been written and had
caused a considerable sensation there were, of course, individuals who
praised it as the greatest work of art of all time. This always happens.
The opinion expressed by an esteemed Austrian critic[10] is rather nice
— I mean 'esteemed' in inverted commas: 'This novel is the most
important event since 1871, which could bring France and Germany
closer together again.'

You see how much truth lies hidden in these things! Yet we are
dealing here with a man who is highly praised today, and I have no
intention of raising even the slightest objection to his outward activities
during wartime. However, what is said in this 'world famous' novel
provides plenty of material for slogans and leading articles in the
periphery. What I have read aloud to you today may indeed be admired
— with all due respect to the hacks of the periphery — at any time
in those leading articles. These things were written long before the
war, as that Austrian critic said 'to bring France and Germany closer
together', and may be found in Romain Rolland's novel *John
Christopher*.

Here you have an example of somebody who excludes the spirit,
who does not want the spirit, and therefore fails to see what is essential
in the events and situations of the present time. What can someone
who writes such things possibly really know about the German
character? We have a right to speak in this way because the subjective
judgements of the author are here dressed up in the guise of an inferior
novel. It is my personal opinion that this novel is one of the worst.
As you have seen from the opinion of the critic from Vienna, it is
held to be one of the best. Internationally, too, the critics have hailed
it as one of the best. If we did not hold the opinion — which is not
all that unjustified nowadays — that anything the critics praise must
of necessity be rubbish, we might even have a certain respect for
something they tell us is the foremost and greatest achievement of
our time. From the viewpoint of cultural history, however, this is
a good example for us of how impossible it is for people today to
draw near to the task set for mankind by the fifth post-Atlantean
period. For this reason alone, karma will have to fulfil itself. It is

our task, however, to think about these things impartially. Above all
we should not accept or parrot without criticism what is said out there
in the materialistic world, but should strive instead to form our own
judgement about these things.

What I have read aloud to you today was written many years ago,
but now it provides marvellous slogans for the leading articles
perpetrated by the journalists of the Entente. Its tenor is terribly anti-
German, but that is not the point, for any point of view has its validity.
It is, however, a strange distortion of the truth to praise a book as
something new when it was in fact written years ago, even though
the final volumes have only recently been published. Other strange
things happen in this way, for instance in connection with quotations
which keep appearing and are said to stem from Nietzsche or
Treitschke[11] and others. In the case of Treitschke you can search his
works in vain for the passages, and in Nietzsche's case the passages
have the opposite meaning to that claimed today by the journalists
of the Entente.

I used to be acquainted with Nietzsche's publisher[12] and discussed
a number of matters with him. At that time the man who translated
the whole of Nietzsche into French[13] wrote to that publisher every
few days from Paris. Nietzsche was a god to him. Today he abuses
him mightily. You can have the strangest experiences in such connections. You will search the works of Treitschke and Nietzsche in
vain for anything that could have been said in that book, for when
they are quoted the texts are taken out of context, and furthermore
they are also mutilated; the beginning of a sentence is quoted, the
middle is torn out, and then the end is quoted. Only by doing this
can they quote these writers.

But they can quote Romain Rolland unabridged. I have read to you
only a few short passages from his novel. There is no need for you
to judge it by these passages, though they could be augmented by
countless others. You could, however, judge it on the basis of the
ending, which shows that the whole novel is riddled with the attitudes
revealed in the quoted passages. None of this is intended as a con-
demnation of the person himself. However, it is essential to illuminate
clearly the poison seeping into our lives today.

LECTURE FIFTEEN

Dornach, 6 January 1917

In order to arrive at a view of the world fitting for today, we need wider horizons than those available to mankind in this materialistic age. This applies especially in connection with spiritual science, and I have already referred to this necessity repeatedly in the preceding lectures. By wider horizons I mean that to comprehend today's world, and in particular human events, we shall have to have recourse to concepts which originate in spiritual science. The fact that the greater part of humanity has so far rejected such wider conceptual horizons in relation to all fields of life and knowledge is connected with the karma of the present time.

With these wider concepts in the background we can characterize one aspect of our life by saying that, objectively, evolution has out-distanced mankind in the nineteenth and twentieth centuries. Today's events most thoroughly demonstrate this situation. One of the most prominent events of the age of materialism is material progress, that is, progress involving all the things that can be accomplished in the world by material means. This material progress is served by the sciences of the age of materialism. And it is especially typical of these sciences that they are growing ever less and less interested in the spiritual world; they strive more and more to become a mere summation of concepts and ideas which can be applied to external material phenomena.

The course of this development finds its strongest expression in the most external of all material matters: mechanical procedures. Factories, industry, machines, these things have attained the highest degree of perfection during this age of materialism. And it is in the very nature of these things that progress in these fields has been non-national — you could say, international; it is world progress. For whether a railway or something similar is built in England, Russia, China or Japan, the laws which have to be taken into account, the knowledge needed, are the same everywhere, since everything is accomplished in accordance with mechanical requirements which are detached from man. In these fields an international principle has indeed taken hold in the widest possible manner.

Over the years, during our lectures on spiritual science, we have often said, in connection with one aspect or another, that there is a body on the earth, a body which is spread over the whole earth. This body needs a soul, and this soul should be equally international. Spiritual science was claimed to be this soul, for it comprises knowledge which is not bound up with any particular individual or group on the earth but can be understood by every single person, wherever he may be, just as physical things in external, material culture — such as a railway or a locomotive — can be understood. We have often stressed that a blessing and salvation for human evolution can only come about if the development in the bodily realm is accompanied by a development in the realm of soul and spirit. For this to take place it would be necessary for people to make just as much effort to understand spiritual matters as external circumstances force them to make — they would far rather be forced than use their freedom — to understand the demands of material progress. So far this has not happened, but it will obviously have to come about as human evolution proceeds. However long it is delayed, it must happen in the end. However much disastrous karma is conjured up because human beings do not want to make the effort, it will happen in the end, for what is to happen will indeed happen.

It is because material progress has run ahead of the good will for spiritual knowledge that mankind has been outdistanced by this material progress and everything it contains by way of passions and urges in human souls. Externally this shows most emphatically in the fact that it is not ideas which strive towards harmonious co-existence of human beings on earth — in other words, not Christian ideas — which are uppermost, but those which, in utmost excess, divide mankind and lead back to cultural periods which one might suppose to have been long overcome. The monstrous anomaly lies in the way nationalism was so forcefully able to take hold of the nations as they lived side by side in the nineteenth century. This shows that in their soul development human beings have not kept pace with material progress.

When people at last come to accept spiritual science on a wider scale, not only in theory but as a fulfilment of their total soul need, then they will, of necessity, have to arrive at different concepts. And such different concepts will help them to comprehend things which cannot possibly be comprehended by materialistic thinking as it is at present. Some matters can only be understood on the basis of corresponding ideas. But, like anything else, ideas must live in order to grow, which means they need soil in which they can flourish. And the soil in which ideas can flourish is nothing other than an attitude of soul prepared by spiritual science. Were materialistic progress to continue its development along the lines of the nineteenth century, people would grow ever poorer in ideas. Put simply: No ideas suitable for comprehending the world would occur to people. Any thoughts they might have about the world could only be stimulated by means of experiments, or by what they could see with their own eyes. The modern insistence on experimentation is nothing other than a paucity of ideas. If the present trend were to continue, mankind would grow ever poorer in ideas. But since a certain intensity of spiritual life is necessary, since human beings must develop some degree of intensity in certain impulses, they will have to discover these impulses in other sources if they cannot find them in the substance of ideas.

When was there an age brimming over with ideas, an age when genuine ideas flourished? You could say that a particularly characteristic and fruitful age was the period extending from Lessing to German Romanticism, to Novalis, or even to the philosophical idealists, among whom we can count Schopenhauer in addition to Hegel and Schelling, as well as those I have quoted in my book *Vom Menschenrätsel*[1] as being the philosophers who sounded a universal resonance which has since died away during the age of materialism. Ideas were truly abundant then. Hence the contempt in which that time is held today! Look at it, so rich and pregnant with ideas, ideas seeking to fathom nature and the evolution of mankind throughout history! Today we gather ideas from the spiritual world about human evolution, about the various post-Atlantean periods and the impulses belonging to them, knowledge which has only become fitting in the present age. Yet just look how close this is to that fertile idea brought forward by Schelling, Hegel, Novalis, Franz von Baader — though it originated with Jakob Böhme. They said that human evolution passed through a period of history — this was as much as they could see without the help of spiritual science — a first period of history in which the principle of God the Father ruled. This was the period characterized in the Bible by the Old Testament and the heathen religions. They called it the Age of the Father. This was followed by the Age of the Son, during which the idea of the Mystery of Golgotha was to become embedded in mankind. Finally, as an ideal for the future, they saw the Age of the Spirit, the Holy Spirit, which they also called the Age of John, for they believed that not until then would the great impulses of the John Gospel be realized.

How infinitely meaningful is such an idea, compared with the desolate, unfruitful talk of human evolution, which is nothing but an abstract idea, in which what follows after is added to what came before as if it were just another link in a chain. How profound by comparison is Schelling's 'theosophy'[2] which he developed on from Jakob Böhme! This 'theosophy' of Schelling attains such lofty heights that, by comparison, the later thoughts of theologians represent a steep decline. Schelling fights his way through to the realization that what matters in Christianity is not so much its doctrine. This doctrine is seized upon by modern progressive theology as if Christ Jesus were no more than a teacher. What matters for Schelling is not the doctrine, but the fact of the Mystery of Golgotha. We must look up to the fact of the Mystery of Golgotha, the fact of the life, the death, and the resurrection of Christ Jesus.

In similar vein we could quote a great many superior, far-reaching ideas originating at that time. With what is the existence of such far-reaching ideas connected? Those who were inspired by such ideas have something in common: They are not narrow-mindedly nationalistic. Their standpoint is that of someone whom they would have called a 'citizen of the world'. I do not know whether this can be understood today, when so many expressions have become empty phrases. How far removed from anything narrow-mindedly nationalistic is, for instance, a spirit such as Goethe! How far removed from anything narrow-mindedly nationalistic is such a work as Goethe's *Faust*! Never mind what its origins were. Of course *Faust* can only stem from the culture of Central Europe. But in the form it has achieved as a poetical work at the hands of Goethe it would be absurd to ask Faust to show you his birth certificate. Yet this absurdity has become a reality, a fact, in our time. Everything that is happening today is, fundamentally, simply a denial of the heights once reached by mankind in such a work as Goethe's *Faust*. Yet such a work shows us that mankind could have progressed further than is the case today, or indeed than will be the case in the near future.

I have told you, however, that the human soul needs a certain degree of intensity in its impulses. If it cannot reach up to ideas, it will take this intensity from elsewhere, from obscure, unconscious soul forces, from forces that rush up from the spirit of the blood. Fundamentally, nationalism is nothing other than a consequence of the lack of ideas. Mankind's primary need now is the will to rise up to ideas. But it has to be said: if this is to succeed, something else will be needed, too: namely, an understanding for the element of grace which can come from the spiritual world. For it is not possible to win through to the spiritual world from a starting-point of a limited sum of preconceived opinions. The spiritual world can only be reached by keeping the soul open for whatever wants to enter in, by desiring not merely to judge, but also day by day to enrich one's ability to judge.

So to begin with it is above all necessary that insight should take hold of human beings. We live in the age which is to grasp hold of the consciousness soul. So this age must strive for insight. But insight can only come about in ideas that span the world; for insight to come about, reality must be filled with ideas. Yet, especially with regard to the most recent events, our age is thoroughly disinclined to accept ideas. An abstract concept, however logical, however convincing, is not an idea. An idea must be born of living reality. Nowadays we see hardly any ideas come into being. Instead we are surrounded by an insistence on abstract concepts. Ideas can, however, become slogans — though if they do, not much damage can be done, because human souls cannot work in slogans that are related to ideas; their absurdity becomes too obvious. But abstract concepts are different. Abstract concepts can become slogans in a very intense way, and their meaning is so obvious because they refer basically to things that are close at hand. So human beings, who are so wary of taking in anything far-reaching, seize on them greedily. But abstract concepts do not have a basis in reality. There are great numbers of them all around us today, but those who can see beyond what is immediately obvious know that their powerlessness is all the greater.

One of the many abstract ideas ruling us today is that of eternal peace. In the way this is handled it is an entirely abstract concept which does not spring from a living understanding of reality, and yet it appears to those who do not desire to widen their horizons as something entirely convincing. These people say: The various states — and they do not wonder whether this expression 'the various states' has any reality — ought to create an inter-state organization, something that stretches across the entire world and is constructed after the pattern of a single state. Furthermore, something called 'inter-state law' is to be established. The idea is beautiful and so everybody finds it convincing. The various states are to commit themselves to keep the peace and they must also create legal norms which can contain their various mutual interests. All very nice! It would be equally nice if, to heat a room, all we needed was the abstract concept of warmth instead of having to light the stove. It is irrelevant whether an idea is nice, or convincing. For what could be more convincing than the thought that our need for stoves and the like really means that nature is a terrible despot!

It is irrelevant whether an idea corresponds to the feeling that it is nice or, perhaps, humane. What matters is whether an idea grows out of reality. But to aim for ideas which grow out of reality it is first of all necessary to study reality. Any narrow-minded brain — excuse the expression — can come up with nice programmes for states to follow in order to achieve peace. But such a brain cannot attain to ideas which correspond to reality and are born out of reality. It does not even feel that the spiritual world is a reality with its own laws, though this is considered a matter of course as far as the material world is concerned. People think the world can be set to rights by means of a few sentences. They have no feeling for the fact that the world is a reality in which all kinds of real impulses work in contrast to one another. And by becoming intoxicated with programmes made up of abstract ideas, they prevent the world from entering into the realities.

Sometimes a fruitful, genuine idea is expressed in the same words as a living idea; what matters is that we should be moved by the way it lives. Today, however, something that is alive appears to people as something utterly paradoxical. Thus, over the course of the nineteenth century, and also in the twentieth century, in various parts of the world the idea of disarmament was born, the idea of limiting militarism. This is a nice idea, but it must not remain abstract if it is to become fruitful! It must take account of reality. For this to happen, reality must be studied. It is all very well to meet somewhere and say: All countries must disarm. This is quite easy, especially as the idea is convincing. But either none of them will actually do so, or some of them will not do so. And even if they all did so, they would very soon start to rearm again if the initial impulse is not truly alive. But if you try to point out only those impulses which are truly fruitful, you are in danger of being considered by most people to be utterly foolish, for these days what is most sensible is considered to be most foolish. When I say 'sensible' in this connection I mean that which is most in tune with reality.

As I said, the idea of disarmament, the idea that all militarism should gradually be dismantled, is a good idea. But it will never be possible to realize it by reaching a formal conclusion about it in some committee of representatives from all states. It can only become reality if a corresponding reality takes hold of it. What do I mean? How can disarmament be achieved? Yes, it is necessary to be very concrete in one's expressions. It is indeed a fact that at a number of points during the nineteenth century it could have been possible to draw closer to the thought of disarmament and transform it into a real idea. How, for example?

Supposing someone had had the idea before the year 1870? How could it have been realized? Before 1870 a step could have been taken towards the idea of disarmament, a step which would have been very fruitful for mankind. But now I have to say something that today would be regarded as utterly foolish: No approach to the idea of disarmament could have been made by means of some kind of treaty between the various states! This is totally fruitless, however nice it may sound. It would, however, have been fruitful if a particular state, one that was in a position to do so, had begun to disarm, had made disarmament a reality for itself. To do this, people would have had to be capable of reckoning with realities.

Let us now look at a few states in Europe in order to point to what is a reality. Can Russia disarm? Certainly not just like that, for beyond Russia lies Asia, and if Russia were to disarm she would have no defences against the invading peoples of Asia, who would most certainly not disarm. So for Russia disarmament is out of the question. There was no German Reich before the year 1870, but how about the entity that did exist at that time? Could it have disarmed? On the eastern border there would have been a state that was not in a position to disarm, so it follows that here, too, disarmament would have been impossible. But there is one state which could have disarmed, thus setting a wonderful example and at the same time bringing into reality in modern times what it is always trumpeting forth with words — and that is France. Before 1870, France was in a very good position to disarm, and in consequence the war of 1870 would never have taken place. Even since then, as regards Europe — not the colonies — France would still have been in a position to proceed with disarmament at any time. This would have been a beginning, and attention could then have been turned to the East.

Obviously, those whose thinking is abstract will object: Ought France to have exposed herself to the danger of attack by Germany? There would have been no such danger, because if a country becomes involved in a war, the cause is invariably the fact that it is capable of war, that is, that it practises militarism. It can be forced to practise militarism. But no country which does not practise militarism would be attacked if its neighbours had no interest in attacking it. Switzerland, of course, has never been in a position to do without militarism. You cannot apply the conditions of one situation to those of another. Equally you may not say in the abstract that Germany would in any case have coveted Alsace-Lorraine. This is nonsense. Why should she have coveted Alsace-Lorraine under any circumstances? Bismarck said that to annex Alsace-Lorraine merely because some of the population were German was an impossible and crazy academic theory! The only reason there has ever been is one of military security. For so long as France is a military power in possession of Alsace, you can reach Stuttgart more quickly from France than you can from Berlin. The only reason there has ever been for attaching Alsace to the German Reich is that of achieving military protection on the western frontier. This may seem to be a paradoxical idea at first, but for our abstract thinking, which is the twin brother of materialism, realities do indeed appear to be paradoxes.

If you picture to yourselves that France started to disarm before 1870, you will begin to realize just how much could have been set aside, if only thinking at that time had been based on reality. By considering such ideas, a thinking based on reality could be greatly expanded. Naturally, ideas based on reality do not always come to fruition, for the simple reason that other impulses might be stronger. But this says nothing against reality. A flower will grow entirely in accordance with its own real laws. But if a cartwheel flattens it, it cannot develop. Our thinking must be true, and if an idea fails to come to fruition at some point, this is of itself no proof that it was not based on reality.

This is what I wanted to say about saturating ideas with reality. It is as pointless to have a wonderful idea about some machine, if you lack the mechanical knowledge with which to construct it, as it is to have all sorts of ideas about states and the like if you are incapable of gaining insight into the real impulses, which in this case could be attained through an understanding of the spiritual realm, the spiritual world. This, then, is one of the points to be made: the saturation of ideas with reality.

The other concerns the extent of the horizon, the will to extend one's view to wider horizons. In the last lecture I read to you some of the judgements on the nature of the German people expressed by

someone who is, after all, an important personality, judgements which
he expressed in a long novel about recent times, which caused a very
considerable stir. But all these judgements derive from a narrow
horizon, an attitude of not wanting to look further than a few inches
beyond the end of one's nose. Living with such narrow horizons brings
about disharmony in the world. You can have the most beautiful ideas
about the peaceful co-operation of the nations, but if your horizons
are narrow, then those beautiful ideas will stand for nothing, or at
most will work destructively. For what you really think, has the
opposite effect of what you are saying with your beautiful ideas. The
important thing is to make for reality. One reality which faces us at
the moment is what — in our idle way of expressing ourselves —
we call the present war. In reality it is no longer a war, though in
some ways it can still be compared with events which in the past were
described as wars. This war came about, of course, as a result of
the most varied impulses, but to gain insight into them we simply
have to form ideas which are based on reality.

The time which should be used for working on ideas based on reality
is used today instead to show that the world in most recent times has
forgotten everything that took place during human history up to the
time when today's tragic events commenced. Of course it is reasonable
to talk in connection with such events of all sorts of horrors and
atrocities. But these ought to be taken for granted if you consider the
experiences of mankind throughout history. Such things really ought
not to be used to deafen us in relation to more profound matters with
which we are faced and the recognition of which could alone bring
people to a point of view that is fruitful.

Let us today turn to something which can easily be recognized by
anyone who grasps matters externally, on the physical plane, but which
is illuminated more clearly if it is considered in conjunction with ideas
put forward in the lecture cycle on the folk souls. Among the various
causes which have led to today's tragic events, there are a number
which could become increasingly clear — to those also who consider
the external world by itself — if only people would be willing to extend
their horizons. The British Empire possesses one quarter of the entire
land surface of the globe. The British Empire and France and Russia
together possess one half. A coalition between Russia, France, the
British Empire and America would account for approximately three
quarters of the earth's land surface. So there would be one quarter
left over. This figure ought of itself to speak volumes to those who

work with reality. Let us, however, look at that quarter which is contained in the British Empire.

Here we have, to start with, the quite small territory covered by England, Scotland and Ireland. England, Scotland and Ireland by themselves in no way constitute the British Empire. To speak of these three territories is to speak of a region of the world which gave birth to that great man Shakespeare and also to incomparable thinkers and, in earlier times, great statesmen. Only good aspects are to be found. All that we find here is supremely suited to play a great role in the fifth post-Atlantean period. What we do not find is the British Empire: namely, those three island regions attached to Europe, together with all that can be called their colonies in the widest sense. Especially in recent decades the impetus for the whole development of this British Empire comes from the relationship of the motherland to the colonies. You can discover what endeavours are being made thus to shape the relationship between the motherland and the colonies.

What the British Empire is striving for is a close-knit relationship between the motherland and the colonies. I have told you about the application of occult forces, and it is these forces that are being used to achieve this goal. If these forces were allowed to work in their own region, no possible harm could come of them. But if the goal is something egoistic, whether for an individual or a group, then their effects cannot but be harmful. It is not at all easy to achieve this relationship between motherland and colonies. Those who imagine that world peace can be achieved by means of programmes and an interstate organization obviously have no idea what forces have to be used in reality to achieve a welding of the British motherland to her colonies in a way that will create the kind of totality which suits the British Empire. At the basis of this endeavour is what they there call imperialism. This is what has always been striven for in recent times, though out of entirely materialistic impulses — but this is what has been striven for. Every means that might serve this idea has been found acceptable from a certain point of view. It was necessary for the British Empire to achieve closer links with its colonies. To make this possible an impulse was needed that would steal into people's hearts and turn their minds towards something they would not otherwise have found acceptable. It is with this that the war in Europe is connected, for out of the mood of this war certain impulses will arise which the British Empire needs in order to create a uniformity between the motherland and her colonies. For those who study the processes of the physical plane it is not only interesting but extremely important to note how all those who think along abstract lines have been mistaken with regard to what I am saying.

Read what these 'clever' people wrote while this war was approaching — I mean clever in the sense in which I frequently use this word. They all reckoned with a defection here and a revolt there and another there, if war were to break out. But nothing of the kind has happened — indeed, the exact opposite has come about. If people's thoughts had been based on reality they would have said: If the British Empire wants to draw its colonies closer together, if it wants to generate impulses there which will tend towards going along with the motherland, then it needs a war, and this war is the means to that higher, so-called end desired by the state. And wherever such thoughts are thought, the end sanctifies the means.

Now is the moment when this fact should become particularly obvious to people. Speaking at present about the evolution of the British Empire, we should always take two significant streams into consideration. The one is the more or less puritanical stream — this word only describes one element of it, though probably correctly — which comes into its own in all that is excellent in the British nation. This puritanical stream was to a great extent dominant in British politics right up to the nineties of the nineteenth century. But during the nineties a change came about, when the imperialistic stream became stronger and more important than the puritanical stream.

Certain people had a good feel for the approach of imperialism — indeed, it is remarkable how good this instinct was. Let me draw your attention to a curious incident which shows rather clearly how these things are linked. While we were in London, shortly before the founding of the German Section of the Theosophical Society, Mrs Besant[3] was then by no means the person she later became. As you know, she always had the tendency to be whoever she had to be, depending on which influences had a hold over her. She was extremely popular in the circle of those who were called the theosophists in London at that time. Anyway, there were various sides to her. At that time — it was the beginning of the century — she gave a lecture on theosophy and imperialism. The imperialistic impulses were developing rapidly. Mrs Besant's line of argument was rather against imperialism. And we could see how, from that moment onwards, she was finished in London, even among those who were then theosophists. A few personal friends stood by her, but everybody else was through with her because she had dared to say something against imperialism. In such things are revealed the forces which, if you can penetrate them, bring you to the point at which you can see how things are interconnected at a higher level. Until quite recently a remnant of the puritanical element was still at work in England. Though politics were being led by puppets, marionettes, there was nevertheless something puritanical about these marionettes, about Asquith[4] and Grey.[5] This had to be removed so that the impulses I was speaking about could come into their own; and what now came was the most willing marionette of all with regard to everything I have described to you. But there is nothing puritanical left. Let us look first at the negative side: the cynical rejection of the idea of peace with the hypocritical justification that it is being rejected because what is wanted is peace. Nowadays the craziest things can be said with impunity and without being taken amiss. That is the negative side. On the positive side we have an event of the greatest imaginable importance: the gathering of colonial ministers, which is one of the first actions of this man who has been placed by a negative miracle in one of the highest positions in the world. At last the public is beginning to notice what is going on. But the public did not notice until it had had its nose rubbed in it, whereas those who live in ideas based in reality have seen it clearly for some time.

It is impossible to find your way about in the realm of reality if you have no inclination to accept genuine ideas. Only then can you look at the world in such a way: You see something which you consider is insignificant; then you see it again, and yet again and still consider it insignificant; but on the fourth and fifth occasion you realize that it is important because it is a significant symptom of future events. Not everything is equally important, but you have to have a sense for what is important, and this sense can only be gained if you take into your soul those impulses which can only come about on the basis of spiritual science.

In the last few days somebody handed me a most interesting essay by a very popular British writer[6] who is now a journalist. He is connected with the military, and in everything he writes he reveals how he is linked with the threads that are being spun. The essay he wrote recently in *The London Magazine* is significant enough. It was handed to me, as they say, by chance. But there is no chance in such occurrences. It is most interesting what this military author, linked as he is with the threads that are guiding events, has to say about the current situation:

'Our people had, and have, the will to conquer . . . In that grand spirit the war has been fought, and the memory of our unquenchable determination to conquer will be the noblest heritage that we shall bequeath to our successors, the sons and daughters of England and of her glorious Dominions . . . We shall have a million square miles of German colonial territory in our hands. We shall have many million veteran officers and men. We shall have greater naval predominance than before. The world will possess indubitable proofs that our Empire is one and indivisible, that its spirit is unconquerable, and that the martial qualities of the race are worthy of its glorious past . . . We have all the moral and material attributes of power on a scale hitherto undreamed of . . . But the war will end one day, and then how shall we stand? Taking Army, Navy, and resources together, we shall be the first military Power in the world.'

Is not a peculiar impression given when someone believes so urgently that he must fight against 'militarism' and then states what a lofty ideal it is to be the predominant military force in the world!

'We shall be recognised as the mainstay of the Alliance.'

This ought to be read in France.

'We have taken the leading part in the Alliance, and the leadership of Europe belongs to us of right.'

Now he takes Kipling's words, 'We have the ships, the money and the men', and makes them his own.

' . . . and if Parliament would vote supplies for a couple of years and then adjourn *sine die*, most of us would be content.'

Such things are an expression of those impulses and instincts which are connected with the strings that are being pulled. They may be observed entirely objectively, without taking sides in the way in which no doubt well-meaning, though short-sighted, patriots tend to take sides. Why should such things not be observed? They are objective facts! The impulses that live in mankind are objective facts which historical events bring to the fore.

While it is essential for us here to avoid taking sides at all costs, it is equally important, especially in lectures, to strive to speak with the utmost objectivity. As you will see, as soon as you speak with the utmost objectivity, the facts themselves provide you with proof. It is impossible to gain an understanding of the world without being willing to take note of facts. This so-called answering note from the Entente,[7] this New Year's Eve gift to the world — my dear friends, it is unlikely that a document composed as this one is will be found again however far you search in history, and this applies both to the basis on which it is written and to the way it is set out and composed. What is written there will have the direst consequences, yet the best way to read it is to skip every single sentence and to realize: Nothing that appears in writing in this document matters! What matters is that behind it there stands what I have been describing to you, and that it is this that is the aim. Of course nobody would dream of saying so in a note. And if you ask whether it can be achieved by means of negotiations, the answer is, obviously, No. Of course such a thing cannot be achieved by means of peace negotiations. It can only be achieved by creating guarantees, and guarantees are contained in dominance. Guarantees mean that the one who wants the guarantees is the only one who can decree what they shall be and that all the others no longer have any say in the matter, and all this is brought about by the interrelationships of power. At present there is a long way to go before this can be achieved. But to live under the illusion that this is not the goal would mean a great lack of responsibility towards the sense for truth that human beings ought to have.

Let nobody suppose that what I have said is directed against the British people, for I make a distinction between this British people and those who pull the strings — if I may use this expression — those who stand behind the events in the way I have frequently described. Neither is it necessary to identify oneself with such impulses, though obviously it cannot be my task to prevent someone from doing so. Also, I shall not prohibit, either in thought or feeling, anyone within our Movement from identifying with such impulses. But let such a one say what is true and not that he is identifying himself with the ideal of the rights of small nations and the like. Let him be clear that he desires to dominate the world. Then we shall be understanding one another in the realm of truth, and that is what matters. We shall make progress if human beings are true. If they say what is really true, we shall make progress. However terrible the truth may be, it will get us further than what is untrue. This is what we should inscribe on our hearts. We make better progress with this than with what is untrue.

Obviously, it would be foolish to imagine that a world power could be moved by all kinds of persuasion or by all manner of propositions to give up its aims. Obviously, it would be foolish to adopt an attitude of high-handed morality and apply all kinds of moral yardsticks. I told you the story of the Opium Wars[8] expressly to turn you away from moral yardsticks. What matters is to speak the truth, to say what is true. It would be far better for the world — though not for those who pull the strings — if we could all say baldly and cynically: This is what is wanted.

This, then, is the meaning in this particular field, of our guiding line and goal: 'Wisdom lies solely in truth'.

LECTURE SIXTEEN

Dornach, 7 January 1917

These lectures on the theme of current events are particularly suited to helping us realize what we can gain for our soul by striving to acquaint ourselves with spiritual knowledge. I have often stressed that this spiritual knowledge must not remain merely theoretical. We must make it come alive by filling it with those hallowed feelings and other impulses which belong to it, so that it can give to our souls that impetus and mood which will enable us as scientists of the spirit to relate to events in the human realm in a manner differing from that of someone who is not a spiritual scientist.

We have reflected in various ways on how individual human beings belong to particular nations, nationalities. But what the individual bears within him that belongs to mankind as a whole — that part of him which is not specialized and individualized with the characteristics of a particular nation — it is of this that spiritual science helps us to become fully aware, for the main content of anthroposophical spiritual science is valid for every individual human being, regardless of any differences among various groups. Indeed, even the national differences are seen differently from an anthroposophical point of view since, in contrast to the non-anthroposophical point of view, we are able to consider objectively what constitutes these differences — the various aspects can be seen objectively.

We are familiar with the threefold nature of our soul in that it consists of the sentient soul, the intellectual or mind soul and the consciousness soul, all three being filled, spiritually permeated, enlivened by our egohood. When the Italian folk soul works into individual human beings, it is the sentient soul that is influenced by the forces and impulses with which it works. In the French individual it is the intellectual or mind soul, and in the British individual the consciousness soul through which the folk soul works. For the folk souls of Central Europe it is the ego that is receptive, and for those of the Slav peoples the spirit-self. If we could fill ourselves with an understanding of this, we should no longer be tempted to form judgements in the way in which they are so frequently formed.

A certain person heard this and was furious, because he understood anthroposophical spiritual science to be saying that in the German nation the folk soul works through the ego, as if this was something higher than a folk soul working through the consciousness soul. This was his own misunderstanding! For in spiritual science different aspects of knowledge are viewed objectively, side by side. The folk souls have tasks to do and to accomplish them they have to work into their nations. But as regards the working of the folk souls in human souls we must realize that in our fifth post-Atlantean period a certain development has to take place. And those who are drawn towards anthroposophical spiritual science ought to feel themselves in the forefront of this development.

How does the folk soul work down into the human soul and mind? To start with we have to note that this working is subconscious and only partially rises up into consciousness. The individual human being feels that he belongs to one nation or another. On the whole, the folk soul works on the individuality via the maternal principle. It is the maternal principle that is embedded in the realm of the folk soul. The effect of the paternal principle is to detach the individual, as a physical and etheric being belonging to nature, from the group. I have frequently discussed this in past years. In the Christian world view this is even expressed in the Gospels. This, too, I discussed some time ago.[1] As things are today, it is in the first instance through the blood that the folk soul works into the individual, and also through what corresponds in the etheric body to blood. Naturally, this is more or less an animal impulse, and it remains at the animal level for by far the greater part of mankind today. Through his blood the individual belongs to a particular nation. The mysterious forces and impulses working in the blood are very difficult to describe since they are extraordinarily complex and manifold. Suffice it to say that they lie beneath the surface of consciousness.

People are far more conscious in all those aspects of their make-up which belong to mankind as a whole, irrespective of national differences. That is why the pathos, the passion, the affectation of belonging to a particular nationality bursts forth with a kind of elemental force. People do not attempt to apply logical reasons or judgements when it is a question of specifying or sensing their attachment to their nationality. It is his blood, and his heart which is influenced by his blood, that bind the individual to his nationality and let him live within it. The impulses in question are subconscious, and it is a good step forward if we can at least succeed in recognizing the subconscious nature of this situation. It is important especially for those who are approaching spiritual science if they can undergo this development in themselves and come to feel about these things in a way that differs from the way the rest of mankind feels.

When people who do not belong to spiritual science are asked what binds them to their nation they will — indeed, they must — answer: My blood! This is the sole idea which they are capable of forming about their sense of belonging to a particular nationality. A student of spiritual science, however, ought gradually to reach a point at which he is able to give not this, but a different answer. If he cannot gradually develop to a point where this different answer is possible, this means that he sees spiritual science as something purely theoretical, not practical and living. Someone who does not study spiritual science can only say: I am connected to my nationality through my blood, through my blood I defend what lives in my nation, it is my blood that obliges me to identify with my nationality. One who does study spiritual science, however, must answer: I am connected with my nationality through my karma, for this is a part of my karma. As soon as concepts of karma are brought into the question, the whole relationship becomes much more spiritual. Someone who does not follow spiritual science will summon his blood to account for the pathos, the impulsiveness of everything he does as a member of a particular nation. But someone who has developed through spiritual science will feel connected to one nation or another through his karma.

The matter becomes spiritual. Externally such a person might act in the same way; even if he feels this more spiritual aspect he might do the same things. But inwardly he will feel, spiritually; his feeling will be quite different from that of a person who feels his links with his nation purely at an animal level.

Here you see one of the points at which belonging to spiritual science changes the soul, brings a new mood into the soul. But at the same time you see how much the general consciousness of our time is lagging behind what could already be known by those who want to know it. In the general consciousness of our time the individual's attachment to a particular nation can only be seen as something that lives in the blood, or in that which is not at all of the blood but which is regulated in connection with the blood and out of this perception of the blood. A far freer view of nationality will gain ground once the whole matter is viewed as a matter of karma. Then certain delicate concepts will arise for someone who perhaps attaches himself consciously to a certain nation, thus bringing about a change of karma.

But however we view the matter, whether in the less complete sense shared by the greater part of mankind today, or in the more complete sense that can be attained through the study of spiritual science, nevertheless the fact remains that the general situation of the world today means that mankind is differentiated into groups. Nothing could make us more painfully aware than current events that this differentiation into groups is still for the most part prevalent. In addition, this differentiation into groups is mingled with quite other conditions and facts because it is to be even more difficult for human hearts and souls to gain an understanding of the reasons for the painful enmities, the painful disharmonies that have arisen amongst mankind today.

In short, we are touching on something pervaded by tragedy which should have nothing to do with ordinary logic or ordinary, superficial judgements. For whether these things are seen as a matter of blood or as a matter of karma, blood lies below, and karma above, logic. As a result, what we have been discussing must of necessity result in conflicts in human coexistence and these conflicts must be seen to be necessary. To believe that these conflicts can be judged in accordance with those concepts that apply to individual human beings must lead to the greatest errors. The widespread discussion of conflicts among nations in the same terms as those applicable to conflicts between individuals is the gravest mistake. I have already said that concepts such as justice and freedom apply to individual human beings. To claim them as parts of a programme for nations proves from the start a lack of knowledge about the characteristics of nations and a lack of will to enter into the question of national characteristics.

For those who understand these things and are capable, through spiritual knowledge, of seeing what is factually and naturally necessary, there is something paradoxical about the belief expressed in so many publications today, for it is comparable with the shark who makes a pact with the little fishes which he normally eats, saying: It is utterly inhumane to eat little fishes; I shall cease doing so! By saying this, he is condemning himself to death, for it happens to be the way of the world that sharks eat little fish!

It is necessary to come to a profound sense for the fact that it is not possible to understand the world without seeing the reality of the necessary conflicts leading to all that is tragic in the world. And to believe that something like Paradise is possible on the physical plane shows a total lack of comprehension of the peculiarities of the physical plane. Paradise does not exist on earth. There can be no comprehension among those who strive to realize the new Jerusalem as a Utopia on earth or who, like the social democrats, want to bring about some other satisfactory solution. There is a profound law which says that human beings, in so far as they live here on the physical plane, can only reach a satisfactory view of reality if they are aware that higher worlds also exist, and that they are connected in their souls with these higher worlds. Only if we understand that we are citizens of higher worlds can a satisfactory view be attained. Therefore, when spiritual consciousness was extinguished, a time had to come when mankind could no longer understand why so much disaster, so many conflicts, are present on the earth. These conflicts can only be resolved when we feel ourselves not only to be living in the physical world, but also in the spiritual world. Then we may begin to grasp that just as man cannot always be young but has also to grow old, so there has to be a breaking down of what was once built up — conflict and destruction as well as creation. When you understand this, you also understand that conflicts have to arise between groups of human beings. These conflicts are the tragic element of world events, and they must be seen to be something tragic.

In order to conjure up before your soul the living concept, the living idea that I am trying to describe, let me remind you of a rather caustic remark once made by the poet Friedrich Hebbel.[2] He was, as you know, a genius of a somewhat ponderous caste, one who wrote rather laboriously, despite a considerable fund of worldly humour. I told you on another occasion that he was not at all far from a view of the world which would have accorded with spiritual science. Thus he once jotted down in his notebook the following theme: Plato, reincarnated, takes his place in a secondary school where the teacher is dealing with the subject of Plato. He cannot understand a word of what Plato is supposed to have said and the teacher scolds him severely for this. Hebbel wanted to work this idea into a dramatic episode. He never actually did so, but you see that he did indeed consider bringing the idea of reincarnation into a play.

Hebbel was a contemporary of Grillparzer[3] and knew him. As I said, Hebbel was a somewhat sombre, melancholy genius, but after he had seen Grillparzer's plays *The Golden Fleece*, *Thou shalt not lie!* and *A Dream is Life* and so on, he said — and this is most interesting: Grillparzer depicts tragic conflicts, but only those of which it can be said that, if people were clever enough to see through the situations, it would be possible to resolve them in the end. According to Hebbel, the tragic circumstances in Grillparzer's plays only come about because the characters are not clever enough to see through the tragic situations. This, he says, is not really tragic. Real tragedy among human beings only comes about when those involved are as clever as anything and yet none of their cleverness and caution can help them, so that conflict becomes inevitable.

What Hebbel as a dramatist calls real tragedy is something that we ought to introduce as a concept into human evolution, human destiny, so that we do not continue for ever to form the naive judgement that one thing or another might have been avoided. Situations which lead to conflicts such as the present one cannot be avoided. And all those declamations about blame are totally out of place in face of a truly penetrating judgement.

It was for this purpose that I arranged these lectures which we have been conducting over the past days and weeks. I arranged them in order to demonstrate clearly that even in the case of an event such as the Opium Wars it is impossible to speak of blame in the way blame is meant in situations involving individual human beings. Concepts such as guilt, freedom, and so on, which can be applied to individual human beings, cannot be applied to souls living on other planes, and folk souls do not live on the physical plane but only work into the physical plane through individual souls. Their abode lies in other spheres, on other planes.

Such things are sensed nowadays by some isolated individuals. But they are not understood when we judge events on the basis of concepts which are customary today, instead of making the effort to take into account the actual evidence. To stand up today as a member of a nation and pronounce judgement on other nations in a manner that is only justified when referring to individuals proves nothing except one's own backwardness in the ability to judge. It is, though, a historical necessity, because certain statesmen are backward in relation to what could be known today, that this backwardness, this ignorance, is brought to bear even in the most terrible historical documents, as a result of which infinite rivers of blood will flow. On the other side stands the possibility of stressing again and again, for those who want to hear it, that the progress and salvation of mankind depend on finding judgements from the realms of spiritual life.

There is indeed a sense in some quarters for that which is necessary as a basis for judgement; but it cannot be brought into consciousness. I shall give you an example, for if I may say so, spiritual science will only be absorbed into our very flesh and blood if we learn to observe ordinary, everyday reality from the viewpoint of spiritual science. In England, in the seventies and eighties of the nineteenth century, the historian Professor Seeley[4] was active. What he taught was in many cases decisive for what later came to live in many souls. Seeley was perhaps the first English historical imperialist. His imperialism was historical and his history imperialistic, for he viewed British history as it had developed over the centuries from the point of view that the trend had always been towards the foundation of the great British Empire which now covers one quarter of the habitable surface of the earth. His lectures appeared in print in the seventies and were frequently reprinted; sometimes there was a new edition every year, for he had very many students. In these lectures he sought to gather up all the separate facts which made the British Empire what it is today. He saw it as something in the nature of divine providence that all the different pieces came together in the way in which they did, as a result of different impulses. He even asks: How did it all happen? And answers expressly: No individuals decided all these things, performed all these actions at just the right moment, which joined yet another portion to the British Empire with the aim of creating the greatest *imperium* that had ever existed; no, all this happened in earlier times as though by instinct.

The various parts came together by instinct and in Seeley's view there is a divine and spiritual order in the way they did so. Now, he says, it is our task to lift up into consciousness what has hitherto taken place instinctively and to round off what arose thus instinctively with our consciousness into an *imperium* such as has never existed on the earth before. He saw it as his task as an imperialistic historian consciously to penetrate what had come together unconsciously. Seeley intends, as it were, to bring into the present consciousness of the fifth post-Atlantean period all that contributed to the rise of the British Empire out of the still-atavistic forces belonging to the laws of the fourth post-Atlantean period. But as we have pointed out, it was not only reasoned, intellectual thinking which took hold of the instinctive coming-together of the different parts. As I have told you, during the final decades of the nineteenth century certain members of occult streams began — not with ordinary consciousness, but with occult consciousness — to expand this British Empire by placing before their souls, and the souls of their pupils, maps[5] which showed what still had to come about if the British Empire was to beam its forces over the whole world. In these occult circles the following idea was consciously cultivated: The fifth post-Atlantean period belongs to the English-speaking peoples. Based on this, all the arrangements were carried out and all the details elaborated. No doubt the Regius Professor was not aware of this; but others were and used all of it consciously in their impulses. This needs to be recorded.

We shall speak more about what it was that they were aware of. But when people are not aware of something it nevertheless creeps into their soul and occupies them in a certain way. Thus, in our time, an extraordinary collaboration came about between something occult hovering in the background and pulling strings, and something of which people are unaware, but which lives in the forefront of events on the physical plane.

One must know such things if one wants to form judgements in the proper way. Over the last few weeks I have quoted a number of peculiar incidents, such as the matter of the *Almanach of Madame de Thèbes*[6] and others. No doubt you remember. Now consider the following quite objectively without taking sides in any way. It is something extraordinary even for somebody who only thinks in the ordinary way; but for those who observe spiritual connections it is something that demands more than mere consideration, it demands to be meditated upon and taken into one's impulses: Is it not extraordinary that as early as the nineties of the nineteenth century an English book[7] should have been published that was written by three editors of *The Times* and given the title *The Great War of 189-*? The timing was handled in a somewhat dilettante fashion. Though the date suggested is rather earlier, the reference is to the present war. This book contains a small error, for we are told that the war will break out as a result of the assassination of the Bulgarian Prince Ferdinand and that it will then escalate into the European conflagration covering the world. What is foretold in detail about this European conflagration covering the world is remarkably prophetic and has been confirmed in the main by subsequent events. We can truly say that the book's greatest error is the confusion between the Bulgarian Prince Ferdinand and Franz Ferdinand of Austria, and the placing of the assassination in Sofia instead of Sarajevo. I consider that there is a significance which should not be underestimated in the appearance of a book in 1892 which so remarkably accurately portrays a future event. Only by endeavouring to form judgements which are not abstract, but founded on what actually exists, can we develop the capacity to see the hidden configuration of things.

Naturally enough, even those who were able to see what was to come misplaced certain details — this is inevitable when speaking about such things. It is not always possible to foresee everything accurately. But we ought to ponder on the fact that there were people at that time who had such strong reasons for going into these matters that they even went as far as publication. I am telling you all this, especially in connection with all that we are considering, so that you can sharpen your capacity for forming judgements. It is essential to have the will to look facts in the face and see how they relate to one another. In earlier lectures here[8] I said: In the fifth post-Atlantean period we can only make progress if we strive on the one hand to achieve Imagination, and on the other to let the facts speak for themselves. All preconceived judgements are doomed increasingly to become empty phrases. Least of all can abstract thinking — as opposed to thinking that is bound up with actual facts — lead to judgements about the tragic conflicts in the world, the tragic play of impulses which work in the way I have described.

There exists today a knack, linked with world history, a knack of saying things which seem very convincing to many people but which, in fact, reveal nothing on which it would be worth basing a judgement. Let us consider a judgement such as the following: Those in power in the British Empire did not want war. To back this up, suitable correspondence, telegrams, letters and so forth, about all sorts of proposals for conferences and so on are are quoted. People who judge, not on the basis of reality but abstractly, can indeed be convinced by these things, because the material available to back up such a statement can sound very convincing. But for a judgement to be valid it must not only be convincing or correct in the abstract, it must live in reality. It is perfectly possible, under certain circumstances, to prove that those in power in the British Empire — or rather those who mattered — did not want a war, and with such proof the greatest impression can be made in the whole of the periphery. In order to prove it — I say 'prove' — it is not even necessary to speak a direct untruth; yet in reality it remains an untruth. Why? Because it is, in fact, true and can be proved to be true, and yet this truth is not worth a snap of the fingers and is totally irrelevant.

You may be certain that those in power in the British Empire would very much have preferred to prevent the conflict in so far as the British Empire is a participant. But what those who matter wanted to achieve by means of the war — this they certainly desired with every ounce of energy at their disposal. Had it been possible to achieve this without a war, they would obviously greatly have preferred it, and from the beginning it was not at all out of the question that these aims might have been achieved by means other than war. To do this it would have been necessary to create some sort of substitute, some international arrangement, by means of which representatives of the various states could have come together to decide certain matters. If you take care to ensure in advance that you have a majority in such a body, then of course you can achieve your aims without a war, as long as the minority are prepared to go along with you.

So you see, in the last resort it is not a matter of whether one wanted to wage or prevent war, but of what one's aims were in the first place. And the objective observer cannot fail to see that the aim was indeed the one about which I have given you a number of hints — it is only possible to hint. As always, I beg you to take into account that I am not passing a judgement on moral grounds, but placing the concept of tragedy on the scales; I am saying that when conflicts are tackled by means of battles, when much blood is spilt — this stems from the tragedy of those conflicts. In contemplating this tragedy externally, we must, of course, have the will to be affected by these things in a way that differs somewhat from the ordinary.

How often do we hear: A share of the blame for this war must be laid at the door of those opinions, sensations and feelings which such people as Treitschke and Bernhardi[9] spread among the German people. It can be quite grotesque, for the names of these writers have often enough been cited as belonging to deceivers, even by people who are convinced in the most honest way that this hits the nail on the head. Sometimes Nietzsche is included,[10] sometimes others as well. There is much to be learnt by taking into account what such things are based on, in what I might call 'the realm of what is true'. But before going into this from the spiritual point of view — for much can be learnt about the spiritual realm by attending to ordinary things — let me draw your attention to the way in which just such phenomena as the German historian Treitschke can illustrate for us everything that is so tragic in human evolution. The only thing is that one must not make judgements of an utterly superficial kind.

Had I been inclined to make judgements of a superficial nature, I should for some time now certainly have looked upon Treitschke as a social monster. I only met him once, at a time when he was already totally deaf. You wrote your questions on scraps of paper and he then replied. When I was introduced to him, he asked: Where are you from? I wrote down that I was an Austrian. He replied: Well, well, — he was loud-spoken, since he could hear nothing — Austrians are either geniuses or rascals, one or the other; and so forth. With Treitschke it was always like this: If you did not want to count yourself a genius, you had had it. He was a vivacious man with considerable depth of character, and he often expressed himself in sharply defined terms. He wrote a much cited history of the German people.[11] It is quoted in a certain way, but it could easily be quoted in another way, too, for anyone who wanted a collection of anti-German vulgarities could just copy them straight from Treitschke. However, this is not what people do. Instead, they seek out passages which are far less frequent than those in which Treitschke tells his people the truth about themselves. They seek out passages which are written, so they think, in a 'Prussian and militaristic' manner.

In this connection I want to introduce you to a rather interesting judgement. It stems from a man who was quite justified in forming it, because he, too, was a historian. He was also particularly interested in Treitschke's definite antipathy towards more recent history and developments in England. Treitschke certainly entertained this antipathy and it soon became obvious when you got to know him.

This historian, who knew Treitschke well, wrote that Treitschke's dislike of modern England was based partly on historical, and partly on moral grounds, for

'Britain's world-predominance outrages him as a man almost as much as it outrages him as a German. It outrages him because of its immorality, its arrogance and its pretentious security. And not without justice'

please note this

'he delineates English policy throughout the eighteenth and nineteenth centuries as aimed consistently at the repression of Prussia, so soon as English politicians discovered the true nature of that state and divined the great future reserved for it by destiny. Had not England been Prussia's treacherous but timid enemy in 1864 and 1866, and again in 1870-71, and, above all, in 1874-75?'

This is what this historian says in his discussion of Treitschke's antipathy towards England. The strongest point he makes in Treitschke's favour is his

'conviction, which becomes more intense as the years advance, that Britain's world-predominance is out of all proportion to Britain's real strength and to her worth or value, whether that worth be considered in the political, the social, the intellectual, or the moral sphere.'

He continues:

'It is the detestation of a sham . . . That which Treitschke hates in England is what Napoleon hated in England — a pretentiousness, an overweening middle-class self-satisfaction, which is not really patriotism, not the high and serious passion of Germany in 1813 and 1870, but an insular, narrow conceit; in fact, the emotion enshrined in that most vulgar of all national hymns, "Rule Britannia".'

He goes on:

'. . . But Treitschke is seldom witty, though often grossly if unintentionally offensive. He is as unable as Heine to see anything fine in the English character.'

You see, this is another judgement about Treitschke. And while we are just discussing this historian, let me read to you a judgement he formed about someone else, much-maligned Bernhardi:

'But what marks out this work'

the book in question is the one which is constantly quoted these days as being particularly abominable

'from all others of the same kind, giving it something of the distinction of a really epoch-making book, is that it represents a definite attempt made by a German soldier to understand not merely how Germany *could* make war upon England most effectively, but why Germany *ought* to make war upon England.'

All this is written about Treitschke and Bernhardi by the English professor Cramb,[12] who from his own point of view could be called the
English Treitschke. If you delve into the matter, you will find an
extraordinary similarity between the tone of Cramb and that of
Treitschke, for Cramb, equally, is utterly preoccupied with making
clear that the British Empire must dominate the world and that
everything must be done to bring this about. You could say that he
speaks about England in the way Treitschke speaks about Germany,
allowing of course for the differences between an Englishman and
a German. Here you see how one of two men — each of whom, speaking from his own point of view, must needs say the opposite of the
other — is nevertheless capable of appreciating what the other says.
In a certain sense a point had been reached at which what had to be
laid aside could indeed be laid aside, in order to come to what is above
the individual and belongs to history.

It is therefore an extremely depressing relapse, a backward step
for people, to find that now, even in the most weighty documents,
judgements come to expression which are utterly inapplicable. There
is really no need to go at all far in order to find tangible truths. But
to do so one needs the keen sense which today can only be maintained
through some connection with spiritual science. On another front there
is something equally grotesque: The Russian plan to gain possession
of the Dardanelles and Constantinople has existed and been admitted
for centuries; yet at the same time the Russians claim to be entirely
blameless, absolutely blameless. Here, in a historical document of
the first water — the Tsar's decree that has recently been going round
the world — we have the juxtaposition once again: We are absolutely
blameless, but we mean to conquer, yet we are blameless. In Russia,
too, people have not always held the opinions they hold today.

Take Kuropatkin for instance.[13] In 1910 he published a book *The
Tasks of the Russian Army*. In this book there is a remarkable passage
which those who speak of Russia's great blamelessness could do well
to mark and digest. It says:[14]

'If Russia does not bring to an end her interference in something
foreign to her, yet of vital interest to Austria, then a war over
the question of Serbia can be expected to break out in the twentieth century between Russia and Austria.'

The Russian general Kuropatkin wrote this in 1910. Of course he had in mind what existed on the Russian side that could lead to a war with Austria over the Serbian conflict.

The question now arises: Why is the truth being so distorted at present? The answer is that something has got to be said, yet it is not as easy as all that to speak the truth. I hinted at this yesterday. The things that are said are intended to spread a fog over the truth so as to distract people's attention from the truth. That is why arguments are chosen which will have an immediate sentimental appeal for those who lack the will to get to the bottom of things.

If only people could come more and more to understand above all the full significance of the many unconscious or subconscious untruths. I have often pointed out that it is no excuse to say that one believes something just because so and so said it. Of course I do not mean that many people do not believe in what they are saying, but this is not the point. These things work in the world, and those who make statements have a duty to take the trouble to find out the truth; merely believing something is not enough. Someone might speak quite truly when he says that he wanted to prevent the war. But this truth is not worth a fig in view of the fact that he intended to use other means instead to achieve his desired aim, the aim he is striving for with all his might. To reverse the truth in this way, whether unconsciously or subconsciously, is something much worse than an untruth, even though it appears to be the truth.

This is now the immensely difficult karma of mankind: that people do not feel in duty bound to pursue the actual, real truth and truthfulness that lives in the facts — indeed, that the very opposite of this seems to have started to rule the world and to be all set to do so ever increasingly. External deeds are always the consequence of what lives in mankind in the way of thought. They are the consequence of untruthfulness, which may indeed appear in the guise of truth because it can be 'proved', though only superficially. What lives in the judgements of human beings can become, on another plane, the thundering of cannon and the spilling of blood. There is certainly a connection between the two. The conclusion we have to draw from this is that we must enter ever more deeply into the facts, that we must develop a sense which can lead us to see in the appropriate places those things which can really throw light and reveal what is essential.

50

LECTURE SEVENTEEN
Dornach, 8 January 1917

When, after repeated requests, I decided to speak about some aspects of most recent history leading up to the present, I expressly stated that my concern was the understanding of the facts and that there was no question of entering into politics or anything to do with politics. I frequently repeated this statement. Despite this, it seems to me that a definite carelessness — not to use a stronger word — is gaining ground amongst us in this respect. People do not consider that when someone is speaking the truth with the intensity that has been the case, he has a right to claim that attention is also paid to the manner of its expression. It appears that here and there people have been speaking about these lectures as if they were political lectures. Lack of consideration has for a long time been the order of the day among some of our members — only a few, of course; I refer only to those who are meant. Everything I have said and repeated over and over again out of anxiety for our concerns has fallen on deaf ears in some quarters. It is perfectly apparent that again and again the matters we speak about here are reported to outsiders in the strangest manner.

As such, I have nothing against reports if they remain within the obvious bounds. But it is clear from various recent publications — among them a most scandalous compilation from the Vollrath[1] camp — that matters are not reported in a manner befitting the way they are discussed here, but in a manner — perhaps from want of a better understanding — that enables the most horrible distortions to be fabricated. I know very well that the source of this is to be found in our midst, and if again and again I hold my peace and refrain from taking steps against those so-called members who behave in this way, it is out of love for our whole Movement and our whole Society. It is surely not possible to hold a constant succession of hearings. It would, however, be possible for members who understand what is going on, to approach in a suitable manner those of whom it is known that their attitude to the spiritual content given here is not what it ought to be. I do not even want to maintain — though sometimes it is indeed the case — that there is a direct lack of morality in people's behaviour, but there is certainly a lack of insight into the way one might behave. If someone wants to speak about what he has heard, it is incumbent upon him to ask himself with honest — let me say — self-knowledge, whether he has really understood it in a way which enables him to pass it on.

It is necessary, unfortunately, to draw attention to this from time to time. I assure you that I am not doing so without good reason. If things go on as they are, it will become necessary to remain silent about certain matters, and it is easy to see what would then become of our Movement. And a share in bringing this about would lie with those members who again and again fail to prevent themselves from using the most awful expressions which can then lead to frightful distortions. Surely it is not necessary to speak about these things in places where they can be overheard by people who do not belong amongst us, and to use expressions which might come easily to the tongue, but which in no way correspond to the whole purpose on which these lectures are founded!

I must admit that having decided after repeated requests to give these lectures, I can only view as entirely personal attacks the instances in which they have been described as 'political lectures'.

Now that we have discussed the many considerations contained in the lectures of the past few weeks, it will today be possible to draw some of them together in order to throw light on aspects which can help us to understand what is happening today. I shall first endeavour to recount quite baldly, in the most external fashion, the historical sequence of events as they occurred, and then, on the basis of the insights gained over the past weeks, I will point out some of the deeper-lying causes. I want to state expressly that, particularly today, I shall attempt to weigh carefully every single expression so that each one provides an exact delineation within which the view it expresses can come to light. Let me start, then, by describing quite externally and briefly certain events, viewpoints and impulses.

As you of course all know, the present painful events have come about in connection with the murder in June 1914 of Franz Ferdinand, heir to the Austrian throne. This assassination was followed in the whole of Europe by a newspaper campaign which showed, in what might be called surging waves, the degree to which passions had been aroused in every quarter. All this led to the well-known ultimatum from the monarchy of Austria-Hungary to Serbia which, in the main, was rejected by Serbia; then on to the Austro-Serbian conflict which was intended by the leading Austrian statesmen to consist of a military entry into Serbia, without any annexation of Serbian territory, for the purpose of exerting military pressure in order to force an acceptance of the ultimatum. The purpose of the ultimatum was to prevent Serbia from inciting unrest against the stability of the Austro-Hungarian monarchy via Austria's southern Slav population. As you know, Austria comprises quite a number of nations — there are thirteen recognized languages and many more than thirteen distinct peoples. In the southern region the population is Slav; more to the West are the Slovenian Slavs; to the East, adjacent to them, the Dalmatian, Croatian, Slovenian, Serbian, Serbo-Croat population; then also the various groups who live in the territories of Bosnia and Herzegovina which were annexed by Austria in 1908, though occupied by her long before that. Serbia borders on the territories populated by these southern Slavs. Austria believed it could be proved — and evidence of this proof can be found all over the place by anyone who cares to seek it — that Serbia was inciting unrest with the aim of founding a Southern Slav kingdom under the sovereignty of Serbia and entailing the detachment of the southern Slav population of Austria.

At all costs the assassination of Franz Ferdinand had to be linked with these things, for the following reason: From 1867 onwards, the monarchy of Austria-Hungary was a dual state comprising, in accordance with a not very concise description 'the kingdoms and lands represented in the *Reichsrat*', and secondly 'the lands of the Holy Crown of St Stephen'. Among the lands represented in the *Reichsrat* were Upper and Lower Austria, Salzburg, Styria, Carinthia, Carniola and Istria, Dalmatia, Moravia, Bohemia and Silesia, Galicia, Lodomeria and Bukovina. To the lands of the Holy Crown of St Stephen belong first and foremost the Magyar regions to which was annexed what had formerly been Transylvania, which is inhabited by a number of peoples; further, Croatia and Slavonia, the latter enjoying a kind of limited self-government within the Hungarian state. A dual monarchy, in other words.

Now it was known that Franz Ferdinand, the heir to the throne, wanted to overcome the drawbacks of the dualism of Austria-Hungary and replace this dualism with a 'triadic' reorganization. This triadic structure was to come about by making the southern Slav territories belonging to Austria self-governing, in the way the lands and kingdoms represented in the Reichsrat and also the lands of the Holy Crown of St Stephen were self-governing. This would have put a triadic structure in place of the existing dualism. You can see how, had it been realized, this would have led to an individualization of the separate southern Slav peoples within a kind of southern Slav community in the Austro-Slav regions. It would have meant a step closer to the aim of assimilating the western Slavs with western culture, thus working against what I have called Russianism in these lectures. This could quite well have worked out, for the structure of the Austrian state is entirely federalistic, not centralistic, and before the war it tended anyway increasingly to grant federal status to the different peoples. From 1867 to 1879 centralism was the aim; from 1879 onwards the efforts to centralize had to be seen as a failure, and from then on federalism was the aim.

In opposition to this were the efforts on the part of Serbia to found a confederation of southern Slavs under the hegemony of Serbia. This did not arise from within the Serbian people, but I have described to you how peoples are, in a way, led simply by means of suggestion. For this to happen, the southern Slav territories would, of course, have to be wrested from Austria-Hungary.

This concludes my brief summary of what lies behind the Austro-Serbian conflict. What I have just been telling you is all to do with the Austro-Serbian conflict. It is thinkable that this conflict could have been 'localized' — I have used this expression once before. Had this come about — I am speaking hypothetically — the European world war would have been avoided. What would have happened if the strictly circumscribed intentions of the Austrian statesmen had been realized? Part of the Austro-Hungarian army would have marched into Serbia and stayed there until Serbia agreed to accept the ultimatum which would have quashed the possibility of a southern Slav conferation under Serbian hegemony, and, of course, Russian supremacy. If no other European power had interfered in this matter, if they had all done nothing more than stand to attention, as it were, then nothing would have taken place except the acceptance of this ultimatum. For Austria had guaranteed that she had no intention of annexing any parts of Serbian territory in any way. As a result, such assassinations as took place many times — that of Franz Ferdinand was only the last in a whole sequence incited by Serbian agitators — such assassinations would not have taken place, and without such agitation the establishment of a southern Slav confederation under the supremacy of Russia is, or rather would, of course, have been impossible. If events had taken this course — I speak hypothetically again — this war need never have broken out.

So what is the connection between this Austro-Serbian conflict and the World War? To comprehend this connection it is necessary to pass beyond an understanding of the external situation and, if I may say so, enter the deeper secrets of European politics. It is not politics we want to enter; we want to understand in our soul what it was that lived in these politics. I want to answer the question: How did a European conflict arise out of the Austro-Serbian conflict? What is the link between the Austro-Serbian question and the European question?

We must turn our attention to what I have just said about the southern Slav confederation. It was the British Empire, the more it took on a conscious form, that was interested in a southern Slav confederation, independent of Austria, but under the supremacy of Russia. In the societies I have mentioned it was the establishment of what was termed the Danube confederation — by which was meant this southern Slav confederation, which was to comprise the southern Slav peoples together with Romania and include the southern Slavs of Austria — that was expressly discussed. In the nineties of the nineteenth century we find everywhere in the occult schools of the West, under the direct influence of British occultists, indications that such a Danube confederation would have to come into being. Attempts were also made to manipulate the whole of European politics towards the creation of this Danube confederation, which would entail the relinquishing of the Austro-Slav territories.

Why was the British Empire interested in this Danube confederation, a project which was anti-Austrian and pro-Russian? The powers which have been in opposition to one another most strongly in recent times as a consequence of the imperialism which has broken out across the world, those powers which actually coexist with the greatest hostility, are the British Empire and the Russian Empire. Such hidden hostilities can indeed manifest outwardly as friendships and alliances. When there is such bitter hostility between countries outwardly coexisting peacefully, a certain consequence results from the fact that our earth has a specific characteristic: namely, that it is spherical in shape. If our earth were a flat plain stretching in all directions, such conflicts could not come about. But since our earth is round, not only do we eventually arrive back at our starting point if we walk long enough in a straight line, but something else also happens: Expanding empires come up against each other at a certain point, and when they collide they have to follow through with their opposing interests. This occurred between the British and the Russian Empires. Among many other situations, it became most obviously apparent when they collided with great force in Persia. The question was: Should Russia succeed in moving down against India and there gradually hem in the British Empire, or would the British Empire erect defences?

When your aim is to gain sovereignty, you can pursue it by means of war, or by other means, depending on which seems the most favourable. For the British Empire it seemed for the moment — in the case of states, only limited periods of time are reckoned with — more favourable to prevent Russia from proceeding against India by providing a different channel, by diverting her attention in another direction in which she could achieve the satisfaction of her natural ambition. Empires are always ambitious. This was to be brought about by conceding to Russia the sovereignty over the so-called Danube confederation. Thus the British Empire was indirectly interested in making the Danube confederation as extensive as possible, for the Slavs in the South wanted to belong together, and this feeling of belonging was stirred up in the way I have described to you. Thus the confederation of southern Slavs was to be played into Russia's hand so that she might withdraw her attention from other directions. This was why the confederation of southern Slavs, to be set up under Russian sovereignty, was in the British interest. It was a long story, prepared well beforehand.

Here we see one of the threads linking the Austro-Serbian question to the question of sovereignty on a world scale. This is how the whole relationship between the British and the Russian Empires was drawn into the matter. It was not a matter of Austria and Serbia, for the whole Austro-Serbian question necessarily became the question: Should Austria take the step towards a triadic structure, thus diverting the confederation of southern Slavs from its path, or should steps be taken towards a Russian-dominated southern Slav confederation? In this way the Austro-Serbian question became coupled with the European question.

When such situations exist — for what I have just described lived in human beings as absolutely real impulses — it is like an electric charge which will at some point have to be discharged. This, then, was one of the threads.

It is still, however, highly questionable whether the Austro-Serbian conflict would have led to the World War, if there had not been further aspects in addition to those we have just discussed. Indeed, it is highly unlikely that it would have done, if there had been no other causes.

But there were plenty of other impulses, all of which reinforced the situation. First and foremost among these was the Franco-Russian alliance within the general European situation. This Franco-Russian alliance had existed since the nineties of the nineteenth century and, looking at the situation objectively, it could not have been more unnatural. No one will doubt that France had entered into this alliance with a view to winning back Alsace-Lorraine, for there is no other imaginable reason for this alliance. All other reasons would only have spoken against such an alliance. In the end, though, those other reasons carry little weight in comparison with the driving forces, for the fact is that an alliance such as this exists; through its very existence it represents a real force. It is there. Much more important than the actual aim of this alliance is the fact that here are a western and an eastern state who in combination constitute a monstrous military power. And between them lies Germany who could not but feel permanently threatened militarily by the scale of this combined French and Russian military might. It was this encirclement of Germany to West and East by the Franco-Russian alliance which became one of the driving forces in European affairs.

To discover further influences which played a part we must look at the following: In recent decades, imperialism has led to a general desire for expansion. You need only look, for instance, at the monstrous growth of the British Empire. Or think of France, whose territorial expansion over the last few decades has been incomparably greater than at any earlier time, when France, as she herself said, marched at the head of European civilization.

The events of recent decades have been like a chain reaction: In every case what came next could not have taken place without what had gone before. The most recent point of departure — of course we could go back further — lies in the British Empire's seizure of sovereignty over Egypt. For today's way of thinking it is perfectly reasonable to justify such an action by claiming the necessity of rounding off and securing one's assets. The expansion of British sovereignty over Egypt was justified by saying that a bridge to India was needed. The hope was that Arabia could be gained too, thus creating a direct link with India.

The expansion of the British Empire to include Egypt provided, to some extent, a protective barrier against any awkward expansion of the Russian Empire westwards; any such expansion westwards need not have harmed the British Empire to any great extent if Egypt had been able to provide the necessary link with India.

Now since the earth is spherical, there is insufficient territory for unlimited expansion outwards by empires because eventually they will clash. In consequence the expansion of one empire generates in the other an equal lust for expansion. Thus the expansion by France to include Morocco, in two stages in 1905 and 1911, was nothing other than a consequence of the expansion of the British Empire to include Egypt.[2] The mutual recognition of these expansions — France's recognition of British dominion over Egypt and British recognition of France's dominion over Morocco — provided the threads with which an Entente Cordiale between the French and the British Empires could be spun. But because Germany was in the middle, efforts were made, as you know, to establish the Triple Alliance: Germany, Austria, Italy.

However, the distribution of Morocco and Egypt, and what followed this, meant that, at the Algeciras Conference,[3] and particularly with the help of an elderly Italian politician who was well versed in these things, Italy was even then successfully drawn into the sphere of influence of the western entente between France and England. After the Algeciras Conference sensible people in Central Europe no longer believed that Italy would be able to remain faithful to the Triple Alliance. Because of the way she had behaved there had to be consequences for her, resulting from the seizure of Morocco by France. And the consequence was that Italy was permitted to establish herself in Tripoli. In effect this meant that Italy had been given permission by the West to wage war on Turkey. So Egypt led to Morocco, and Morocco to Tripoli. Then, because Tripoli meant a new weakening of the Turkish position, Tripoli led to the Balkan War. These events took place like a chain reaction, Egypt-Morocco-Tripoli-Balkan War; each is unthinkable without its predecessor.

Turkey having been weakened by the Italo-Turkish, or Tripoli War, the southern Slav peoples, with the others in their wake, and also the Greek peoples, believed themselves strong enough to win the Balkan peninsula for themselves. As a result of this, the trend towards a southern Slav confederation became linked with the national aspirations of the Balkan countries. The linking of these two chains gave the Balkan War an outcome in which Serbia was the strongest winner. Serbia has grown very powerful, incomparably more so than she was before. In consequence there came a revival of the ideal of founding the southern Slav confederation under the hegemony of Serbia and the overall sovereignty of Russia. This led to the agitations which culminated in the assassination of Franz Ferdinand, which in turn led to the Austro-Serbian War. Now we have brought the two links together: The Austro-Serbian question was linked with the European question as a consequence of the whole historical process. Those who followed these events with understanding were able to see under these circumstances many years ahead to the coming war, hanging like a sword of Damocles over European culture and civilization. Wherever these things were discussed you could hear how people realized that Russia's pretensions would lead to a conflict between Central and Eastern Europe. This conflict was inevitable. No one who studies the realities of history will say that this conflict between Central and Eastern Europe was not based on what may be called a spiritual necessity. Just as in ancient times conflict arose between the Roman and the Germanic peoples, so in modern times there had to be conflict between Central and Eastern Europe. There were manifold forms it could have taken, but conflict there had to be. Everything else, in so far as it had to do with the East, was included in this conflict.

It was the pretensions of Russianism that led to the expectation that somewhere or other these pretensions would lead to an attempt by Russia to impose sovereignty on the Balkan league. This was expected. The geographical situation made it inevitable that there would be a clash between Russia and Austria. And when this clash occurred — so said all those who had been contemplating these things over the years — everything else would automatically follow.

How, it was asked, would the situation be shaped by the existing structure of alliances at the moment of Russia's attack on Austria? Obviously no one expected Austria to attack Russia of her own accord. This was unthinkable; Austria could not possibly find herself in a position to launch an attack on Russia. It had to be supposed, therefore, that matters would arrange themselves in a way that would enable Russia to attack Austria. Well and good! Because of the alliance between Austria and Germany, Germany could be expected to stand by Austria and attack Russia in her turn. And as a result of Germany's attack on Russia — I am telling you what was presumed — the Franco-Russian alliance would come into action. France would be obliged to take Russia's side and attack Germany. And because of the relationship between France and England — whether laid down in a treaty or not — England would have to join in the attack on the side of Russia and France. These things were foreseen. The structure of treaties and alliances would automatically lead to a sequence of events.

In the end, the sequence was not quite what had been expected by those who concerned themselves day in, day out, with the future of Europe. What form did it take? Let us see. I have already described to you the history of the ultimatum, the rejection of the ultimatum, the resulting insistence by Austria on acceptance of the ultimatum. But the European powers did not remain indifferent to all this, for Russia immediately made ready to enter the fray as Serbia's protector. This made the localization of the Austro-Serbian question unthinkable. From the British quarter came all sorts of meaningless suggestions of the kind made by those who either want to take a hand in affairs without thinking things through properly, or who want to build up for themselves from the start a world-wide reputation of having endeavoured to settle the matter by peaceful means. This is not actually the aim, but it has to be possible later on to say that it was.

So the meaningless suggestion was made to call a conference made up, of all things, of England, Germany, France and Italy, to decide about the questions pending. Just imagine what would have been the outcome of such a conference! A majority verdict would have been required on whether Austria's demands to Serbia were justified or not. On the basis of the real situation, imagine, please, how the voting would have gone! Italy had inwardly deserted the Triple Alliance, France was on Russia's side, Russia was obviously only satisfied if Austria was refused the right to insist on acceptance of the ultimatum, England was in favour of the Danube confederation. Leaving aside Austria, the majority would have gone to Italy, France and England. Germany would obviously have been out-voted at all costs. This conference could not possibly have led to anything other than a refusal for what Austria, from her position, was compelled to demand. That means that if this conference had been held it would have been nothing but a farce, for Austria would either have been forced to give up her pretensions, or, regardless of the outcome of the conference, she would have continued to demand acceptance of the ultimatum. In other words, the conference would have been nothing but a bluff, as they say. A thorough study of the documentation reveals, however, that from the start Russia's pretension was to interfere in the Serbo-Austrian question. So it is really irrelevant whether the World War came about as the result of an automatic sequence of events or of deliberate scene-setting leading inevitably to the War.

It was the scene-setting that took place for, in addition to the various impulses, you must also take into account a quite particular mood.

Maybe no other world event, no other historical event but this, has ever been quite so dependent on a certain mood. The mood of soul of those participating in the outbreak of the War at the end of July 1914 was certainly one of the most important causes. Of course there were also agitations at the outbreak of earlier wars, but they did not sweep in with such stormy, such hurricane force, as did the events between 24 July and 1 August 1914. Within a few days a monstrous agitation had gathered over the participants, an agitation in which was concentrated all the accumulated anxiety of the many years during which this coming event had been foreseen. This mood must definitely be taken into account. Those who do not do so can only speak in empty phrases.

All kinds of points could be brought in to characterize this mood, but I shall draw your attention to only one. An event had taken place which was indirectly, though in fact very strongly, connected with the outbreak of the War. If it is to be evaluated properly it will, and must, be seen in its proper place amongst the other events in Europe. This was the German defence bill,[4] laid before Parliament after the Balkan War, which budgeted for an enlargement of the German army by means of a single large defence payment. This enlargement of the German army, which, by the way, was not anywhere near completion by the time the War broke out, can be studied by anyone in connection with the results of the Balkan War. These results showed that for an uncertain time in the future the clash between Russia and Austria was being manipulated. It was only because of certain situations, which I do not want to go into here, that Russia was prevented as early as 1913 from attacking Austria in order to gain sovereignty and dominion over the Balkan confederation. The enlargement of the German army was undertaken for no other reason — as I said, I am choosing my expressions very precisely today — than the threatened dispute with the East. Yet the French reaction followed promptly: If Germany is enlarging her army, then we must do something about strengthening ours. What this means is that the destiny, the inevitable necessity for Central Europe to take precautions with regard to the East, always produced reinforcements in the West, which naturally produced further reactions in their turn.

In this way matters progressed. In particular, everything connected with the defence bill after the Balkan War generated terrible anxiety in Central Europe because the whole of the European periphery was seen to have turned against Central Europe. Opinions differed only in the matter of Italy: Some still thought she would somehow throw in her lot with Central Europe, while others no longer held this to be possible.

Let us still assume — hypothetically — that the World War did not break out. There was only one precondition that could have prevented it. Russia would have had to refrain from immediate war threats — in other words mobilization, which under the prevailing circumstances could only be regarded as a war threat. Central Europe could not for one moment have thought that France would not go along with Russia, so an assault on two fronts had to be reckoned with. The only course of action open to those in positions of responsibility was to paralyse this assault in some way. No one in a responsible position could have thought: Let us spend the next fortnight at a conference! Not only could this conference have led absolutely nowhere, as I said, but it would have meant certain defeat. But no one can be expected to accept certain defeat from the outset. So the only possibility was to match the monstrous military superiority of West and East by means of speed.

For this the only possible course of action, as I showed earlier, was to violate international law and march through Belgium. Any other solution could only have led to the involvement of most of the German army in a long war of defence in the West while leaving the way open to invasion from the East. This was one of those historical moments at which — whether you can express it aptly or not — a state is forced to enter into a breach of the law in self-preservation. There is no other course of action open to those responsible for that state. In Central Europe it was — and I am choosing my words very carefully today in order to make my meaning quite clear — for some of those in responsible positions utterly monstrous to attempt war on two fronts at once.

So the attempt was made to restrict the matter to a single front. Careful, carefully intentioned, attempts were made to keep France neutral, and it was believed that France could be induced to remain neutral. No one in Central Europe had any intention of harming France. With a feeling of total responsibility it is possible to say that absolutely no one in Central Europe, no one in Germany, had any intention of harming France. What was done was done only with a view to tying matters up as quickly as possible in the West in order to prevent the threatened invasion from the East. It therefore never ceases to be astonishing that so much talk persists in the world about all the atrocities Germany has committed towards the West. None of the atrocities would have occurred if only France had declared her neutrality. France was perfectly capable of protecting herself and Belgium against any attack. That France was forced to keep her agreement with Russia is her own affair and should not be trotted out in the same breath as the atrocities committed by Germany, for the allegiance of one state to another is no business of her enemies.

Since it proved impossible to keep France neutral by direct means, the attempt was then made via England — here, too, without success. I have touched a number of times on how England could have saved Belgium and, equally well, France. These things must be viewed absolutely objectively. Please accept as totally objective the statement that, once the war between Austria and Serbia could no longer be localized because Russia would not allow this, every effort was made at least to prevent it from spreading to the West. Truly, no one in Central Europe was seized with the madness of wanting to make war on two fronts, let alone subsequently on three.

That all the other universal untruths followed on from this is really not surprising now, when every day astonishes us with new lies, spoken, written and printed. Before coming here today I found someone had put on my desk a pamphlet by one of the participants engaged in the neutrality debate with Georg Brandes. Here, on the English side, you have William Archer, in whose pamphlet[5] you find juxtaposed the black infamy of Germany and the pure innocence of the allies. Ten points illustrate the black infamy, and the angelic, utter innocence of the allies; we need consider only one of these, the second. The second point states that in Germany there exists a notable faction which is openly agitating for further territorial expansion, either in or outside Europe. In contrast it is said of the allies — in English, mark you: The allies have no desire for any territorial expansion, least of all at Germany's expense; even France's feelings for Alsace-Lorraine are exclusively peaceful.

My dear friends, much can be both printed and spoken these days! The other nine points are in similar vein. Just think of the expansion undertaken by England and France over recent decades; and then read that these countries have no desire for territorial expansion. It is quite possible nowadays to say and print the exact opposite of the truth, just as it is possible for countless people to believe it. People do indeed believe these things.

Here, then, you have the historical view of these events. Now we must link this external historical process with what we can discover through our knowledge of the impulses from the West which have been at work for a long time. Not all the impulses that make use to a greater or lesser degree of occult forces — such as we have discussed — are included in what might be called the outer ramifications: namely, Freemasonry, though as we have seen, a great deal is indeed brought about by western Freemasonry. Many strings are pulled by those involved there. And as I said, account is taken of long stretches of time.

Now add to the points I have been making the fact that modern Freemasonry undergoes a process of consolidation in England at the beginning of the eighteenth century, on foundations, of course, which are older. Within Britain, not the Empire, but the United Kingdom, Freemasonry remains — let me use the correct expression — essentially respectable in the interests it pursues. But everywere else, outside Britain, chiefly — or indeed exclusively — political interests are pursued by Freemasonry.

Such political interests, to the most marked degree, are pursued for instance by the French *Grand Orient*, and also by other Grand Lodges. You could ask: What business is it of the English if political trends in other countries are pursued by certain orders of Freemasonry which possess an occult background? In reply you might remind yourself that the first Grand Lodge in Paris was founded under the jurisdiction of England, not France! Englishmen, not Frenchmen, founded it; and then they let the French in. Then also remind yourself that after the founding of this Grand Lodge in Paris in 1725, this *Grand Orient* in turn sanctioned the founding of a lodge under its own jurisdiction in Paris in 1729. There were, under the jurisdiction of England, foundations in Gibraltar in 1729, Madrid in 1728, Lisbon in 1736, Florence in 1735, Moscow in 1731, Stockholm in 1726, Geneva in 1735, Lausanne in 1739 and Hamburg in 1737. I could carry on for a long time with this list. I could show you how a network was founded of these lodges, which were to act as the external tools for certain occult, political impulses. They differed in character from those in the United Kingdom itself. In addition to the breathtaking sequence of changes as we see them in history, such as the Jacobins and the furore they created, the Carbonari and their political activities, the Cortes in Spain and others, they also have a strong influence on the culture of their time and send out shoots which even show in the works of the greatest spirits of their time. We need only think of Rousseau's natural philosophy, or the critical philosophy of Voltaire, which became ever more cynical though its aim was to enlighten, or the efforts of the Illuminati, who wanted to overcome the prevailing cynicism, and similar circles. These progressive circles were crushed by reactionary streams, but continued to work in manifold ways underground.

So here you have the source of much that I have been describing. And you must attach a degree of importance to the following: The English Freemasons can maintain today that their lodges are entirely respectable and that any others are none of their business; yet if you look beyond the historical connections and the interplay of opposing currents, you are sure to find high-level British politics hiding in the background.

To understand the deeper meaning of these politics it is necessary to draw a little on recent history. Preparations having been under way from the sixteenth century onwards, there has been a tendency ever since the seventeenth century towards the democratization of society — in some countries more quickly, in others more slowly — by taking power away from the few and giving it to the broad masses. I am not here involved in politics and I shall not therefore express myself in favour of either democracy or anything else. I simply wish to state facts. The impulse towards democracy is having its effect in modern times at varying speeds, and so different streams are coming into being. It is a mistake, where several streams are apparent, to follow the course of only one. The way streams flow in the world is such that one always forms a complement to the others. Let us say a green and a red stream are flowing along side by side. Nothing occult is meant by these colours — it is simply to illustrate that there are two streams flowing side by side. Usually people are, let me say, hypnotized into looking at only one of the streams, while they fail to see the other flowing beside it during the same period in history. As you know, if you push a hen's beak into the ground and then draw a line leading away, the hen will always walk along this line. In the same way people today, especially university historians, see only the one side, and can therefore never really understand the historical process.

Parallel with the democratic stream there came into being the use of occult motives in the various secret societies — in isolated cases, also Masonic orders. In their purposes and aims these are not, of course, spiritual, but there developed, let us call it, a spiritual aristocracy parallel to that democratic stream which was at work in the French Revolution; the aristocracy of the lodges developed. To see clearly as a human being today, to be open to the world and to understand the world, it is necessary not to be dazzled by democratic logic — which has a place only in its own sphere — by empty phrases about democratic progress and so on; it is necessary also to point to that other stream which asserted itself with the intent of gaining power for the few by means that lie hidden within the womb of the lodge — the ritual and its suggestive influence. It is necessary to point to this also.

This has been forgotten during the age of materialism, but before the fifties of the last century people did point these things out. Study the philosophical historians prior to 1850 and you will see that they pointed to the connection between the lodges and the French Revolution with all that followed it. During the period that can be seen as preparatory for today, western historical development, the western world, never emancipated itself from the lodges. The influence of the lodges was always strongly at work. The lodges knew how to find channels through which to impress certain directions on people's thoughts. Once a web like this has been spun — of which I have shown you merely a few strands — the button need only be pressed for things to be set in motion.

Emancipation from all these situations, and the impartial embracing of humanity as such, only really came about under the influence of such great spirituality as developed in German philosophy beginning with Lessing, and developing through Herder and Goethe. Here you have a spiritual stream which took account of all that lives in the lodges, but in such a way that the mystery was brought out of the obscurity of the lodges and transformed into a purely human matter. You need only glance at Goethe's fairy tale *The Green Snake and the Beautiful Lily*, at *Wilhelm Meister* and other of Goethe's writings. This was material with which the step to emancipation could be taken and which still today makes emancipation possible. So you may view that whole part of German cultural history portrayed in my book *Vom Menschenrätsel*[6] as a forgotten reverberation which is entirely independent of all the intrigues of the lodges.

In western culture over the last few centuries preceding our own day you will easily find many ways of demonstrating how the character of ideas in the exoteric world stemmed from the esoteric thinking of the lodges. Obviously this does not apply to the time before Queen

Elizabeth and Shakespeare but it is certainly true of what came later. But the spiritual culture linked with Lessing, Herder and Goethe has no such connections. You might ask: What about German Freemasonry — in Austria it is proscribed, so there is none there — or Magyar Freemasonry? Well, the others did not allow them to join in. They are quite an innocuous crowd. Though they might appear as thick as thieves with regard to their secrets, this is nothing but show.

The real, mighty impulses emanating from the quarters I have described to you are truly not found in German Freemasonry, which I have no wish to offend. So you can easily understand how it was possible for some rather strange occurrences to take place. Suppose, for instance, someone were to make known in Germany the things I have told you about societies, their secret connections and their external branches — the lodges of Freemasonry. It could be rather useful to make these things known there, but what would be the consequence? Experts would be asked to corroborate these things, and in this case the experts are the Freemasons themselves. But it would never occur to any Freemason in Germany to say anything other than that the English lodges do not concern themselves with politics, that they are concerned only with entirely respectable matters. This is all he knows, for he is ignorant of anything else. You can even be told — and this has actually happened — if you ask about specific names, that they are not on the list of members. They have the list but are unaware that perhaps the most important of all are not included in the list. In short, German Freemasonry is a quite innocuous society.

This does not alter the fact, though — and this may truly be said without any kind of arrogance or nationalistic affectation — that the spiritual life cultivated by certain western secret brotherhoods actually stems from Central Europe. Look at this historically. Robert Fludd:[7] pupil of Paracelsus;[8] Saint-Martin in France: pupil of Jakob Böhme. The origin of the movement itself is to be found in Central Europe. From the West comes the organization, the establishment in degrees — some western lodges have ninety-two degrees; just imagine how elevated you can become if you rise to the ninety-second degree — the use of knowledge for political aims, and the introduction of certain external elements.

We have just had an example which is quite typical, one to which I drew your attention. I am only describing these things in order to make you aware of their objective nature, just as the facts of natural history can be described; not from any nationalistic affectation. I drew your attention to the recent appearance of a book by Sir Oliver Lodge,[9] in which he reports on communications he has received through various mediums from his son who was killed in action. A book like this, written by such a distinguished scientist, is sure to cause quite a sensation. Now that I have read the book there is no need for me to retract anything I said to you a little while ago. I said at the time that I would return to this subject. The strongest proof offered by Sir Oliver Lodge is the following: Seances with various mediums result in the manifestation of the soul of Raymond Lodge, who died in action. These seances tell us nothing people do not know already and would be unlikely to make any strong impression on anyone. But one thing did make a strong impression on the eminent scientist Sir Oliver Lodge and his whole family, who up to that point had been very sceptical about such things. At one of the seances a group photograph was mentioned, showing Oliver Lodge's son together with other people. This photograph, one of several, was described as showing the same people at the same place, but in varying arrangements; the same people are seen, but with differing gestures. Raymond Lodge described this photograph through the medium at that seance in England. But Sir Oliver Lodge and his family knew nothing about this picture, for it had been taken at the Franco-Belgian front at the end of Raymond Lodge's life and sent by him to his family, though it had not yet arrived. So this medium described a group photograph which existed but was unknown to the family: the participants in the seance. They only saw it after it had been described by the medium.

For those who dabble in the occult, this is naturally tremendously convincing. What should you make of the fact that a group photograph is described at a seance, the participants of which know nothing about it? The family, the participants in the seance, know nothing of it and nor do the mediums, because it has not yet arrived in England. It is still on the way. It only arrived later. Yet an exact description is given of where Raymond Lodge is sitting in relation to the others and even of the way he has laid his hand on a friend's shoulder. What could be more convincing than this?

However, Sir Oliver Lodge's interpretation can only have been reached by someone who merely dabbles in the occult. If he had known nothing much but had investigated the literature — for instance Schubert[10] or similar people who still wrote about such things in Germany around the first half of the nineteenth century — he would have found countless examples of something that every genuine occultist knows: When consciousness is damped down even slightly, future events can be seen. The most simple case of seeing a future event is when someone experiencing a moment of lowered consciousness sees a funeral procession which will not take place for several days. A person has not even died, yet someone sees his funeral. Something in the future is seen. This is quite normal when consciousness is lowered. So this is what took place: A photograph has been taken in Flanders and is on its way to England. The time will come when the family will focus their eyes and their understanding on it, when they will bear it in their thoughts. The medium foresees it as an image of the future. Whether you foresee a funeral procession, or whether you foresee how a family receives such and such a photograph of their son in a few days' time — it is the same phenomenon: that of seeing a future event in advance. This is just a phenomenon.

If he had known something about real occult facts, he would not have interpreted the event as he did. Such an interpretation arises because occult values, occult laws, are seen from a materialistic standpoint. It comes about because people avoid undertaking that form of development which would enable them to comprehend the spiritual world in an inward process. Instead they want to see the spiritual realm by laboratory means, purely materialistically. The spirit is made materialistic, whether by Sir Oliver Lodge or anybody else. But this is only one example of what happens to everything that is spiritual. These things can be observed, just as you can observe the progression from Paracelsus to Fludd, from Jakob Böhme to Saint-Martin; everywhere the spirit is made more materialistic.

As the Anthroposophical Society we only succeeded in saving ourselves from becoming materialistic by emancipating ourselves from the Theosophical Society. For impulses emanating from the kind of society I have described penetrate deeply into the social fabric. Naturally, here again I must beg you not to misunderstand me. I am not saying that this is a natural characteristic of the western nations. But it exists and has succeeded in influencing the course of history and is not even without influence on the untruthfulness which is now playing such a devastating part.

It is particularly to this untruthfulness that I am obliged to draw you attention, for this untruthfulness always takes the form of accusation, of blaming others. That dismal New Year's Eve note[11] is really nothing but an accusation based on a distortion of the facts, just as is the article by Mr Archer which I read to you here. But you see such things are beginning to be believed, they are beginning to play their role. In a few weeks' time people will have long forgotten that an opportunity to achieve peace was present in a form that could not be overlooked by the world, and that this opportunity was thwarted by the powers of the periphery. People in Europe will once again begin to believe that the offer of peace was refused by the powers of the Entente on purely humanitarian grounds, on the basis of the extraordinary reasoning that if one wants peace one must prevent it from coming about. Even such grotesque untruths as this are believed nowadays. That they can be believed at all derives from preparations made by the kind of occultism I have been describing to you. It is indeed a sign of an arrant corruption of the soul when it becomes possible to write down side by side the two sentences I mentioned about the black and the white raven. And this corruption of the soul comes about as a consequence of an atmosphere tampered with by organizations such as I have described.

In this connection, too — I can say this quite objectively — there has been a tendency for Central Europe to emancipate itself. In all the Central European spiritual life thrown open by Lessing, Herder, Goethe, such as we have spoken about during the course of our anthroposophical life, you have seen clearly enough how the direction was towards a gradual evolution into the spiritual world. What it is not inclined to do, is enter into any kind of permanent compromise with what lives in the western streams such as those I have described to you. This is impossible. That is why things appear in a different way.

Let us look back for a moment to Fichte,[12] so disparaged in the West today; let us turn to his *Reden an die deutsche Nation*. What is Fichte aiming at? That the German nation should educate itself! What he says in *Reden an die deutsche Nation* is not aimed at other nations; he is endeavouring to inspire Germans to improve themselves. But others seem to have what we might call a real 'genius' for misunderstanding whatever comes into being in Germany. That harmless national anthem *Deutschland, Deutschland über alles*, which, if you take the trouble to read the next few lines, speaks of nothing more than loving one's fatherland above all others — for only the different parts of the fatherland are named — is made into something utterly grotesque. In the same way, if one wants to, one can misunderstand Fichte, since he begins *Reden an die deutsche Nation* with the words 'I speak for Germans as such, and about Germans as such'. Why does he say this? Because Germany is divided into a whole number of small individual states, and he does not want to address the Prussians, or the Swabians or the Saxons, or the people of Oldenburg, Mecklenburg or Austria and so on, but Germans as such. He wanted to unite all the individuals. So he is talking to Germans and only to Germans. I do not want to praise the Germans, but such things may justifiably be included in a description of them.

I have brought up this matter today because there is definitely a tendency to sound a note in the centre, a note differing from that of the periphery. And if our anthroposophical work can contribute to this other note, there is no reason why we should not say so amongst ourselves. Just today I received a pamphlet by our friend Ludwig von Polzer,[13] who as you know worked here: *Thoughts during Wartime*. Whether you agree in detail with what he says or not, it is interesting to note that he is not particularly concerned with attacking and insulting others but rather with reading the riot act to his Austrian compatriots. It is to them he speaks. Obviously he has come to be an Austrian as a result of his karma, but he nevertheless reads the riot act to his Austrian compatriots. He does not say: We are blameless, we never did this or that, we are pure white angels and all the others are black devils. No, he says:

'Why does mankind hate itself and tear itself to pieces? Are external political differences of opinion really the cause of so much suffering? Every party to the fray claims to know what it is about, but in reality none of them know.
A declining, decadent culture is fighting its deathly struggle. The Central Powers, who are fighting for the first germination of a new culture, have not recognized it as yet; they fight for something they do not know, for something unknown to them; and they are themselves still filled with the convictions against which their own soldiers are bleeding in battle.
The old degenerate ways must be, as it were, vomited forth and that is why in their final fling they are running so wild.
Do we not come up against it amongst ourselves wherever we turn, this attitude of the Entente which bears the old, decadent culture? Has it not infected us as well? We see it on the streets in the latest fashions, it is embodied in modern architecture, it grins down at us from the hoardings, in commerce it runs

to orgies, it inflates itself in bureaucratic madness, in its self-important untruthful humanism it lies to itself, our press seeks to outbid its colleagues of the Entente in devotion to the truth, and so on.

The Entente is here among us, fuming and raging, claiming to work for our honest soldiers and compatriots, almost all of whom have meanwhile died a sacrificial death.

All these things running so horrifyingly wild in our own country — let it be hoped for the last time before the end — are not *deutsch*.'[14]

So all those things worthy of censure in his own country he calls 'not *deutsch*'. His main aim is to appeal to the conscience of his own compatriots. There are further, similar passages in this booklet. It is good that such a thing is said for once in connection with our own endeavours. There is no need for us to be in total harmony with every sentence that is written amongst us. The most wonderful achievement will be to work on all these things independently, preserving our individuality and taking nothing as dogma or as the word of a higher authority. Those things which are meant to come to the fore are quite able to do so without the help of any authority. But to give our Society meaning we need to stand together in unanimity. In part this means, of course, that we should be alert to what goes on amongst us and should recognize those who work alongside us and who endeavour to place before the world what goes on within our Anthroposophical Society in such a way that it really reflects the intentions of our Society. The main thing we can do to help our age is to work with understanding through the impulses of this age from our viewpoint. We need not lose heart, for however unfavourable conditions become in time, we may recall Lessing's words: Is not the whole of eternity mine?[15] This is a thought that concerns every single human being.

We should be particularly careful to develop good practices with regard to the proper evaluation and estimation of all that comes to the fore amongst ourselves. In this connection I hope you will not mind my mentioning something, without wishing to say anything unpleasant to anyone. The periodical *Das Reich*, produced by Alexander von Bernus,[16] makes every endeavour to move within our stream. So what does it matter if we agree or disagree with one or another of the articles it publishes? It is quite possible to disagree with a good deal. But many mistakes have been made on the part of our members with regard to this periodical. Seeing how it has been berated from all sides, I have to say that it is really not right to throw obstacles in the path of efforts which genuinely endeavour to work in harmony with our Movement. Of course everybody is entitled to his own opinion about the verses which Alexander von Bernus composed in connection with certain historical occult teachings which may be found amongst us. But I do consider things have been taken too far when floods of blatantly rude letters start to arrive from our members. Where will it lead if we ill-treat those who are on our side while taking very little notice of those who insult us, just letting them go on doing so?

I wanted to bring up the matter of this periodical *Das Reich*, which strives to promote our endeavours, because I want to reply to the question that could be asked: What can we do? The very reason why these lectures have been given is to find a reply to this question: What can we do? What we can do is maintain an understanding attitude, in accordance with our anthroposophical spiritual science, towards everything going on at present! For what would be the significance of this spiritual science for us if we could really not transcend the attitude prevalent all over Europe today of people who speak of national aspirations and the like, and shape events in accordance with these national aspirations. Within the Society which serves anthroposophical spiritual science no one need become a faithless son of his nation, or deny anything he ought not to deny because he is firmly united with a particular nation as a result of his karma. But no one can be a true anthroposophist if he turns a blind eye towards the enormity of what is going on just now and allows himself to be deafened by all those means which some of those in power use today to stun us in order to avoid having to state what they are really playing at. So let me point out those things that are easily believed when they come towards us in a sentimental form, whereas what has always been hidden by the screens behind which occult events take place still has to remain hidden away behind these screens.

It must become clear to us that a time could come again — I am choosing my words very warily today, so I say *could* come again — in which the battle grows extremely terrible because peace is definitely not wanted. It could grow even more terrible than it has hitherto been if something is not introduced from one side or the other which can prevent this terror. Then there will once again be an opportunity to speak about the atrocities of Central Europe; then under the rubble and ashes will be buried the fact that these atrocities could have been prevented if people had not roared like a bull against moves towards peace. It was within the power of countries of the periphery to bring about peace. Yet the time will come — it is by no means unlikely that the time will come — when it will be said once again: The Germans are doing this or that and flouting every international law.

Indeed, my dear friends, it is once again fashionable for the encircling powers, having failed to bring about what could have held such actions in check, to accuse those who are encircled of protecting themselves on all sides. We must come to see this clearly in all its enormity. Beside all that may very well have happened, for instance in Belgium, must be placed the fact that the British Empire could have prevented all that has happened in Belgium.

Harsh though it might sound, it has to be said that it is untruthful to speak about the atrocities in Belgium without taking into account how easily they could have been prevented by the English. And it goes without saying that we feel the tragic destiny of France. Yet France was truly in a position which could have enabled her not to participate in the war.

The Central Powers were not in a position to avoid waging a defensive war once it became obvious that France would take part in any case. It is all very well to say the two could have faced each other, frontier to frontier. This is the very thing that was not possible, because Franco-Russian militarism so greatly outweighs what is called Prussian militarism.

However strongly we feel we belong to one group or another, we can surely resolve to look at these things squarely — I say 'can', not 'must'. Then, when we work through this and make it a part of our lives, each in his own way will be able to do whatever he wants to do, in answer to the question: What can the individual do? Unless ever more and more people come to nurture the idea of making a united European stand against the belligerence of powers now at work invisibly, the collapse of European culture will indeed be inevitable. Even now a belligerent wave from the East is threatening to engulf us — from Japan, where a form of imperialism is in preparation which might turn out to be far mightier than any imperialism the world has so far known. The will to conquer is expressed in the cry of the new national anthem[17] which, reminiscent of the English hymn, 'Rule Britannia', now resounds in 'Rule Nippon'. To show you that the powers of Europe would have good reason not to mock the word 'peace', not to mock the content of the peace idea, let me read to you this hymn, now quoted in Japanese newspapers:

When Nippon, at the Lord's command,
Rose from the sea at dawn,
There sounded throughout all the world
A call from heaven's blue dome:
Born, Japan, are you to rule.
Rise proudly with the morning sun:
You I choose to rule the world.
Torn by hate and blinding rage
Europe drowns in her own blood,
But you, devoid of blame or fault,
Shall be the guardian of the earth.
Born, Japan, are you to rule.
Rise proudly with the morning sun:
You I choose to rule my world.

This is what is now booming across the world from the East. This is the Orient's answer to Europe, bathed in blood. Yet despite this, there are people in Europe who want to scorn the call for peace! This is a fact to which we cannot give too much thought.

LECTURE EIGHTEEN
Dornach, 13 January 1917

It seems to me today more then ever necessary that the members of
our Movement should be knowledgeable about what is going on in
the world. Indeed this purpose has been served to a greater or lesser
degree by the discussions we have been having here. To speak of
spiritual science in the way we understand it means to fill ourselves
with knowledge of how our world, which we observe with our physical
understanding and senses, is in fact a revelation of the spirit. As long
as the spiritual world is taken in the abstract, as long as the human
being is divided up into his constituent parts, as long as all kinds of
theories about karma and reincarnation are expounded — something
we have really never done here in such a theoretical way — spiritual
science cannot become fruitful for life. That is why I have been direct-
ing your attention in all kinds of ways to external reality, whereby
I never lost sight of all that stands behind this external reality, either
by way of direct occult factors, or by way of impulses being used
in one way or another by human beings.

Those who understand the true situation today to some extent will
find it becoming increasingly obvious in future, when looking back
at this time, that the old way of looking at history is no longer sufficient
for an understanding of the present. Circumstances will make certain
occult teachings necessary for the increasingly mature understanding
of human beings, and those who shut out such possibilities will in
future have to bear the mark of ignorance, of lack of understanding.

Since the nineteenth century it has been the custom to construct
history purely materialistically, on the basis — as people put it —
of the available documents. Today it is not yet realized that this does
not lead to a true depiction of historical impulses, but merely to a
description of materialistic spectres — paradoxical though this may
sound: a description of materialistic spectres. Even in the best history
books, the description of people and events of the past right up to
the present shows nothing but spectres without any real life, however
realistic it is meant to be. It can, indeed, only be a description of spectres because all reality is founded on spiritual impulses, and if these
are omitted, what remains are spectres. Thus up to today, the recoun-
ting of history has been spectral, yet in a certain way it has satisfied
human souls; it has worked in a certain way.

In many respects, today's great tragedy is the way in which karma is lived through in such untrue, spectral ideas which people have gradually amassed. But within our Movement, too, we must not allow the process of history to fall into two disconnected halves — though there are some among us who would like this: On the one hand to luxuriate in so-called supersensible ideas, which remain, however, more or less abstract concepts, and on the other hand to become firmly stuck in habitual opinions, no different from the ordinary vulgar understanding of external reality viewed entirely materialistically. These two aspects, external physical reality and spiritual existence, must unite, that is, we must understand that in place of traditional historical methods something must be developed which I have called symptomatic history, a history of symptoms which will teach us that the historical process expresses itself in some phenomena more strongly than in others.

Recently I have perhaps described things rather too realistically, though only for those whose feeling makes them ask: Why is he telling us things we anyway hear elsewhere? Look more closely, however, and you will find that you do not, actually, hear them elsewhere in the way they are described here. You do not find them juxtaposed as they are here, as symptoms in which various characteristic details unite to form a living concept of reality. The obvious question now is: How do symptoms such as the ones I have quoted come about? Let me go a little further into this.

During the course of these lectures I have mentioned a whole series of facts, some of which people might well consider excessively minute, such as that of the descendant of the Voidarevich family, the voivodes of Herzegovina, or that matter of the Russian-Slav Welfare Committee and so on. Such things could, in one way, be viewed as utterly insignificant. In another way, though, you could say: What is the connection between such things? What is this way of looking at history that collects widely different and separate details and then endeavours to fit them together in a total picture? A more direct way of asking me this question could be: How has it come about that as you have gone through life you have collected and know all about just these particular events, which have to be seen as characteristic of our time? I should like to answer this question in a way which I hope will give you a living idea of how spiritual science can intervene in life.

During the course of life one comes to know about certain things if one's karma leads to them, and if one's karma is allowed to take its course honestly and truthfully. Many people believe they are giving their karma a free reign, or are surrendering themselves to their karma, but this can be a great illusion. No one can follow external events in such a way that the truth is revealed to him, if he fails to surrender himself genuinely to his karma, if he fails to leave much in the subconscious realm, if he fails to let much pass unnoticed before his soul, for every morsel of sympathy or antipathy clouds free vision. Nothing is more likely to cloud free vision than what is today called the historical method. This historical method brings spectres into being because today's historian is unable to surrender himself to his karma. Obviously if he did so from his earliest years, he would fail every exam. He is not allowed to surrender himself to his karma and thus learn to know those things to which his karma leads him; he has to learn to know what the exam regulations and so forth require of him. But they require all kinds of things which of course tear his karma to shreds, and he can never arrive at the actual truth if he follows the stream of those requirements.

The actual truth can only be reached if these things about which spiritual science speaks are taken as seriously as life — if they are not taken as mere theories but as seriously as life. Another way of not taking them as seriously as life is to allow one's view to be clouded by all kinds of sympathies and antipathies. You have to approach things objectively, and then the stream of the world will bring you what you need in order to reach an understanding.

Now one aspect of surrendering to one's karma with regard to present events may be found in the fact that you, my dear friends, have been brought into the Anthroposophical Society by your karma. So it really should be possible in the Anthroposophical Society to speak about the facts without being hampered by sympathies and antipathies. If not, it would mean that, even within this Society, karma was not being taken as seriously as life.

I wanted to give you this introduction to what we still have to discuss because I wish to show you certain important spiritual facts which cannot, however, be understood unless we can link them to life, and unless we can penetrate the really tangled undergrowth of untruths which today buzz about in the world. The world today is filled with untruthfulness, and the sense for truth must be cultivated in the Anthroposophical Society for as long as it exists — and regardless of how long it is likely to exist under present circumstances — if it is to have a real meaning, a real sense for life.

I have — you could say — burdened you with a great variety of things recently, not simply to throw light on them in one way or another, but because I am filled with the conviction that it is important to correct certain concepts. Those who believe that I say these things from any kind of nationalistic feeling, simply do not understand me.

Terrible accusations are being continuously hurled at the centre from what is today the periphery, all of which end, in some form or other, in the phrase: Never mind, the German will be burnt. Of course, people are ashamed to quote this directly. Among these insults is the fact that in the widest circles certain personalities, whose works are of course not known or understood, are pilloried as being the despoilers, the corrupters of the German people. One of those brought to the forefront in this way is the German historian Heinrich Treitschke.

Now, as I have said, I should like to view such a personality not from a national, but from a purely human standpoint. I told you that I never had much to do with Treitschke but that I did meet him once. I said that he was a somewhat blustering character. Today let me add that at that meeting I did form a picture of his being and his character, for we covered much more than just those first few words which I have already quoted to you. We spoke about historical interpretation, about publications on history which were causing rather a sensation then, in the nineties, and there was time — banquets usually last for several hours — to go into many questions of principle with regard to scientific history. I was well able to form a picture of this man at the end of his life — he died soon afterwards — quite apart from the fact that his work as a historian is very well known to me.

The main thing I want to say is that Treitschke is a personality who gives us cause to approach him to some extent from an occult standpoint. Socrates spoke, in a good sense, of a kind of *daimon*. In the case of Treitschke you could say that he was indwelt by a form of *daimon*; not an evil demon, a kind of *daimon*. You could sense that he was not merely driven by considerations of the materialistic intellect but that his driving force came from within, from what Socrates called the daimonic forces. I could even say that this is what led him throughout the course of his life. This man from Saxony was an enthusiastic champion of the nascent German state; for he worked in a most significant way even before this state was founded. His *German History*,[1] though, was written after its founding. In a manner characteristic of Central Europe, there lived in him something that is not known in the periphery, not only not wanted but also not known, something which people do not wish to understand. This was a sense for reality, for what is concrete. There lived in him a certain aversion to abstract theories and to everything expressed in empty phrases. This aversion was present with daimonic force to such an extent that you could look, you might say, through the personality to the spiritual forces speaking out of it.

In addition to this, Treitschke went profoundly deaf very early in life, so that he heard neither his own voice nor that of others, but associated only with his own inner being. Such a destiny turns a person in upon himself. The complete absence of a sense of hearing, far more than the absence of one of the other senses, brings a person who is so inclined into contact with occult powers which are at work and which usually remain unnoticed because people are distracted by their sense-perceptions from what speaks to them over and above their senses. So there is definitely a significance in a karma which makes a person totally deaf early on in life, and it is connected in this case with what I have called a daimonic nature.

This nature, this human being, in contrast to many — indeed most — people today, was formed and shaped as a whole. His intellect never worked in isolation; his whole soul was always involved. There are plenty of plain truths in the world, truths which can easily be confirmed by 'logical proof'. But special note should be taken, whether one agrees with them or not, of truths with which human blood accords, truths filled with warm human feeling. For the human being is the channel linking the physical world with the spiritual world, and we approach the spiritual world not only by studying the theories of spiritual science, but also by acquiring a sense of how each individual represents a channel between the physical world and the spiritual world.

Above all else, Heinrich Treitschke was a personality who strove to form his knowledge and his thoughts on the basis of a broad understanding, an understanding always founded on judgements of the soul and not of the intellect. His judgements were always warm because they were formed by the critical faculty of his soul. They may have had a blustery quality, but they were always warm through having been formed by his critical faculty of soul. From this angle Treitschke always placed at the centre of his considerations the question of human freedom, which — since he was a historian and prepared himself early on to become the historian of his people — for him was always linked with the question of political freedom, freedom from the state.

There is among German literature a work which deeply penetrates the question of the relationship between the overall power of the state and the freedom of the individual, not only the freedom living in the individual soul, but freedom as it can be realized in social life. I know of no other work in world literature which penetrates so deeply into this question. It is entitled *The Sphere and Duties of Government* and is by Wilhelm von Humboldt,[2] the friend of Schiller and brother of the writer Alexander von Humboldt. This work, written at the turn of the eighteenth to the nineteenth century, defends most beautifully the human personality in its full, free unfolding, against every aspect of state omnipotence. It is said that the state may only intervene in the realm of the human individual to the extent that such intervention leads to the removal of obstacles standing in the way of the personality's free unfolding.

This work stems from the same source as Schiller's wonderful *Letters on the Aesthetic Education of Man*.[3] I could say that Wilhelm von Humboldt's work on the limitations of the state is the brother of Schiller's *Letters on the Aesthetic Education of Man*. It stems from an age when people were endeavouring to assemble every thought from cultural life capable of placing the human being firmly on the soil of freedom. For various reasons it was not much used during the nineteenth century, yet it was often enough consulted by those who, during the course of the nineteenth century, were endeavouring to reach an understanding of the more external aspects of the concept of freedom. Of course the nineteenth century was in one way the time when in many respects the concept of freedom was laid in its grave. But people were still keen to come to an understanding of the concept of freedom, and in this connection Wilhelm von Humboldt's work *The Sphere and Duties of Government* gained a degree of international importance in Europe.

Both the Frenchman Laboulaye[4] and the Englishman John Stuart Mill[5] took it as their point of departure. This work was an important point of departure for both these thinkers. Both, in their turn, and each in his own field, endeavoured to come to grips with the concept of freedom. Laboulaye considered that the institutions of his country, in so far as they concerned the relationship between state and individual, were suited only to the smothering of any true freedom, any free unfolding of the personality, by the state. John Stuart Mill, once he had discovered Wilhelm von Humboldt's work, took his departure from it and argued forcefully, in his own work on freedom, that English society could only undermine a true experience of freedom. With Laboulaye it is the state, with John Stuart Mill society. John Stuart Mill's work poses the question: How can an unfolding of the personality be achieved in the atmosphere of unfreedom generated by society?

Then Treitschke, with the critical faculty of soul I mentioned just now, and linking his work to that of Laboulaye and Mill, himself wrote about freedom[6] at the beginning of the eighteen-sixties. Treitschke's paper on freedom is of particular and special interest because as a historian and as a politician he is immersed in that schism which invades the human soul when, on the one hand it recognizes the necessity of a social structure called the state and, on the other, is filled with enthusiasm for what we call human freedom. In this way, in the sixties of the nineteenth century, Treitschke set himself to discuss the concept of freedom on the basis of Laboulaye and John Stuart Mill.

In this paper *Freedom* he endeavoured to work out a concept of the state which, on the one hand, does not deny the necessity of a state structure, yet, on the other hand, does make of the state something that is not the gravedigger of freedom, but its cultivator and guardian. A state structure that could achieve this was what he had in mind. This was the time, remember, when a German, asked to name his fatherland, might easily have replied: Schwarzburg-Sondershausen, or Reuss-Schleiz,[7] or something similar. At the beginning of the sixties what we now call the German Reich did not yet exist. At a time when a great many people were thinking about bringing together in some way all the individual groups in which Germans lived, Treitschke, too, was thinking about the necessity of a state structure. But for him it was axiomatic that no state should be allowed to come about which did not guarantee, to the human personality, conditions in which it could unfold as freely as possible. Even if it cannot be maintained that Treitschke achieved any rounded-off philosophical concepts, nevertheless his paper on freedom does contain many points worth considering very deeply.

In appreciating Treitschke and taking into account those aspects which are important for an occult understanding of him, we must not forget that he was a fearless person willing to serve no god other than truth. Many things that are said today without any objectivity about Treitschke are the height of stupidity. Such judgements buzzing about in the world today cannot be given even the flimsiest of foundations, for the simple reason that something is missing. I mentioned it the other day when I said that if people were willing to investigate what spiritual science has to say about the differences between the folk spirits, then fewer stupid statements would be made. I said this apropos of various stupid remarks made both by and about Romain Rolland.[8] I had to say it because a really penetrating view of what is called a folk spirit can only be undertaken through spiritual science. Those who do not want to become involved in this can only reach subjective and therefore stupid judgements such as those of Romain Rolland.

Those who are willing to take into account what arises out of a spiritual scientific view of the folk spirits must be clear above all about one thing: that a person who is typical of his people will bear certain traits characteristic of that people. What made Treitschke typical was his daimonic nature. And it is true to say that to understand Treitschke is to understand much — not all, but much — of what was characteristic of the German people in the second half of the nineteenth century. Those for whom it is possible to gain a point of view from spiritual knowledge must investigate — not through cosmopolitan, but through national individuals — the fundamental difference that exists between western European and Central European judgements.

This cannot be taken into account for matters which are general and human, but they are relevant in so far as the daimon of a people lives in the folk spirit. With this reservation I shall say what I now have to bring forward. When the characteristics of a people are seen working through individuals it is possible to say what a certain American said. It is better if I tell you what this American said, because if I use my own words they might be taken amiss. He said: A French judgement, if it comes out of the nature of the people — not an individual, whose judgement might indeed be cosmopolitan — a judgement that comes out of the very substance of the French people lives in the word; an English judgement lives in practical political concepts; and a German judgement lives in an a-national, a non-national, search for knowledge.

This was said by an American travelling in Europe. It means that certain judgements formed in the West turn into something different when they are taken into the substance of the German people. In the West they are abstract in character. But a German belonging to the German people tends to translate judgements into their concrete components. He thus calls many things by their true name which are never touched upon by their true name in the West. Let us take a concept we have been discussing: the concept of the state.

In his lectures on politics,[9] which were later published, Treitschke spoke about the state. Of course very many people speak about the state; but let us for the moment consider only what it means when someone speaks about the state by drawing on the very substance of the people to whom he belongs. In the West people tend to speak about it by using the state as a hook from which to suspend all sorts of concepts which, for one reason or another, they want to link with the concept of the state. Thus they attach to it such concepts as freedom, justice and many others, and they might even come up with the peculiar statement: The state must be divested of any concepts to do with power; the state must be a *Rechtsstaat*, a state subject to the law. You can say this only so long as you are not obliged to look squarely at the concept of the state.

But if you approach the concept of the state in the way Treitschke did, you discover the mystery of the state. Instead of demanding that the state must be based on the principle that power is above the law — an assertion slanderously attributed to Treitschke — you come to realize that the concept of the state is unthinkable without the concept of power. Power is simply a truth in this situation because it is impossible to found a state except by basing it on power. If you refuse to admit this, you are quite simply not representing the truth. So Treitschke could not avoid speaking about the state in connection with power. This is then distorted by those who claim Treitschke to mean that in the German concept of the state, power is above the law. Yet there is no question that Treitschke ever thought like this. His soul was far too strongly imbued with the meaning of what Humboldt said in his *Sphere and Duties of Government*. Just because the state cannot avoid unfolding a certain power, it must not be allowed to become omnipotent. A *Rechtsstaat*, a state subject to the law, is a contradiction in terms, like saying — perhaps not iron made of wood, but certainly iron made of copper. The two concepts are disparate, to use a term from the sphere of logic; they have nothing to do with one another. But this conclusion can only be reached by one who takes things really seriously.

From the same viewpoint Nietzsche arrived at his concept of 'the will to power'. Again, it is nothing but a monstrous defamation to impute that Nietzsche defended the 'principle of power'. The only thing he defended was the need to consider how far power is indeed one of the basic drives of human beings. It is quite in character that Nietzsche should postulate the following. He says: There are people who from certain principles of asceticism defend the thesis that power should be opposed. Why do they do this? Because by their very nature they can achieve quite a degree of power by means of opposing power! To oppose power is their particular will to power! To stress powerlessness is merely their particular will to power! To stress powerlessness in an ascetic way gives them in their own way a particular power! What lay at the foundation of what Nietzsche said, and also what pervades Treitschke's considerations is: not to try and convince oneself that black is white; to see things as they are in very truth and not to turn out empty phrases.

So you see, neither Treitschke nor Nietzsche intended to introduce into social life any kind of principle of power. Their concern was simply to show that power lives wherever the state manifests, and that it would be untruthful to maintain anything different. One could say that the karma under which Treitschke worked was: to come upon the idea that it is a monstrosity to live with the illusion of abstract, empty concepts which one trumpets forth into the world. He wanted to take a straightforward hold on reality and this is what is so attractive about his writings. From the same standpoint he could say of the concept of freedom: The question as to whether the state exists in order to promote, or not to promote, freedom, is no question at all. In other words, his object was to seek things where they live in their reality. I do not want to defend this, but simply to describe it.

Surely a fearless human being who only wanted to state things as he saw them with his sense for truth cannot be weeded out by means of inciting opinion against him. And yet everywhere these days people are weeded out by means of incitements against them. Treitschke is a fearless spirit whose aim, no matter what he is discussing, is truly never to mince his words. It would be far more to the point — I really must repeat this again — to indicate how Treitschke was in reality a kind of teacher for those who wanted to listen to him. There were not nearly as many who listened as is claimed nowadays. When Treitschke speaks about freedom he does this far less as a critic of other nations than as an educator of his own. I should now like to read you a passage from his article *Freedom*, which ought to be at least as well known as so much that is quoted out of context and which cannot possibly be understood without proper context. Having first discussed what aspects of society promote freedom, Treitschke writes:

'It is still most timely' — he is speaking in the eighteen-sixties — 'to speak of class prejudices. How truly discouraging to discover that this great civilized nation' — he means the Germans — 'continues to acknowledge the legal concept of misalliance in marriage, a concept thrown overboard by the ancients at the beginning of their rise to civilization. We do not, of course, refer to that crude titled gentry who hold a career in the stable to be more respectable than a scientific calling, and the rule of the fist more noble than the free citizen's respect for the law. That caricature of aristocracy has had its come-uppance. But even the motley crowd of the so-called educated, well-to-do classes cherishes a multitude of unfree, intolerant class conceptions. How hard are the loveless judgements passed on the shamefully misnamed dangerous classes! How heartless the deprecation of "luxury" for the lower orders, when a free and noble individual ought to be overjoyed to see the poor beginning to take some pride in themselves and the decency of their appearance! What abject fear at every sign of defiance and of self-respect among the lower classes! German goodness of heart has perhaps preserved our educated classes from developing this attitude in a form as crude as that held among blunter Britons; but so long as aristocratic interests, of which the cleverer among us have never been entirely free, take these forms, there is not much hope for our inner freedom.

We enter a field in which unfreedom and intolerance flourish in abundance when we enquire after the class concepts of that most mighty and exclusive of all "classes" — or whatever else you would like to call this natural aristocracy — the male sex. Unbelievably widespread amongst us, lords of creation, are the ramifications of a silent consipiracy, thoroughly to defraud women of a portion of harmonious human culture. For women gain a part of their culture only through us. Yet we take it for granted amongst ourselves that religious enlightenment is a duty of the educated man but a bringer of corruption to the populace and to women. Indeed, how many of us find a woman most particularly winsome the moment she displays some glaring superstition. And as for "politically-minded females", they are an abomination we prefer not to mention. Is this indeed our manly faith in the divine nature of freedom? Is religious enlightenment really only a matter of sober understanding and not to a far greater degree a need of the soul? Yet we imagine a woman's warmth of heart might suffer if we let her take her own delight in the great spiritual works of the last hundred years. Do we truly understand German women so little as to imagine that they could ever become "political" and start to worry their heads over ground rents and commercial agreements? Yet the political poverty of our people has to it a human side which might be more deeply, more delicately, more intimately understood by women than by ourselves. Of this abundance of enthusiasm and love, which we so often confront with coldness, inner poverty and heartlessness, could not a small fraction be reserved for our fatherland? Must the shame of the French occupation return once more if our women are to feel themselves, as do their neighbours in East and West, daughters of a great nation? With our unfree lack of magnanimity we have maintained silence towards them for far too long about what stirs in our breast; we felt that they were great enough to be told no more than the most trifling of trifles; and because we were too small-minded not to begrudge them the freedom of culture and education, there is now only a minority of German women capable of understanding the earnest gravity of this momentous era.'

You see how it is possible to quote from Treitschke passages which refer to matters of general humanity, even though on his part he wrote them out of a national spirit for his own nation. If any of the nations who today abuse Treitschke had among them a spirit who meant to them what he means to Germans, you would see that they would place him on the highest pedestal. Imagine an Italian Treitschke. What would the Italians say if the Germans were to speak of their Italian Treitschke in the way they and many others speak of the German Treitschke. The infinite tragedy of our age is that it is stamped with ignorance and with all that counts on ignorance. It would be utterly impossible for such untruths to buzz about in the world today if it were not at every moment feasible to count on people's ignorance. By ignorance I do not, of course, mean the fact that not everybody has time to inform himself about everything. What I do mean is that a little self-knowledge is what is needed.

Of course certain situations cannot be judged if certain things are not known, and judgements born of ignorance, made about whole nations, work in the most terrible way. Today so very much is born out of ignorance. This is, as a matter of fact, caused by that black magic — I have described it like this on other occasions too — known today as journalism. It is a kind of black magic, and there was a certain truth in the way folk legend felt the inventors of the art of printing — with all the perspectives this opens up — to be black magicians.

You might now exclaim: As if there were not enough follies and oddities in anthroposophical spiritual science — now the art of printing is described as black magic! But I did only say 'a kind' of black magic. I have often stressed that it is wrong always to say: I must not let Ahriman anywhere near me; away with him! I must not let Lucifer anywhere near me; I only want to have dealings with the good gods! If this is what you want, you can have no dealings with the world, for whether you like it or not, the world hangs in the balance between Ahriman and Lucifer. It is impossible to have dealings with the world if you have this attitude of mind, an attitude which appears particularly frequently in our circles. One must achieve truthfulness even in the smallest matters. This must be the practical outcome of our efforts in spiritual science — the practical outcome. You can feel this in yourselves: If you cannot develop the urge for truthfulness in yourselves, you will always be open to the danger of being infected, influenced, by the untruthfulness that lives in the world.

That is why I said the other day: In future all the efforts that have been made towards peace will be forgotten, and in the periphery the only thing to be remembered will be the shouting-down of peace; but it will not be remembered as a shouting-down but as something that was justified; everything else will be forgotten. This is sure to be what will happen. So at least our discussions here should be a contribution to making it possible to sense the truth of the situation. For today one of the foremost demands made of those who are truly concerned with the welfare of mankind and the progress of mankind is that they should not allow themselves to be taken in by untruthfulness.

Let us look at one of the facts of today totally *sine ira* but not *sine studio*; without sympathy and antipathy but with a basis of facts. You have, I am sure, all read the note from the Entente to President Wilson.[10] From a certain standpoint this note, in contrast to all the earlier ones, could be regarded as a favourable symptom for the future. For if things are taken too far, if the bowstring threatens to snap, then there is once again hope, the hope that if spiritual powers are challenged, then the blow will also be returned by the spiritual side. This note certainly outdid all the earlier ones.

Let us now look at the facts. Here, roughly, is Austria-Hungary as it is today. [The lecturer drew.] Here is the Danube and this is where Vienna would be. Now assume that the demands of the note from the Entente are met. It says that the Italians — that is the Austrian Italians — want to be liberated. The worst thing about this note from the Entente is that it suffers from that inner untruthfulness which arises out of total ignorance. That is why it is difficult to make the drawing I now want to make. There will be difficulties, as you will see. Assume that the Italian Austrians are liberated. Now the southern Slavs are also to be liberated. This is rather difficult. If the southern Slavs were liberated, the map would look like this, for they live everywhere over here.

Further it is said, funnily enough: The Czecho-Slovaks are to be liberated. We know the Czechs and also the Slovaks. It goes without saying that only the Entente has heard of Czecho-Slovaks. Let us presume that it is the Czechs and the Slovaks who are meant. If we go by what the Czechs themselves think, the result would be like this. Then on to the liberation of the Romanians. This is what it would look like. Also to be liberated, as the note says '. . . in accordance with the will of His Majesty the Tsar', are the Poles inhabiting Galicia, but this is to be done by Austria herself. In the end, Hungary would look something like this, and Austria something like this.

This map is the result of carrying out what is said about Austria in the note from the Entente. And at the same time it is said that there is no intention of doing anything to the peoples of Central Europe!

The whole note demonstrates, for instance, a total lack of awareness of the difficulties of managing all this *here*, where the Slavs are in the majority, compared with *there*, where they are a tiny minority. The whole note lays bare the most arrogant, unscrupulous ignorance of the situation! With this ignorance, historical notes are written. And to add insult to injury it is further said that the only intention is . . . I really don't know, for it is almost too repulsive to repeat these empty phrases.

What could be better proof than this note from the Entente of the fact that Austria was forced to defend herself? What could give better proof? In short, this note can only be seen as something pathological. It is a challenge to truth and reality. It is taking things too far. So let us hope, since it is a challenge to the spiritual world, that this spiritual world will find it necessary to put things right, even though, of course, human beings will have to be the tools with which the spiritual world will work.

It really is time for an illustration such as the one I have sketched here to be shown all over the world in order to demonstrate this utter historical ignorance and lack of understanding about Central Europe. Obviously, where power rules, reason cannot have much effect. But a start must be made by understanding that, when rights and freedoms are mentioned, power is meant, actual power. Things must be called by their true names. This is what our time is suffering from: That people cannot bring themselves to call things by their right names, that people cannot make the resolve to call things by their right names. Many people fail to understand a great deal. When you come up against something like this absolutely idiotic division of the Austrian nations, it becomes perfectly obvious that this note stems from people who know nothing of what exists in Central Europe, yet who possess the arrogance to judge things about which they know nothing and who want nothing other than to extend their power over these territories. They could not care less what the real situation is.

But you do have to ask how such things could come about in the first place. For instance in some versions it says: Liberation of the Slavs, the Czechs and the Slovaks. But the Swiss newspapers, whose translation is probably more accurate, speak about Czecho-Slovaks. You will agree, if someone makes a correct statement, you are not curious about the source of his information; but when someone speaks absolute balderdash, such as the description of the nations in the note from the Entente, you do begin to wonder about its source. It is indeed not uninteresting to take note when situations seem to run, in a way, parallel, though of course without basing any hypothesis on this, or drawing any conclusions. I naturally asked myself: What is the source of these nonsensical terms? I repeat: Without forming any kind of hypothesis or conclusions, let me give you an *aperçu*.

In the last few days — I am not judging the fact, but simply telling you this — a sentence passed in Austria on the Czech leader, Kramar,[11] has been made public. He was for a long time one of the most influential people in Austria. He was sentenced to death, and this sentence was then commuted to fifteen years hard labour. The wording of the sentence also includes the statement that certain articles that had appeared in *The Times* — in English, of course — had been found in the possession of Kramar in his own language. Now Dr Kramar has a friend, the university professor Masaryk,[12] who has fled from Austria and now lives in London and Paris. So let us consider certain sentences from Kramar's programme which were the basis on which he was sentenced. If you understand nothing about the situation in Austria and you read these sentences in *The Times*, or wherever else — they also appeared in Paris in *Revue tchèque* — and play about a little with the wording, not forgetting that Kramar of course uses the proper terms, you arrive, curiously enough, at the sentences about the peoples of Austria as they appear in the note from the Entente. And if the term 'Czecho-Slovaks' is indeed used, you gain the strange impression that Kramar was hoping to found a state consisting of Czechs and Slovaks, which would be meaningful. But those in western Europe who know nothing about the actual situation would make of this: 'Czecho-Slovaks'.[13]

It is indeed necessary today, when so many underground channels play their part, to clarify certain questions about interconnections. I do not want to build any hypotheses, nor draw any conclusions in connection with what I have said, but the fact remains that a curious conformity exists between the sentence that was passed and the text of the note from the Entente. Obviously you can have different opinions about this sentence, depending on your point of view. Kramar could be seen either as a martyr or a criminal. But I do not want to pass judgement. The important thing is to be in a position to observe this curious conformity. As I said, I simply noticed this when I was puzzling about the origin, apart from everything else, of the stupendous ignorance on which the note is based.

We must certainly speak about this stupendous ignorance. For it is significant, and is one of the characteristics of our time, that on a basis of this kind of reality an opinion is expressed by those who dominate one half of the habitable earth. It is a challenge indeed to the spirit of truth.

[The next few sentences in this lecture refer to a quotation from an 'article' dated 25 July 1914 mentioning Rasputin, which the stenographer unfortunately did not record. Since they are meaningless without the quotation, they have been omitted. Ed.]

It will always be possible, if one has the power, to give the facts an impudent slap in the face — and the periphery does have this power. But you cannot slap truth in the face. Truth speaks and will — let us hope — also be an impulse which, when things are at their worst, can lead mankind to some kind of salvation.

We shall continue tomorrow.[14]

LECTURE NINETEEN
Dornach, 14 January 1917

The nature of man is complicated, and very much of what actually goes on within the human being remains more or less beneath the threshold of consciousness, merely sending its effects up into consciousness. True self-knowledge cannot be won without first obtaining insight into the working of the sub-consciousness weaving below the surface in the impulses of soul. These, it could be said, move in the depths of the ocean of consciousness and come to the surface only in the wake of the waves they create. Ordinary consciousness can perceive only the waves that rise to the surface, and on the whole one is not capable of understanding their significance, so true self-knowledge is not possible. Merely pondering on what is washed up into consciousness does not lead to self-knowledge; for things in the depths of the soul often differ greatly from what they become in ordinary, everyday consciousness. Today we shall look a little into this nature of man in order to gain, from this point of view, an idea of how the subconscious soul-impulses in the human being really work.

In this field we can, of course, to a greater or lesser extent, speak only in pictures. But if you bring together much of what we have hitherto discussed within our Anthroposophical Movement, you will be able to understand the realities that want to speak through the pictures. We can say: The invisible nature of man, his ego, his astral body, his etheric body, work through his visible nature, so what is not manifest works through what is manifest. However, the manner in which what is evident works through what is not evident is very complicated. But if we work our way bit by bit through the various parts of this complicated process, and place them all together, we shall, in the end, attain an overall view of the being of man. Even this, though, will always remain incomplete, for the being of man is infinitely complex. But at least we can gain a certain basic knowledge of human nature as a valid foundation for self-knowledge.

Today we shall examine how the separate components of man's nature express themselves in a more or less pictorial or formalized manner through physical life. Here is a human being. To illustrate what I want to tell you, I shall start with what we recognize for earthly man as the aspect of which we are conscious: the ego. I must emphasize that pictorial explanations can very easily lead to misunderstandings, because things said earlier seem to contradict other things said later. Follow carefully, and you will soon notice that such contradictions are, in fact, non-existent.

So let us start with the ego-nature of man, with that component we call our ego. This ego-nature is, of course, entirely supersensible; it is the most supersensible part we have as yet acquired, but it works through the physical. In the intellectualistic sense the ego works in our physical being chiefly through the nervous system which is called the system of ganglia,[1] the nervous system radiating from the solar plexus. Diagrammatically we can indicate this nervous system, this system of ganglia, this system of the solar plexus, thus (see diagram, dark shading). It is active in a way which, at first glance, does not appear to have much to do with what, in a materialistic sense, we could call the life of the nerves. Yet it is the actual point of contact for real ego-activity. This is not a contradiction of the fact that when we begin to see ourselves spiritually, we have to seek the centre of the ego in the head. Since the ego-component of the human being is supersensible, the point at which we experience our ego is not the same as the point at which it chiefly works in us.

We must be quite clear what we mean when we say: The ego works through the point of contact of the solar plexus. What it means is this: The ego itself is equipped with only a very dull consciousness. The ego-thought is not the same as the ego. The ego-thought is what is washed up into consciousness, but the ego-thought is not the real ego. The real ego intervenes as a formative force in the whole human organism through the solar plexus.

Certainly you can say that the ego distributes itself over the whole body. But its main point of contact, where it particularly intervenes in the formative element of the human organism, is the solar plexus. A better expression would be the system of ganglia, because all the ramifications are part of this process — the system of ganglia. It is a process that lives in the subconscious and works in this system of ganglia. Since the system of ganglia plays its part in the circulation of blood as well, this does not contradict the fact that the ego expresses itself in the blood. The exact meaning of everything that is said must be considered. It is one thing to say: The ego intervenes through the system of ganglia in the formative forces and in all the life processes of the organism. But something else is meant when we say: The blood with its circulation is an expression of the ego in the human being. The nature of the human being is, as I said, complicated.

To understand the significance of what has been said, it will be useful to answer the following question: What is the relationship of the ego with the system of ganglia and all that is connected with it? How is this ego anchored, as it were, in the abdominal organs of the human being?

When the human being is in a normal state of health, the ego is chained to the solar plexus and all that is connected with it. It is bound by the solar plexus. What does this mean? This human ego, given to man during the course of earthly evolution as a gift from the Spirits of Form, has been, as we know, subjected to the temptation of Lucifer. The ego, as it now exists in man, and because it has been infected by luciferic forces, would be a bearer of evil forces. The truth of this fact must definitely be recognized. The ego is not a bearer of evil forces because of its own nature, but because it has become infected with luciferic forces through the temptation by Lucifer; it is in fact the bearer of truly evil forces, forces which, because of the luciferic infection, tend to distort the thought life of the ego towards evil. Since the moment when the ego was given to him, man has been able to think. If there had been no luciferic temptation, man would think only good thoughts about everything. But as the luciferic temptation did, in fact, take place, the ego does not think good thoughts, but thoughts infected by Lucifer. This is a fact of earthly evolution: the ego is malicious and dastardly. It thinks only of showing itself in a good light and consigning everything else to the shadow. It is infected with all kinds of egoisms. This is how it is, because it is infected by Lucifer.

Now the system of ganglia, the solar plexus, is something in man that has come over from the Moon incarnation of the earth. It is a kind of house for the ego; the ego fits into it in a certain way. In fact, it can be held a prisoner there. So we have the following state of affairs: Because of its luciferic infection, the ego tends all the time to behave in a dastardly, lying manner and place itself in the light, while consigning everything else to the shade. But it is held prisoner by the nervous system of the abdomen. There it has to behave itself. By means of the nervous system of the abdomen the properly progressing forces, which have come to us from ancient Saturn, Sun and Moon, compel the ego not to be a demon in the bad sense of the word. So the manner in which we bear our ego within us is to have it bound by the organs of the abdomen.

Assume now that these abdominal organs are unhealthy in some way, or not in a normal state. Not to be in a normal state means not to want to take in fully what fits into them spiritually, what spiritually belongs to them. The ego can be somewhat freer in its activity if the abdominal organs are not quite healthy. If this freeing is brought about by some physical hyperactivity, this can express itself in the human being in that the ego is let loose on the external world, instead of remaining bound. When the ego behaves freely in this way, we have a case of psychological illness: the human being displays the characteristics of the ego infected by Lucifer. The characteristics of the ego of which I have spoken then make their appearance. There is certainly no need to be a materialist in order to understand fully the manner in which the spiritual — in this case the ego — can be bound to physical organs in life between birth and death, though in a way that differs from what is perceived by a materialist. There is no need to be a materialist to see how, in a manner of speaking, the devil can throw off his chains and break loose. This is one instance of psychological illness.

The freeing of the ego, however, is not necessarily a question of psychological illness, because another state of affairs is also possible. In such an instance it is not a question of illness in the abdomen but rather a 'switching off' of its normal activity. This is what happens in the great majority of cases of hypnotic consciousness. The functioning of the system of ganglia in the abdomen is put into a state — either by natural causes or by all kinds of mesmeric effects — in which it is unable properly to keep the ego under control. Thus in this way, too, the ego has an opportunity to become more involved with its environment. It is not embedded in the system of ganglia and is therefore free to make use of channels to the outside world which enable it to perceive from a distance all kinds of processes in space and time which, when it is embedded in the system of ganglia, are processes which it cannot normally perceive.

So it is important to know that a certain relationship exists between the hypnotized state, which in a mild way switches off the normal activity of the processes bound to the system of ganglia in ordinary consciousness, and certain forms of madness, where the switching-off is caused by deformation or illness in certain abdominal organs. If the ego is freed, if it feels, you might say, free of its chains and is linked, not with its body but with the spiritual forces in its environment, this is always, in a way, a pathological state, just as is also the case in madness. That is why some forms of madness are characterized by the appearance of spite, mendacity, cunning and craftiness — everything that comes from luciferic infection; the urge to place oneself in the light and consign others to the shadow, and so on.

Now you will understand why a person's constitution of soul depends on the very way the shell which binds his ego is fashioned. In order not to focus too closely on the human being and perhaps offend some human souls, let us instead look for a moment at a lion, a savage carnivore, and how it compares with a bull or an ox. You can see the difference. Even though the lion has a group ego while the human being is endowed with an individual ego, we can still use this comparison. What is the difference between the lion's nature and the ox's nature? The lion is definitely a carnivore while the ox is for the most part a vegetarian. The difference is this: What in the lion corresponds to his group ego is less bound; the forceful activity suitable for his abdominal organs makes the ego freer, lets it loose more on its environment, whereas in the vegetarian ox the group ego is more bound to the abdominal organs. The ox lives more bound up in itself.

You can see why it can be good sense for human beings to become vegetarian — of course, only if they so wish. For what does a vegetarian diet bring about? It makes the abdominal organs even more capable of binding the ego, which, if this does not sound like a paradox, leads to the human being becoming more gentle. His evil demon is more internalized and lives less in the environment. Nobody, however, should persuade himself that he does not possess this demon, for he does, but it is more imprisoned within him. It would be easy to set up an experiment to compare the behaviour of hungry carnivores and hungry vegetarians. When hungry, one is apt to be less inhibited. So it would be likely that the hungry vegetarians, who are in the habit of containing themselves as a result of their vegetarian diet, would be the more savage. For hunger brings about changes in the functions of the abdominal organs, which are then less able to fetter the ego than they are when satiated. I do not mean to be absolute in what I say, because the carnivore in any case binds the ego less strongly than the vegetarian. But I said that, in comparison, the hungry vegetarian, in contrast to his state when satiated, is likely to be far more savage than the hungry carnivore, in contrast to his state when satiated.

Human nature is indeed exceedingly complicated. One very good way of attaining some knowledge as a basis for true, genuine self-knowledge in life is to pay attention to the connection between the spiritual and bodily parts. I should add, though, that vegetarians should take care not allow themselves to become too undernourished. If they are undernourished they are in danger of damaging themselves, and then their chains — the prison for their devil, who shows himself in wiliness, lies and so on — are weakened. They then let their devil out into the environment, and the environment is troubled by their problems. Either that, or else they themselves have the trouble. They fail to cope with themselves, for they either constantly have a mania for manifesting the various bad qualities of the ego, or — if they are well brought-up — they have the urge to keep all this to themselves, in which case, too, it can happen that they fail to cope with themselves. All kinds of dissatisfactions arise in their soul. It is important to see this.

Just as the ego has its point of contact in the system of ganglia, so does the astral body have its point of contact in all those processes which are linked with the nervous system of the spinal cord. Naturally, the nerves run through the whole body; but in the nervous system of the spinal cord we have a second point of contact. Included in this, of course, are once again all the processes connected with this spinal nervous system. I am not speaking of the cerebral nervous system. I mean the nervous system of the spinal cord which has to do, for instance, with our reflex actions and is a regulator for much that goes on in the human body. In the present context we must include all the processes regulated by this nervous system. Again we have to see that the astral body is either bound to everything connected with this spinal system or that it can become free of it, through illness or through partial somnolence brought about by mesmerism or something similar.

The entity which is bound here received its luciferic attributes, which are mingled a little with ahrimanic attributes, as long ago as the time of ancient Moon. Therefore these are weaker than the luciferic attributes of the ego, but they are present in the astral body, too. If you want to turn your soul to a contemplation of the process by which this luciferic infection crept into the astral body, you will have to study what I said in my book *Occult Science*[2] about the separation of the moon from evolution as a whole. This infection made its appearance during the time of ancient Moon. Here you will discover another reason for certain characteristics in the human being, characteristics of a hypnotic nature — higher hypnotic characteristics which are bound, in the main, to the organs of the chest and which bring in higher experiences than do the organs of the abdomen. At the same time you will see that if something is not in order, so that the astral body cannot be bound as it should be, something can again come about which is a psychological illness, a psychological disorder. Just as the ego can be released, causing signs of madness, so also can the astral body be released, which again leads to signs of madness.

When the ego is released, this leads, as I have said, to characteristics such as spite, cunning, wiliness, fraudulence, giving prominence to oneself and putting everyone else in the shade, and so on. When the astral body is released, this leads to volatility of ideas and lack of cohesive thought, manic states on the one hand or, on the other, to withdrawal, depression, hypochondria. Again, these conditions could be brought about by hypnotic or mesmeric intervention; but in this case the organs are not ill, but have had their normal physical function suppressed by the intervention of a hypnotist or mesmerist.

There is much in our human nature which must be held in check, for in a way we do belong to the devil. We are at least partially decent human beings solely because the devils in us are held in check by the divine spiritual forces which have developed in the proper way through the periods of ancient Saturn, Sun and Moon. Because of the various temptations, we do not possess all-that-great an aptitude for decency. A good many bad dispositions and moods of soul life are the result of meeting with the demon in us. The appearance of the demonic element comes about because what is bound can become unbound.

We shall speak on another occasion about what it is in the life between death and a new birth that binds those aspects that are bound by our physical body now, during life between birth and death. You will agree that we owe a great debt of gratitude to the cosmic order that here, between birth and death, we possess our physical organism, for without it we would have no prison for our higher components. When these higher components are set free, after we have laid aside our physical body, different conditions come into operation, which we will discuss another time. Suffice it to say that the higher components still retain some fetters, even then.

Now, just as the astral body is bound in this way by the system of the spinal cord and all the processes of organic life connected with it, so is the etheric body bound by the cerebral system and everything that belongs to it. Therefore, the etheric body has its point of contact by means of the cerebral system. Similar things could be said here, too. In our

head there is a prison for our etheric body. Madness or hypnotic conditions come into operation if the body is not quite well and the etheric
body is let loose. Left to itself, i.e., not enclosed in the prison of
the head, the etheric body has the tendency to reproduce itself, thus
becoming a stranger to itself and spilling over into the world, carrying
its life into other things. This is a description of the conditions that
come about if the prison warder releases the etheric body.

So we have three possibilities for psychological illness, and also
three possibilities of escaping from the physical body. These three
possibilities must definitely be taken into consideration — but of course
in quite a different way — when a person is to become free of his
physical body through Initiation. What we have been speaking about
is a freeing brought about by illness, when the organs of the physical
body do not remain healthy and are then incapable of containing the
higher components. Somnolence of the brain would result if brain
activity were damped down. The etheric body would be freed and
a somnolent condition would take over. But when the brain is defective, the prison can no longer hold the prisoner — that is, the etheric
body — which then embarks on its own adventures, endeavouring
to live and create its own disordered, muddled life by opening out
into the world. So you see clearly that psychological illnesses are,
in the main, caused by a kind of freeing from the physical basis to
which the various higher components of man belong during life
between birth and death.

The etheric body, when it is freed, has mainly ahrimanic characteristics. Envy, jealousy, avarice and similar states will be pathologically
exaggerated, always in connection with a kind of spreading into the
environment, a kind of letting oneself go. Try to understand it like
this: The only point of attraction for the ego is, more or less, the system
of ganglia and whatever is connected with it; the astral body's point
of contact is with the spinal system, but together with the system of
ganglia; and the etheric body is linked with the cerebral system, but
jointly, with both the spinal system and the system of ganglia. So,
from this point of view, the system of ganglia also has to do with
the brain, for instance, in so far as it serves all subconscious organic
processes. If the system of ganglia brings about a process of illness
which runs its course in the brain, then it could be the etheric body
which is freed, even though the root cause lies in the system of ganglia.
You see how very complicated things are.

Psychiatry today has, as yet, no means of distinguishing between these three forms of soul sickness. Psychiatry will only achieve some degree of perfection when distinction is made between psychological abnormalities brought about by the freeing from bondage of the etheric body, or the astral body, or the ego. Then there will be a really significant way of distinguishing between, and assessing, the various symptoms of psychological abnormality — and it will be important to assess them in this way.

You see from all this how self-knowledge can only be built up on a penetrating view of the complicated nature of the human being. Knowledge can certainly have disagreeable sides to it. But knowledge is not supposed to be a toy, for it is the most serious matter in the whole of human life. Someone who knows everything there is to know about human nature — if he is even only somewhat inclined to understand it in a way which is not egoistic, if he is inclined to think and feel about it in an objective way — can have in this knowledge an important healing factor at his disposal. One might be too weak to use this healing factor; but this knowledge is an important healing factor. It cannot be gained by remaining in one's subjective nature; it cannot be gained by failing to extricte oneself from this.

This is a great problem for a movement such as ours. On the one hand it is necessary to strive earnestly for the highest knowledge, but on the other hand not everybody who decides to join such a movement is inclined to accept such knowledge with total objectivity and with full earnestness. Such knowledge brings health to personal life only if one is not constantly busy reflecting upon one's own personality, if one is not constantly wondering: How do *I* feel, what is going on in *me*, how am I getting on in the world, what is living in my soul, and so on. It brings healing only if we free ourselves from all that and concern ourselves instead with the affairs of mankind as a whole, matters which concern every human being. Difficulty arises only if one wants to concentrate on oneself, if one cannot get away from oneself. The more one is capable of turning away from oneself and towards all that concerns people and the world in general, the more can knowledge become a healing factor.

How glad I would be if only you would believe this! A movement like ours gives plenty of opportunity for observing the very opposite of what I have been saying. It is, of course, natural and justified that people who cannot easily get away from themselves should turn to our Movement for comfort and hope and confidence. But if they do not honestly strive to get away from themselves, if they continue to concern themselves with their own head and their own heart — not to mention whatever else very many people in our Movement are concerned with — then knowledge cannot become for them what, in truth, it is. It is possible to be interested in knowledge in such a way that it becomes not only a personal, but also a general human affair. The more personal considerations are involved, the more one is distracted from what is healing in all the knowledge about the deeper aspects of the world.

From the points of view we have now reached we must endeavour to gain clarity about how certain impulses in human nature are connected with the freeing of the soul and spiritual element, either in states brought about by hypnosis or mesmerism, or in madness. A process of freeing is always connected with a merging into the spiritual element. But this is in turn bound up with a certain feeling of voluptuousness, with real voluptuousness, both direct and indirect. For whatever has become free — be it the etheric or astral body, or the ego — in a way pours itself into the spiritual world. And this pouring forth is definitely connected with inner feelings of bliss.

Somebody with a psychological abnormality gains a certain satisfaction from his abnormal soul activity and is therefore loath to depart from it. In every age, those who have concerned themselves with the healing of psychological abnormalities have reported the following experience: When doctors have found a way of healing their patients, it happens that as the moment of health approaches, the patient senses that he can no longer freely merge with his spiritual environment and that he has lost a certain feeling of voluptuous bliss, so he begins to hate the doctor who has taken this from him. Usually those who are not psychologically ill are grateful to their doctor when he heals them, but efforts expended on the psychologically ill are met with the opposite. You will find this documented in the appropriate literature. Doctors have frequently found that when a cure is effected, or even only an attempt is made to overcome the sickness, the patient begins to find his doctor abhorrent because he is taking away what the patient really wants, especially in his subconscious, even if he would consciously deny this.

Such things lead us deep into the mystery of the human being's soul nature. We then also understand that the ego, or the etheric or the astral body, after endeavouring to work with the help of their physical tools, if they then become free, yet are still strong and imbued with the forms they had within their physical tools, can more easily unfold certain forces than was possible for them within the diseased organs. That is why people with periodic illnesses — for there are cyclic, periodic abnormalities of the soul — when they once again leave their organism, often feel that they have capacities which they do not otherwise possess. This gives them great satisfaction, and when they then return to their physical body a certain awareness of what they have experienced remains with them; they can sometimes be very clear about themselves and what has happened.

During the first half of the nineteenth century a well-known physician, Willis,[3] cured someone suffering from madness; that is, he brought him to a point at which he was once more capable of thinking sensibly about himself. And this person, who was intelligent, wrote a kind of review of his madness. If you take into account what I have just said, you will well understand what this intelligent individual wrote. His illness involved the freeing of all three higher components. He wrote 'I expected my fits of insanity with impatience ... with bliss'. Remember, he awaited the moment of leaving his body with impatience because he knew he would then enjoy a kind of bliss.

'Everything appeared easy to me. No obstacles presented themselves either in theory or practice. My memory acquired, all of a sudden, a singular degree of perfection ...'

Someone who understands these things can tell from this that the patient must otherwise have suffered from severe constipation, i.e. an abdominal condition, which led to a dulling of his memory. As soon as his ego tore itself free, his memory was again intact.

'Long passages of Latin authors occurred to my mind. In general, I have great difficulty in finding rhythmical terminations, but then I could write verses with as great facility as prose.'

You see how exactly the patient described himself, and it is understandable that in a certain way he endeavoured to induce the abnormal state. This cannot actually be done, of course, but he was glad when it came, for it brought him voluptuous enjoyment.

This is the main difficulty in the case of psychological abnormalities for, subjectively, the patients have to be led from a happy to an unhappy state of mind, and so they are truly downcast about it. In their ordinary consciousness this is different, of course, but in their subconscious they are downcast if they are cured. Of course they go to the doctor and say they want to be cured; but subconsciously they do not, in reality, want to be cured. This is the difficulty. The freed component or components resist with all their might being torn away from the bliss they enter when they are freed. You see how, by looking at things in this way, we do justice to the material foundation of our physical existence, and yet we do not become materialists.

Take a person who is stupid to a greater degree than is apparent in external life. There are such people. Well, stupidity is only one stage on the way to a certain abnormality of soul: namely, imbecility. The cause is possibly that the otherwise bound etheric body is free because the brain is too compact and cannot achieve sufficient fluidity in the way it works. Perhaps this person shoots himself in the head without killing himself. Someone who knows what to look for might find that this is not a bad thing, as long as he had not done himself any other harm. For the resulting loosening of his compact brain might lead to his becoming clever. There are certainly known cases in which head wounds have led to people becoming more wide awake than they were before.

There is truly nothing in the physically-perceptible world as complicated as the nature of the human being. It is more complicated than anything else in the world. To understand man in his totality you have to view him in the way I have been describing. We have seen, for instance, that in the human being as he stands before us with his head, the activity of this head depends in some degree on the etheric body connecting up in the right way to it. Abnormal activity comes about if the etheric body is freed, if it is unbound. Because of the way the human being is normally organized with regard to his sense organs and the nerves of his brain, the etheric body can have a normal relationship with the ordinary environment. What man is as a result of the special connection between his etheric body and his head makes him into a human being like all others in his existence between birth and death in the physical world. If we had nothing else about us except the normal connection of our etheric body with our head, all human beings would be the same, and there would also be no way of feeling connected with that part of our being that is immortal. For our head brings to us the experiences we have in life between birth and death through our senses, through the nerves of the brain.

Consider this in connection with what I have said about the loss of the head during the course of reincarnation: What is now our head was in our previous incarnation our body, and what is now our body will become our head in our next incarnation. We know about this connection with our immortal part which runs through all births and deaths, even though without the wisdom of spiritual science this knowledge can only take the form of a belief. Through our head we can understand this connection, but we can only have this knowledge because we have the system of the spinal cord as an organ of our astral body. This is where those ideas and feelings are wrought which bring us into a mutual relationship with our immortal, our super-personal, part.

Everything we possess only for this life between birth and death is given to us through the earthly, solid element in our organism. On other occasions I have pointed out that there is indeed very little of the solid element in our make-up, of which ninety-five per cent consists, in fact, of fluid, of a pillar of fluid. The human being is a pillar of water containing only five per cent of solid ingredients. Yet only this solid element can be the bearer of our ordinary thoughts in physical life; and only in so far as we are permeated by the fluid element with its pulsation can we know about our super-personal part. And this fluid element with its pulsation is linked with the spinal system, which for the most part regulates this fluid element and its pulsation.

How all this is related to certain things I have described on other occasions, to the pulsating rise and fall of fluid between the abdomen and the brain, I shall discuss tomorrow, for at the moment it would take us too far from today's theme. Now, because the human being bears the fluid element within him he is linked with his super-personal part. But this fluid element also establishes his specific personality. If we had only heads, we would all think the same, feel the same. But because we also have hearts, the fluid element, blood and other juices in us, we are specific in some degree; for through this element the hierarchy of the angeloi can have a part in our being. The hierarchy of the angeloi can intervene in us via the fluid element.

A third possibility for intervening in our being is given because even with the normal working together of the higher components with the system of ganglia, it is possible for the airy element and everything connected with it to have an effect on us. This happens in the process of breathing. It is very complicated, and it varies depending on where we breathe, on how much oxygen, how much humidity, how much sun warmth is in the air and so on. It is the hierarchy of the archangeloi, the archangels, who work on us via the airy element. And everything that works in us from the hierarchy of the archangeloi — both those who have progressed normally and those who are retarded — works via the system of ganglia. Also this is the route by which the folk spirits work, for they belong to the hierarchy of the archangeloi. The work done by the folk spirits in the human being takes its effect through the organs which are connected with the system of ganglia. This is why nationality is something so far removed from consciousness, something that works in such a demonic way. And for the reasons I have pointed out it is linked so strongly with everything to do with locality. For the locality, the local climate, is far more closely connected with the working of the hierarchy of the archangeloi than one might imagine. Climate is nothing other than what works on the human being via the air.

So you see that by discussing the system of ganglia one is indicating how the impulses of all that belongs to the folk soul work in man's unconscious. You will now also understand why, more than one might ordinarily think, belonging to a particular nation is connected with certain characteristics which are linked to the system of ganglia. More than one might think, the problem of nationality has to be seen in relation to the problem of sexuality. Belonging to a nation has the same organic foundation — the system of ganglia — as the sexual element. Quite externally you can understand this when you remember that you belong to a nation by birth, that is, your body develops inside that of a mother who belongs to a particular nation. This of itself creates a link. So you see what subterranean soul foundations connect the problem of nationality with the problem of sexuality. That is why these two impulses in life manifest in such related ways. If your eyes are open to life you will see a tremendous amount of similarity between the way people behave in an erotic sense and the way they show their connection to their nationality. I am not speaking either for or against either of these things, but the facts are as I have described them. Arousal of a nationalistic kind, which works particularly strongly in the unconscious if it is not brought up into ego-consciousness by making it a question of karma as I described the other day, is very similar to sexual arousal. It is no good glossing over these things by making out that the emotional illusions and longings of national feeling are noble, while sexual feelings are rather less so. For the facts are as I have described them to you.

From all this you will see that a good amount of agreement can be reached amongst people in matters of the head, for in the head everyone is the same. If we consisted of heads only, we would understand one another famously. It is peculiar to say: If we consisted of heads only. But when life has brought one together with all kinds of people one grows accustomed to speaking in paradoxes such as this. In parenthesis, let me tell you that I once met quite an important Austrian poet[4] who also entertained philosophical thoughts and was terribly worried about the way human beings were growing ever more and more intellectual. He said: People are growing more and more intellectual, so in the end the rest of their body will waste away and there will be nothing left but walking heads. He was quite serious.

If, as I said, we were heads, it would be easy for us to reach an understanding about all kinds of things. It is less easy to reach an understanding about matters which have to be comprehended via the tool of the spinal system. That is why people are embattled with regard to their view of the world, their religion and everything else they connect with what is super-personal. And there is no doubt at all that today they are embattled also with regard to everything for which the system of ganglia is the organ. By this I do not mean the external war; I mean the war that speaks in the language of hate against hate, for the external war need not necessarily have anything to do with all that is unfolding in such a terrible way in the form of hate against hate.

It is essential for people to become conscious of these things. Only if people can come to understand the nature of the human being will it be possible to find a way out of that chaos into which mankind has entered. Tomorrow we shall speak more about this chaos. But we must be clear about one thing: The knowledge and understanding we gain about the complicated nature of the human being must be filled with a mood that I described just now as an impersonal mood.

So far I have only described harmless, personal moods such as those in people who cannot cope with themselves, who go on and on about their heart, or one thing and another. But in the world at large we meet with less harmless moods, either personal or belonging to the egoism of a whole group. Occult knowledge is not always applied in a selfless manner, as you saw during our considerations over the past few weeks. We can certainly look more deeply into the impulses at work in human history if we have an understanding of the complexity of human nature. For what we can come to know with regard to the individual is connected in turn with all that happens between people, both on a one to one basis and also between the different groupings that come about during human evolution.

Now I told you that occult knowledge was used by certain secret brotherhoods in order to give a turn to events which would serve not general human aims but the egoistic aims of a particular group. I told you that certain secret brotherhoods entertained views about how Europe ought to be structured and how they could influence that structuring. Today I want to add to what has already been made plain something that has not yet been mentioned. I do this because it seems to me to be a good thing that once at least, in however small a circle, something is said which will certainly be made known in the future, just as the division of Austria has been made known in the note from the Entente to President Wilson. Those who knew about these things could have sketched the division of Austria as long ago as the nineties — I do not want to go back any further — on the basis of the maps I have already mentioned.[5]

Whatever is made publicly known is only a fragment. It flows into external, exoteric affairs at a time when it is considered to be useful; but the rest, meanwhile, is held back. Truly, I say what I am now going to tell you not from the slightest political or inflammatory motive, but solely in order to let you have the facts. They do exist in the world. I am truly very far from wanting to worry anyone, or persuade anyone to believe anything in particular or be anxious about anything; for I am concerned only with knowledge. So let me sketch approximately part of the future map of Europe as it was worked out in those secret brotherhoods. So as not to take too long, my sketch will only be approximate. As I said, this is the form which such secret societies thought Europe should take at some point in the future. [The lecturer drew.]

First they turned their attention to the southern European Balkan confederation. This was to be a kind of bulwark against Russianism. Obviously, in the West, Russianism was considered to be the opposite pole, definitely not something with which to remain linked for ever, but something against which there would always be a need to fight. Since the intention was to weld together the present Kingdom of Italy with the Balkan Slavs and the southern Slavs at present belonging to Austria, this confederation would comprise a large part of the Apennine peninsula, the Italian-speaking part of Switzerland, the southern part of Austria, Croatia, Slavonia and Dalmatia. To this the northern part of Greece would be added. The confederation would also include

Hungary and the Danube estuary. This would be the Balkan confederation. Next to this, eastwards, would be everything belonging to Russia in the wider sense. In the programme shown in these maps it was always — I mention this expressly — sharply stressed that however Poland might behave, it was a necessity of world history that the whole of this country should, whatever the circumstances, be returned to the Russian Empire. From the start the programme said that Poland, including the parts now belonging to Prussia, must once again be included in the Russian Empire. So according to the programme, the Russian Empire would include today's Poland, and also Galicia reaching beyond the Slovaks. The part that I am shading here would dip in like a peninsula. This would be Bukovina. [Drawing was continued].

Then would come France which, starting at the Rhine estuary, would cover the territory over as far as the Rhine and the French-speaking part of Switzerland and would be bounded here by the Pyrenees, and here something like this. Nothing much was said about the Scandinavian peoples. No doubt they have been granted a good long respite.

The rest would be: German-speaking Switzerland with Germany and the German parts of Austria. They would cover this area. And these coloured parts would fall more or less into the sphere of influence, however that may appear, of the British Empire: Holland, Belgium, the coast, Portugal, Spain, the lower part of Italy — we can speak about the islands another time — and the southern part of Greece.

So here we have a map for which the one we tried to draw on the board yesterday is clearly a kind of payment on account. The Central European part looks quite similar to that implied by the note from the Entente to Wilson. This is what was seen to be an ideal structure for Europe. I repeat yet again: This is not something remotely intended to influence anybody. All I want to show is that this structure for Europe, clearly traceable by me to the nineties, or even the eighties, was taught in certain secret societies.

The reasons for wanting to shape Europe like this were also always given. The ways and means — of course the reasons were eminently sensible — for achieving this structure for Europe were more or less described. We shall talk about this tomorrow. Just let me say that I am not making this up. It is something that lived as a powerful impulse in many heads, something that had to be brought about, something that would have to be brought about by every effort. I know very well how ill will could easily maintain that it is improper, in consideration of a particular point, to say such things precisely here, of all places. But I do not want to be inflammatory, nor do I want to set up a picture of the future, either for those nations now at war or for those who are neutral. I have nothing to do with these things. I speak about them merely to show you the impulses which existed in those circles. What we have here is a picture of the future arising from endeavours to use certain impulses in the egoistic interests of a group. Those who are shocked to see what would disappear, might remind themselves that *we* are concerned with the tasks of mankind in general. Things which emanate from the egoistic interests of a group are obvious, and there is no need to regard them as fateful, as pending fate. What I do regard as fatal, however, is the attitude of hiding one's head in the sand, of simply refusing to recognize such facts because they are uncomfortable, with the excuse that such things ought not even to be thought because they might cause disquiet. Of course I know that it could be said: We should not speak about such things because they might upset people who are honestly striving to be neutral. But the foundations on which we stand ought to have enabled us to transcend this kind of upset by now. We should be capable of looking at what is really happening in the world. And when I say these things it is on the assumption that you are sensible enough to take them in the right way.

LECTURE TWENTY
Dornach, 15 January 1917

I pointed out yesterday how the spiritual components of man's being
have their points of contact in his physical organism. Awareness of
this will have to enter into the consciousness of mankind as a whole,
for it is this knowledge that in truth must lead man to the light out
of the darkness of today's materialism, which will last for a very,
very long time. Never, though, must the thread of spiritual knowledge
be lost entirely. At least a small group of human beings must always
ensure that this does not happen. I have already shown how the true
discoveries of material science — which anthroposophical spiritual
science must certainly not fail to recognize — are put in the correct
light when things are seen spiritually, especially the human being.
The examples I started with yesterday can show you how the physical
processes in the human being are fully recognized by spiritual science
— only spiritual science recognizes what is spiritual and investigates
how the spiritual element is anchored in the physical element,
especially, in the first instance, in the human being.

Thus we avoided the pitfall of seeking the spiritual element solely
in abstract concepts which are unable to deal with something that has
been created by it, namely, the material world. What is spiritual must
not live only in a Cloud-cuckoo-land floating above the material world.
It must be so strong and intense that it can permeate the material element and show how spiritual it is and how it has been created by the
spirit. Thus true spiritual knowledge must come to the possibility of
understanding the material world and existence on the physical plane.
It is important now, of all times, to pay attention to the interaction
of spiritual and material elements in the human being, because now
it is necessary properly to understand the intervention of something
not material, namely, the folk soul, in the human being.

I said: Those things in everyday life which we think, feel and will
— not as members of one group of people or another but as citizens
of the earth — are bound to the solid, earthly element. Even though
only five per cent of our body is made of this earthly element, I said
that that in us which gives us in the world between birth and death
our purely personal knowledge, will impulses and degrees of feeling, is bound to the mineral, solid element of the brain; that is where

it has its point of contact. As soon as we progress to what leads us into super-personal or sub-personal realms, we can no longer count on conceptions which are brought to us by the solid element, for conceptions here are brought by the fluid element. And conceptions which take us so far into the super-personal or sub-personal realm that we come to the intervention of the archangeloi in our being are brought to us by the airy element. The airy element is the mediator between these archangel beings and their sphere and everything which the human being experiences in that very subconscious way I described yesterday.

Well over ninety per cent of our physical being is a pillar of water, a pillar of liquid, but this liquid element in the human being, of which very little account has so far been taken by natural science, is the main bearer of life in the human being. I have pointed out how the aeriform element works through the liquid element into the solid element which is anchored in the brain. We breathe in; because we breathe in a stream of air and fill our body with it, the organ we call the diaphragm is pushed down. In this sucking-in of the stream of air and everything that goes with it, down to the lowering of the diaphragm, is to be found that sphere in which the impulses emanating from the kingdom of the archangeloi work. Just as all this remains in the subconscious, so does the real manner of the folk soul's working remain in the subconscious. As I said by way of comparison yesterday, it surges up like waves, in a form that differs utterly from the way it lives down there in the depths. When the diaphragm is pushed downwards it, in a way, dams up the blood in the veins of the abdomen. This pushes the stream of cerebral fluid upwards through the spinal cord so that it pours into the brain, or rather round the solidified mass of the brain. So now, as a result of breathing in, the cerebral fluid is in the brain, has been pushed up. In the way these pulsations of the cerebral fluid work lie all the impulses that come into man from the sphere of the archangeloi, everything man can have in the way of conceptions and feelings which lift him into the realm of the super-personal or sub-personal, everything that connects him with the forces that reach beyond birth and death. And in the brain itself the cerebral fluid comes up against the solid element.

Parallel with this runs the process by which all our ideas and conceptions ebb and flow in the liquid element. These ideas and conceptions are spiritual entities which ebb and flow in the liquid element, and they appear as our everyday conceptions relating to the external world because they come up against the solid element and are mirrored back by this solid element into consciousness.

When we breathe out, a damming-up takes place in the blood vessels of the brain, and the cerebral fluid is pushed down through the spinal cord into the abdomen. There is room for it there because breathing out has raised the diaphragm. So thinking and having ideas and so on is not the mere brain process of which the sciences of anatomy and physiology dream today. What takes place in the brain is a mirroring-back by something solid, and this is connected with what is not mirrored but remains in the fluid element whence, via the detour of breathing, it regulates the influence of the aeriform element. This is also the detour via which everything is mediated to us which belongs to a particular climate, the local soil conditions of a particular terrain and all the other influences connected with breathing. That part of breathing which never enters our consciousness but remains lika an ocean swell, is where spiritual realities surge. Via the detour through the cerebral fluid the breathing process is connected with the brain.

Here you have a physical process belonging to the whole human being, described in such a way that you can recognize it as a revelation of the spirit which surrounds us everywhere, just as does air or humidity. This gives you, through a true understanding of physical processes, an insight into how his earthly surroundings, together with the spirit contained in them, work on man, and into how, as a being both spiritual and physical, man is embedded in his earthly environ-ment, which is also spiritual and physical. The air, water and warmth which surround us are nothing other than bodies for the spirit, just as our muscles and nerves are bodies for the spirit.

I am presenting you with these things now because they show how human life is founded on processes which are not at all obvious to present-day science. It will be the task of the fifth post-Atlantean period to raise these processes to the level of true knowledge. During the course of the fifth post-Atlantean period this realization must enter into everything we do — in teaching, in education generally and in the whole of external life. It must, in due course, be recognized that what is seen as science in materialistic circles today will gradually have to disappear from the life of the earth, together with all the consequences it has for life. All the battles still to be won in the fifth post-Atlantean period will be no more than an external expression of a spiritual battle, just as, in the final analysis, the present battle is an external expression of the confrontation between materialism and spiritual life. Hidden though these things are, behind today's infinitely sad events lies the battle of materialism against spiritual life. This battle will have to be fought to the end. It will take various forms, but it must be fought to the end because human beings must learn to bear everything they need to bear in order to achieve the spiritual view necessary for the sixth post-Atlantean period. It may be said that there must be much suffering, but only out of pain and suffering can arise what truly binds knowledge to our self. For the other side of the coin is that connected with the materialistic view of the world, is the materialistic way of life, which is only beginning today but which will take on infinitely more terrible forms.

The materialistic way of life began when science became willing to recognize only what is material. It has already led to a stage at which people are prepared, in life, too, to accept only what is material. This will be taken much, much further and will become far more intense. For the fifth post-Atlantean period must be lived to the end. In all areas it must reach a kind of climax. For spirituality needs its opposite pole if it is to recognize itself with the intensity that will be needed if mankind is to step with maturity into the sixth post-Atlantean period.

So do not shy away from following the spiritual guidelines offered as a possibility for comprehending the external facts of the world. For it is the prime task and duty of all those who strive spiritually to comprehend the course of human evolution up to the present and also to understand the likely evolution of the future in spiritual directions. We have often spoken of our inheritance from the fourth post-Atlantean period which ended in the fifteenth century, and of the fact that it is the task of the fifth post-Atlantean period to develop to the full the consciousness soul.

Now it is precisely the consciousness soul which will unite man intimately with all material events and everything belonging to materialism. We have seen how, in the fourth post-Atlantean period, from the eighth century BC right up to the fifteenth century AD, the Greco-Latin element gradually came to dominate the world, first in what is usually called the Roman Empire and later in the Roman Papacy which reached the climax of its dominance during the thirteenth and the beginning of the fourteenth centuries. This is at the same time the beginning of the fifth post-Atlantean period. It coincided with the first breaking of Roman Papal dominance. It is also the beginning of those impulses whose influence has brought about the present sad events. In the end no one can understand what is going on today without taking a wider view. For really all the peoples of Europe have contributed their share to the sad events of today's Europe. Those who want to understand things must necessarily turn their attention to impulses which have been in preparation for a long time and which today are being given a kind of first chance to show themselves.

So today we shall bring together what can be seen far in the future with things that are close at hand. First let us remember the description I gave of how the southern peoples, the Italian and Spanish peoples and the various kingdoms they have brought forth, represent a kind of after-effect of the third post-Atlantean period — of course, with the inclusion of the overall heritage of the fourth period. You need only follow the whole structure of Italian-Spanish development as it took place at the turn of the fourth to the fifth post-Atlantean period, in order to see that it still included what was directly justified in the third, the Egypto-Chaldean period. You can see this especially in the way in which, emanating from Rome and Spain, a religion spread which was borrowed from the cults of Egypt and Chaldea. In this you have the continued existence of what had been left behind in Egypt and Chaldea, and this reached its climax in the thirteenth century.

Papal supremacy emanated from the South and reached its climax in the thirteenth century. In order to describe it in a way which is meaningful today and which fits the facts, we should have to say that this papal supremacy, which covered and dominated the whole of European culture, was essentially the ecclesiastical element of cultus and hierarchy. This ecclesiastical element of cultus and hierarchy, which was a transformation of ancient Rome into the Roman Catholicism which streamed into Europe, is one of the impulses which continue to work like retarded impulses throughout the whole fifth post-Atlantean period, but especially in its first third. You could, I might add, work out how long this is going to last. You know that one post-Atlantean period lasts approximately 2,160 years. One third of this is 720 years. So starting with the year 1415, this takes the main period to the year 2135. Therefore the last waves of hierarchical Romanism will last into the beginning of the third millennium. These are echoes in which the impulses of the fourth post-Atlantean period assert themselves in the forms of the third post-Atlantean period. But many things work side by side at the same time, so there are other impulses working together with these. Roman Catholicism had its actual climax in the thirteenth and fourteenth centuries.

Let us now see how it continues. We have to distinguish the way it worked up to the thirteenth century — when it was, you might say, justified, because that was still the fourth post-Atlantean period — and what then followed, when it began to assume the character of a retarded impulse. It seeks to spread. But how? For it certainly spreads significantly. We see that the form of the state, which gradually matures in the new age, is more or less saturated with this Roman Catholicism. We see that the English state as it begins to grow at the beginning of the fifth post-Atlantean period is at first entirely in the hands of this Roman Catholicism. We see how France and the rest of Europe are entirely in the grip of this Roman element of hierarchy and cultus in so far as their ideas and cultural life are concerned. To characterize this impetus we would have to say that there is an impulse on the part of Rome to permeate, to saturate the culture of Europe with this hierarchical ecclesiastical element right up to the bulwark it has itself created in eastern Europe. But it is noteworthy that an impulse like this, if it is a retarded impulse, takes on an external character. It no longer has the strength to develop any inner intensity, but becomes external in character. It spreads out widely on the surface but has no strength to go into its own depths. So we see the strange phenomenon of Roman hierarchism spreading further and further afield yet, in the countries at its core, being unable to give any inward strength, thus depriving its own population of inwardness.

See how such things start. Everywhere Romanism spreads in all shapes and forms, whereas in Italy itself, in Spain, the population is hollowed out. Just think what an extraordinary Christianity lived in Italy when the Papacy was at the height of its glory. It was the Christianity against which the thunderous words of Savonarola were directed. For in isolated individuals, such as Savonarola, the Christ impulse was alive; but these individuals felt impelled to grind official Christianity into the dust. A history telling of what happened at the point from which Christianity rayed forth would have to say: The power of the Roman church element rayed forth, but the Christian souls at the point from which this happened were hollowed out. This could be proved in detail. It is an important truth: Something raying out destroys its own inner core. This is how life goes. Like a human being growing old and using up his forces, so do cultural phenomena, when they spread, use up their own being and hollow themselves out.

On earlier occasions I have shown how the French state was in a certain way a recapitulation of the fourth post-Atlantean period in the fifth. Here we now have a second case of raying forth. For the southern element we used the expression 'ecclesiastical element of cultus and hierarchy' to describe something that strove to found a universal monarchy of the church, a theocracy of Europe. Now we shall endeavour to find an expression to describe that cultural element which bears the culture of the intellectual- or mind-soul from the fourth post-Atlantean period up into the fifth. An expression encompassing all the historical elements, an expression which fits the facts and describes the reality of what is brought into the fifth post-Atlantean period, if we have the good will to find it, would have to be: the universal diplomatic element. Everything connected with this universal diplomatic element is also connected with what grew out of the French state element. It is not for nothing that the French language is the language of diplomacy, even today. Every historical trend is illuminated in detail when you discover that just as the universal theocratic element rays out from Rome and Spain, so the universal diplomatic element rays out from Paris.

And it is remarkable that just as with the Spanish-Italian element — though to a lesser degree because the element being brought forward is less ancient — so also, in the case of the French element, the raying forth is accompanied at its source by a hollowing out. It is particularly interesting to view history in the light of this. Take the way in which great French statesmen, such as Richelieu or Mazarin, inaugurate and carry on world diplomacy by translating old impulses into the diplomatic, political element. The servants of Louis XIV think on a European, not a French, scale and see themselves as the obvious leaders of Europe as regards the diplomatic, the universal, diplomatic element. One element, one impulse, always absorbs the other. It is not for nothing that cardinals practised in politics and diplomacy surround the King of France when the French state is at its zenith.

Studying that time particularly in the history of France, we find that the very concern which sends diplomacy all over Europe withdraws from its own country infinitely great forces in the realm of economics, finance, and also culture in general, hollowing it out down to the fine details. To see things this way, they must, of course, not be viewed in the light of national prejudices, but in all truth, objectively and impartially. This hollowing out is also the source of that uprising of the people into the element of revolution which leads to the exact opposite of what would be the most suitable for the French state: monarchy. In the Spanish-Italian realm there is no parallel to this Revolution, for the reasons I have already given. Yet it is precisely this Revolution which shows how strangely this contrast works in the French element, this contrast between concern for European diplomacy and the lesser concern for one's own country.

For we must not forget that the fifth post-Atlantean period was accompanied by the spread of civilization and culture across the whole earth, which went with the discovery of hitherto unknown regions. We see how, as a matter of course, those states which border the ocean build up their navies. French diplomacy spreads its concern over the whole earth, and at the same time — you can follow this in the various trends of history — the French navy begins to blossom; but this has its opposite in what rages uncared-for within and then comes to expression in the Revolution. It is notable that the more the Revolution proceeds, the more the French navy is neglected. You can observe how, during the build-up to the French Revolution, France's sea power grows ever smaller as her navy is totally neglected.

This has a significant consequence. When the French element withdraws once again from the revolutionary age and returns to what is more suited to it — the emperorship of Napoleon — there develops in the person of Napoleon that significant opposition to the third element, that element which is now suitable for the fifth post-Atlantean period, the opposition of France against England. This had been in preparation for a long time but in the person of Napoleon it took on quite a new character that differed greatly from the character it had had before.

What is most remarkable in all the waves created by Napoleonism? If you investigate what lived in Europe with regard to Napoleon, you find the important opposition between Napoleon and England. But Napoleon lacked something which was missing in the heritage of the Revolution, something which had to be lacking — I speak of a historical necessity — but which he would have needed so that the second element could have asserted itself against the third, the French against the English, namely: a navy! Hypotheses are only justified in connection with history as tools for understanding, but they can indeed make a great contribution. So let us make a hypothesis: If Napoleon had had a navy which he could have joined to those of other countries with which he was allied, he would not have been defeated at sea by England and the whole of history would have taken a different course. But the Revolution had not given him a navy. Here we see the mutual limitation of the two elements, those of the third and the fourth post-Atlantean periods, as they rise up into the fifth. Now we come to the third element, the one which corresponds to the fifth post-Atlantean period and has the task of bringing into being the culture of the consciousness soul: the English, the British element. The sentient soul element, brought into culture by the Italian-Spanish sphere, expresses itself in the theocratic element of the cultus — the sentient soul does not live in consciousness. Similarly the political and diplomatic element corresponds to the French sphere. And now in the British sphere we have the commercial and industrial element, in which the human soul lives fully and entirely in the material world of the physical plane. But we must make clear an important difference. The Papacy could only pretend to world dominance for one particular reason.

Here [the lecturer drew] is the fourth post-Atlantean period. Now comes the first element, A, of the fifth post-Atlantean period, the papal, hierarchical element. It strives for a kind of universal monarchy because in a certain way it is the continuation of the universal Roman Empire.

Here, B, is the culture of the intellectual or mind soul. It also strives for something universal, but it is something universal that is very much in the realm of ideas. The most important consequence of the spread of the French element are not the conquests, which are merely side-effects, but the saturation of the world with the political spirit, with political, diplomatic thinking and feeling — that diplomatic, political thinking found not only in French diplomacy and politics, but also in literature and even the other aspects of French artistic life. A universal monarchy in connection with this could only be described as a kind of universal dream. And the way in which France marched in the forefront of civilization is a very exact expression of this dream.

In contrast, we now come to the third element, C. This, in harmony with the whole of the fifth post-Atlantean period, which has the task of bringing to expression the consciousness soul, is what corresponds to the British element, the special bearer of the consciousness soul in the age which is to develop especially the consciousness soul. Hence the pretension of the British element to universal commercial and industrial world dominance.

My dear friends, things which have their foundation in the spiritual world will run their course. They will, with all certainty, run their course. Do not imagine that you can moralize or theorize about this. They will run their course and become fact. Nobody need believe, therefore, that the mission of the British people will not — out of inner necessity — become fact: namely, the mission to found a universal commercial and industrial monarchy over the whole earth. The pretensions emerge as realities. These things have to be recognized as lying in world karma. And what people express and what they think is only a revelation of spiritual forces behind the scenes. So nobody should believe that British politics will ever be morally reformed and withdraw, out of consideration for the world, from the pretension to dominate the world industrially and commercially. Therefore we need not be surprised either that those who understand these things have founded societies whose sole aim is to realize such aims by the use of means which are also spiritual means.

This is where the forbidden interplay begins. For obviously occult principles, occult means and occult impulses are not permissible as promoters, as driving forces, especially in the fifth post-Atlantean period, which ought to be a purely materialistic civilization. The moment occult impulses work behind the spread of this purely materialistic culture, things become questionable. Yet, as I have shown you, this is what is happening. There are those who want to foster world dominance not only with the forces available on the physical plane, but also with the impulses of occultism, the impulses which lie in the world of the invisible. But these occult means are not used to work for the good of mankind in general but only for the good of a group. If you see the connection between such encompassing viewpoints, given to you from deeper knowledge, and everyday events, you will thoroughly understand a great deal.

There are still plenty of praiseworthy idealists — this is not meant as any kind of mockery, for idealism is always praiseworthy, even when it errs — who believe that the network of commercial and industrial measures, which has been spread by the British Empire over various countries, can only last as long as the war, and that after that people will once more be free to go about their own commercial business. Apart from a few illusions which will be raised by creating some interregnum or other, or by some other means to prevent people from becoming suspicious, all the measures that have been set up during this war to control commercial traffic throughout the world are not intended as something that will disappear once the war is over, but as something which is only beginning with the help of the war and will then continue. The war merely provides the opportunity for noses to be poked into business records. But do not imagine that this poking of noses into business records will cease after the war. I am speaking symbolically to describe something that will take place on the widest scale. What I mean is that commercial world dominance will become more and more thorough.

I am not saying all this in order to be inflammatory, but simply in order to show you what, out of the impulses of world history, really is the case. Only by recognizing what is really the case can people learn to conduct themselves appropriately. That is no doubt why that map of the European world turned out in the way I showed you on the blackboard yesterday. Let me repeat: I have traced this map back to the eighties of the nineteenth century. How far back it goes beyond that I do not know. I state only what I know, only what I can assert with certainty. That is why I have said nothing about the Scandinavian countries, since I do not know whether any plans have been made for them too. I limit myself strictly to what I know, and wish to stress this particularly on this occasion, though it is a principle which I follow on every occasion.

Further, this map — that is, this rearrangement of European affairs — has the tendency to serve the formation of a universal commercial monarchy. Europe is to be arranged in such a way that a universal commercial monarchy can be founded. I am not saying that this is to happen by tomorrow. But you can see that part payments are already being demanded. Only compare the most recent note to Wilson with the map of Europe, and there you have it. Nothing is said as yet about Switzerland. This payment on account will be demanded later. But as the demands appear one by one they will correspond to the map I drew yesterday.

The division of Europe shown there is suited to the founding of commercial world dominance. Study the details of this map and you will see that it is well conceived as a basis for founding what I have just said. I said: commercial world dominance. There is no need actually to possess all the territories, for it is quite sufficient to arrange them in such a way that they fall into one's sphere of influence. It is also very cleverly arranged so that at first those very regions will be drawn into the sphere of influence which I yesterday coloured yellow, as being the ones to be claimed as British: the peripheral territories. Indeed, in order to leave the others a little longer in the warm glow of a certain idealism, it is possible to arrange things in such a way that one practises the commercial domination oneself while leaving the others to play about with territories for a little longer. But the spheres of influence will be established as the drawing shows. It is quite irrelevant whether in the year 1950 there will be a Belgium, or a France extending right up to the border. The important thing is what power Belgians have in Belgium, or the French in France, and what power the British have in Belgium or France. In order to found commercial world dominance it is not necessary to actually possess the territories. What we must be clear about is that this world dominance is to be commercial and industrial. This is the basis for something extremely important.

I should, though, have to give a whole series of lectures if I needed to prove these things to you in detail. This would be perfectly possible, for the things I am saying can be proved very profoundly. Today, however, I can only draw an outline. In order to found a commercial and industrial world dominance, the first thing to do is to divide the main region into two parts. This has to do with the nature of commercial and industrial affairs. I can only explain this by using an analogy: Whatever takes place on the physical plane always requires a splitting into two parts.

Imagine a teacher without any pupils; there is no such thing. In the same way there cannot be a commercial empire without another region which is its counterpart. Therefore if a British commercial empire is founded, then a Russian opposite pole must be founded too. So that a differentiation can arise between buying and selling, so that the necessary circulation can come about, two regions are needed. If the whole world were to be made into a unified realm, it would be impossible to found a universal commercial realm. It is not quite the same, but similar to saying that if you produce something you need a buyer, otherwise you cannot produce. So this twofold split is necessary. And the fact that this has been initiated as a major trend is a great — indeed, a gigantic — conception on the part of those secret brotherhoods of which I have spoken. To create this contrast is a conception of universal proportions, against which everything else pales into insignificance: this contrast, between the British commercial empire on the one hand and, on the other, all that emanates from the Russian sphere involving, through their spiritual capacities, preparations for the sixth post-Atlantean period, together with everything I have described to you. It is a great, gigantic, admirable conception of these secret brotherhoods about whom we have spoken. Put simply, it is hardly possible to imagine a better opposite pole for what has developed in the West — namely, the supreme flowering of commercial and industrial thought — than the future Russian Slav who in times to come is sure to be even less inclined than he is today to occupy himself professionally with commercial matters, and who, just because of this, will be an excellent polar opposite. A commercial empire of this kind will, of course, have to state its own terms. Profound thought on the part of Spencer,[1] and even his predecessor, led them to stress repeatedly: The industrial and commercial element which suffuses a nation does not want to have anything to do with war; it is for peace, it needs peace and loves peace. It is absolutely true: There will indeed be a deep love between the element striving towards commerce and industry and the element striving towards peace in the world. Only this love for peace can sometimes adopt bizarre forms, as witness the present note to Wilson, which certainly contains something peculiar.

Look at what happens to Austria in this map, which is drawn exactly in accordance with the note. Yet this note dares to express something else as well: The common political unity living in the nations of Central Europe is not to be touched in any way. Well, this too is 'gigantic', a gigantically frivolous game with the truth. Usually untruths are not actually put down on paper, but here we have one note which says two different things: We shall dismember the middle realm, but we shall, of course, do it no harm. There is an accompanying chorus from the newspapers too. They write: Let us see whether the Central Powers will agree to these acceptable terms. Everywhere we read: The Entente Powers have stated their terms; now we shall see whether these terms, which ought to be eminently acceptable to the Central Powers, are bluntly rejected or not. Things have come a long way, have they not! For such things are there for all to read.

Now let us see where the thought leads us. We are dealing here with a splitting of the world into two parts, and those concerned are interested in achieving this in such a way that they can say to the world: We want peace, we stand only for peace. The recipe they are following is one which is behind much that is written today. It is like saying: I shall not touch you, I shall not harm a hair of your head, but I shall lock you in a deep dungeon and not give you anything to eat! Have I done anything to you? Could anyone maintain that I have harmed even a single hair of your head?

Many things are shaped in accordance with this recipe. Even the love for peace, despite the fact that it is a reality, is shaped in accordance with it. But if this love for peace is paired with a pretension to commercial world dominance it becomes unacceptable for the other side and it is utterly impossible to apply it. And so the peace-loving commercial empire is sure to find itself in future somewhat disturbed in its love for peace. This is, of course, known to those who divide the world into two parts, and so they need a rampart in between. This rampart is to take the form of the great southern European confederation which also comprises Hungary and everything else I mentioned yesterday. This is supposed to make for peace. Through the sphere of influence I have hinted at, the manner in which the British Empire is behaving towards the Mediterranean shows that it can quite easily give the southern European confederation Constantinople, as well as all kinds of other things. For they cannot go further than the Mediterranean, since the West, if it so wishes, can blockade the Mediterranean at any time.

In short, you can follow in every detail the gigantic, splendid thought on which this map is based. We have not enough time today to go through everything in detail. But it is a gigantic, splendid thought to leave only the southern ports which lead to the Mediterranean open for France, whilst keeping the others under one's own sphere of influence. This means, basically, that the French Empire, which France was anyway only able to found under the protection of the others, becomes an illusion, and can also be included in one's sphere of influence. If you follow all this, you will see in how gigantic a manner is to be realized — out of what belongs to the culture of the consciousness soul — what these occult schools are striving to achieve.

Those things which correspond to certain impulses do come to pass. For necessity governs world history and world evolution. These things do come to pass. But they come to pass in such a way that forces really do mutually affect one another. Just as there can never be positive without negative electricity; where opposites work on one another with varying intentions — so is it also in the events of human history. Therefore we must be careful, when we turn our attention to such things, to apply judgement that is free of moralizing. This also saves us from asking: Why must such a thing happen? For in the mission of one element or another is included the fact that things develop which must develop. And the adversary, the opposite pole must also exist: namely, something that resists whatever it is that wants to come about. This also must exist. So if we now once again take a wide view of all these things, we shall see something working in from the periphery which we have characterized as these three elements.

First let us return to the centre. Our concern here is that the adversary, the opposite pole should be there, so that a kind of brake can always be applied. This brake is just as necessary as the other element. And I blame one as little as I praise the other. I am simply describing the impulses and the facts. I have not the least inclination to pronounce a morally disparaging judgement on something I am describing as a necessity arising out of the whole character of the fifth post-Atlantean period. There is nothing bad about giving the world a materialistic, industrial, commercial culture, for this is a necessity. But the opposite pole must exist, too, for human evolution cannot proceed in a straight line. Opposing forces must clash with one another, and in this clash reality evolves. In Central Europe a collection of impulses has always of necessity existed, some of which worked with those streaming to the periphery in the way I have already described, while others had what was in many ways the tragic destiny of working in opposition to these.

These forces certainly stream outwards from Central Europe and make themselves felt elsewhere in many ways. But if you look closely you will find also in Central Europe the forces that oppose those I have described. Consider, for instance, that the first opposition to the theocratic, cultic element of the Spanish and Italian South came from Central Europe. It reached a certain climax in Luther and its greatest profundity in the mysticism of Central Europe. Not only German elements worked here, for mingled in the Central European stream were also Slav elements. Here there was a desire not for the Christianity of the Papal hierarchy, but for precisely that inwardness that had been hollowed out in the South. Savonarola was, after all, simply executed. This inwardness lived in the Czech, John Huss, and in Wyclif who stemmed from the Germanic element in England, and in Zwingli, and in Luther. Its more profound element is to be found in the mysticism of Central Europe, which, by the way, is very close to the Slav element. Precisely these relationships show how things fulfil themselves in a remarkable way. For Central Europe backed up by the Slav element is, in this, certainly an opponent of the periphery. So although they are in many aspects still disunited politically, Central European influences and Slav influences work together. In an occult sense, too, they work together fundamentally in a wonderful way.

We see how a certain materialistic element develops more and more in the South, reaching a peak in such people as Lombroso.[2] We see this materialistic element setting the tone elsewhere in the periphery, as well. Right up to Oliver Lodge,[3] about whom we spoke recently, we see materialism projecting itself into spiritual life. But on the other hand we also see how this is opposed by something which emancipates itself — to start with, from the Roman, hierarchical element. In this, Copernicus, the Pole, stands behind Kepler, the archetypal German; in this, Slav spirits, in particular, stand behind those who are German spirits. Indeed I could say: On the physical plane we see links between what is Central European and what is Slav; Huss, the Czech, Copernicus, the Pole — others might just as easily be named — these form a link stretching across the physical plane. We see, too, how in Central Europe the Slav element joins with the German element — we see the eastern European Slav element growing together with Europe. This, though, we only see when we consider the occult situation.

Let me give only one example: The soul of Galileo lives again in the Russian Lomonosov,[4] and the Russian Lomonosov is in many ways the founder of Slav culture in the East. In between these two lies the spiritual world, so that we might say: The Central European Slavs are still linked with the people of the West on the physical plane; what lies behind this is linked with the people of the West via the higher plane.

This fits entirely with the fact that the Russian element follows the Slav element; but it also fits with the situation in which the western Slav element must be thought of as having a relationship to Western Europe differing from that of the eastern Slav element. Therefore, only those who do not think in accordance with human evolution as a whole, but solely in accordance with the English-speaking Empire, will want to assimilate Poland in the Russian Empire.

This point in particular gives an example of the difference between the kind of thinking which is concerned only with a particular group and that other kind of thinking which is concerned with the good of mankind as a whole. The thinking which is concerned with the good of mankind as a whole could never include the territory of Poland in the Russian Empire. For in a remarkable way it is precisely the western Slavs with their profoundest characteristics who belong to Central Europe. I cannot speak today about the checkered destiny of the Polish people. But I just want to say that the spiritual culture of the Polish people found one of its culminations in the Polish messianic movement — let everybody think what they like about this reality — which, out of the substance of the Polish people contains spiritual feelings and spiritual ideas belonging to mankind as a whole. We are speaking here, in a way, about that Gnostic element which corresponds to one of the three soul components which are to flow from the western Slavs to Central Europe. The second element lies in the Czech people to whom — not for nothing — John Huss belongs. Here is the second soul component inserted into Central Europe out of the Slav element. And the third component is from the southern Slavs. These three soul components push westwards like three cultural peninsulas and most certainly do not belong to the eastern European Slav element. Externally, on the physical plane, by means of political marriages, but inwardly by means of what I have just been explaining, this Austria has come about whose purpose it is to amalgamate German and western Slav peoples precisely so that the western Slavs can unfold in accordance with their own impulses. This has nothing to do with any principle of dominance! Anyone who has known Austria in the second half of the nineteenth century will regard as utterly ridiculous what is said in the present note to Wilson about Austria and a certain principle of dominance. Of course the situation is difficult. But anyone familiar with the history of Austria in the nineteenth century knows how possibilities were sought which would enable any Slav people, indeed any nationality whatever, to develop absolutely freely in Austria.

However, all kinds of things are contained in this note. You need only glance at an elementary history textbook to see that the territories Italy is now demanding from Austria have never been under Italian rule. Yet the note says: The Italians are demanding the return of territories which once belonged to them.

But truth is not the concern of this note, for its aim is to say what it wants to say while counting on it that the magical power of modern journalism has persuaded people to believe everything. And you can certainly often count on this. The power of journalism is indeed one of the means on which certain societies count. Just because Austria has been preparing — as it were, beneath the surface — for the mission about which I have spoken, she has always been an opponent, an opposite pole, to any Freemasonry of the kind which has developed in the West in the way I have been describing over the last few weeks. Freemasonry has never been allowed to enter Austria. Its presence begins to be felt to some extent — but merely in the way I have described — only beyond the river Leitha.

Of course there are also other impulses which, as you have seen, are the cause for some degree of leniency, so that the peoples of Central Europe will not be utterly destroyed politically. The war aims, and also the peace initiatives which are at present being made, are in accord with this. But the fact that Austria herself is being attacked so viciously is in part explained by the enmity that has always existed between Austria and western European Freemasonry, right from the days of Maximilan I.[5] It is disguised in various ways, of course, and what I am now saying is easily proved wrong, just because on the physical plane things are disguised, are masked.

So we see how Central Europe has to put up a fight on behalf of mankind, for it is the pole which opposes the impulses coming from the West. This brings it about that the evolution of Central Europe does not proceed in a straight line. It fluctuates, for Central Europe always has to take up and bring to a certain climax, a certain intensity, whatever there is by way of opposition to any of the impulses coming from the West. Take the hierarchical, theocratic impulse. While a kind of Christianity is carried into Europe on the waves of the hierarchical, theocratic impulse, opposition begins to build up as early as the twelfth century. Read Walther von der Vogelweide, that great Central European poet, and you will find he opposes the Roman Papacy and indeed everything Roman. What later reaches a climax in Huss, in Luther, in Zwingli and so on, is already hinted at by Walther von der Vogelweide. Then you also find what is developing as a more inward Christianity, parallel with that of the periphery but inwardly intimate, in Wolfram von Eschenbach's Parzival epic.

There, at the very beginning of the fifth post-Atlantean period, you have opposition against the theocratic, hierarchical, Roman element emanating from Spain and Italy. This opposing pole works in such an extraordinary way that intimate inwardness is never denied. It remains. It is confiscated from the principle of power and fashioned into the opposing pole.

I am neither praising the one nor blaming the other, for I am simply quoting facts. After the hierarchical, theocratic principle came the diplomatic, political principle. It is carried over in all its forms and in all its side manifestations. Here, some historical details are interesting. Something that is often said in historical textbooks is not actually correct: namely, that the invention of gunpowder was the origin of modern military forces, in contrast to the armies of the age of chivalry in the Middle Ages. A much more important factor came into play when, at the beginning of modern times in Europe, the barter economy of the Middle Ages was replaced by a currency economy, so that those in power came to be administrators of money, which had formerly not been the case. Until then, barter had been much more to the fore, with money playing only a minor role. The currency economy led to the development of mercenary armies that were no longer compatible with the armies of the age of chivalry which had been adapted to the barter economy of the Middle Ages. This modern military organization started in Switzerland. The Swiss were the first soldiers in the modern sense of the fifth post-Atlantean period. You can follow this in history: It was just because the Swiss became such efficient soldiers that they were able to win all those battles they had to win in order to create a Switzerland which would later be able to withstand the assaults of chivalry. I am speaking to the Swiss amongst us. Basically the Swiss with their armies are the primary, the real, conquerors of chivalry. Chivalry was overcome in Switzerland. It was from Switzerland alone that the rest of Europe learnt how to use their armies of infantry to overcome the armies of chivalry. Study history, and you will find that this is true.

Now let us proceed in history to Napoleon. Why were Napoleon's soldiers and armies superior to those of Central Europe? It was because Central Europe was still working, at the time of Napoleon, not with Swiss soldiers of course, but with the Swiss military principle, whereas Napoleon had under his command a real national army born out of the French nation itself. You will appreciate this if you follow the battles between the Central Europeans and Napoleon in the right way. How the generals of the Central European armies had to keep a hold on their mercenaries — for that is what they really were — even inside their barracks! Thus they never had the possibility of a strategy of long battle lines. Napoleon is the first to be able to use long battle lines because the French army at his disposal is a national army born of the people. When strategy necessitated a wide distribution of his forces, he did not need to worry that the men might desert. The Prussian general, on the other hand — for instance during the famous campaigns of Frederick the Great — was constantly concerned that a troop dispatched to a distant spot would desert, for his was not a national army but a crowd collected and sometimes coerced from all quarters; they came from all over the place, including quite foreign parts. The national army was invented in France, and this meant that Central Europe, starting with Prussia, also established national armies modelled on that of France. The Central European national armies came into their own when they assumed a French character.

So we see how even in this field things work parallel with the periphery. When it is a matter of armies, obviously the opposition takes the form of waging war. This is not the point I want to make, however, for I want to lead on to a similar contrast in another field. So far we have seen that the hierarchical, theocratic, Roman character met its opposition in Central Europe in everything that culminated in the Reformation. The diplomatic, French character made its way into Central Europe up to the time of Frederick the Great, right into the eighteenth century. Lessing was still in a position to debate whether he might, indeed, write *Laokoon* in French. Read the published correspondence of the eighteenth century. In Central Europe people wrote excellent French and poor German. The French element flooded the whole of Central Europe. We can say that what the Reformation had done to what came up from the South, Lessing, Herder, Goethe and those who came after them did in relation to the French, diplomatic element. Here, in Central European literature, Goethe, Schiller, Herder and Lessing emancipate themselves from the West, just as, in the Reformation, Central European Christianity emancipated itself from the South. But this process of separation goes hand in hand with one of combination. In his youth, Lessing still wrote a great deal in French. Leibniz wrote the whole of his philosophy, apart from what he wrote in Latin, in French, not German. In both these fields there was at the same time a working together and a standing in opposition. It is quite correct to summarize as follows: The South and Central Europe — opposition; the West and Central Europe — opposition.

With the third element, the British, it is the same. At first there is some kind of a parallel course. This is expressed especially in the fact that, from the eighteenth century and during the course of the nineteenth century, the great Shakespeare becomes a thoroughly German poet, for he is totally absorbed into German culture. He is not merely translated, he is totally assimilated and lives in the spiritual life of the German nation. For obvious reasons, I do not want to say that he still lives more in the spiritual life of the German nation than in that of the British nation. But look at the whole development, starting with Elias Schlegel,[6] who first translated Shakespeare into German, and on to Lessing's subtly spiritual penetration into the spirit of Shakespeare; the enthusiasm for Shakespeare felt by the German Naturalists of the eighteenth century, and also by Goethe; the absolutely outstanding — not translations — assimilations into German of Shakespeare by Schlegel and Tieck,[7] and so on, right up to

the present. Shakespeare lives in the German nation. When I went
to Vienna and sat in on the literary history lectures in addition to my
scientific studies, the first I heard were by Schröer,[8] who announced
he would be speaking about the three greatest German poets, Schiller,
Goethe and Shakespeare! Of course Shakespeare has not been captured
in the sense that it is claimed that he is actually German. But this
one example shows how standing in opposition can at the same time
take the form of an absolute working together. Thus it was with regard to the diplomatic, political, French element.
And so it happened also with regard to the British element. At the
same time the opposite pole must be present as well. The third element
has not yet found a form in Central Europe. The first was all that
led to the Reformation; this was in opposition to the southern, hierarchical element. The West is opposed by what culminated in Goethe's
Faust. And what we now hope for in Central Europe is the development of the element of spiritual science. In consequence there will
arise the sharpest opposition between Central Europe and the British
realm, an opposition even sharper than that of Lessing, Goethe and
their successors, with regard to the diplomatic, French element. Thus,
what took place between us and the followers of Mrs Besant[9] and so
on, was no more than a prelude. These things must be seen from wide
points of view.

I hope you know me well enough not to think that I speak out of
any petty vanity when I say certain things. But I do believe that the
great opposition is to be found between what works with experiments
on the physical plane — even to proving the existence of the spirit
— on the one hand, and on the other hand what in the human soul
longs to rise up to the spiritual world. There is no need for anything
as coarse as the declaration of an Alcyone[10] as the actual physical
Christ, for the more subtle descriptions by Sir Oliver Lodge would
be quite sufficient. One senses what is intended. Well, I suppose there
is no harm in saying these things. There is indeed a kind of opposition
between two things that came into being more or less simultaneously
when, on the one hand, Sir Oliver Lodge pointed to the spiritual world
in a materialistic way, while at the same time I was writing my book
Vom Menschenrätsel,[11] in which I endeavour, in a totally Central
European manner, to point to the paths which are being taken in Central Europe by the human soul to the world of the spirit. There is
no greater contrast than that between the book by Oliver Lodge and
the book *Vom Menschenrätsel*. They are absolute opposites; it is
impossible to conceive of any greater contrast.

This very clear differentiation only began more or less at the commencement of the fifth post-Atlantean period. Before that, things were still rather different. At first the universal Roman realm exercised its power, even as far as England, and the sharp differentiation between England and France only really came to the fore with the appearance of the Maid of Orleans. But then everything began, everything which was to happen within the context of these differentiations. The remarkable thing is that, even within this context, the impulse appears which says that a link ought to be created with the opposite pole. Thus, as I have often shown, we see the utterly British philosopher Francis Bacon of Verulam, the founder of modern materialistic thinking, inspired from the same source as Shakespeare, working across so strongly into Central Europe, in the way I have described. Jakob Böhme, too, was inspired from the same source. He transforms the whole inspiration into the soul substance of Central Europe. And again from the same source comes the southern German Jesuit Jakobus Baldus.[12]

You see, beneath the surface of what takes place on the physical plane there works what is to bring about harmony. But one must see things as clearly differentiated and not let it all disappear into a nebulous jumble. One of the greatest, most gigantic spirits of the British realm stands quite close to the opposition against what is merely commercial within the British commercial empire, and that is James I. James I brings in a new element by continuously inoculating into the substance of the British people something that they will have forever, something that they must not lose if they are not to fall utterly into materialism. What it is that he inoculates into them is something that is linked by underground channels to the whole of the rest of European culture. Here we are confronted by a significant mystery.

You will agree — neither one thing nor the other can be called either justified or unjustified; things simply have to be comprehended as necessary facts. But we must be clear that we surely ought to understand these things properly. It is easy to ask the question: What can I myself do in these painful times? The first thing one can do is to endeavour to understand things, to really see through things. This brings up thoughts which are real forces and these will have an effect. What about the question: Have the good forces no power against the evil forces we see all around us? To answer this we have to remember how difficult human freedom makes it for the spiritual world to assert itself amid the surging waves of materialistic life. This is what it is all about. Is it to be made so very easy for human beings to enter fully into the life of the spirit? Future ages will look back to today and say: How careless these people were with regard to adopting the life of spirit! The spiritual world is sending it down to us, but human beings resist it with all their might. Apart from all the sadness and suffering holding sway at present, the very fact that all this does hold sway is in itself a destiny signifying a trial. Above all it should be accepted and recognized as a trial. Later it will become apparent to what extent it is necessary for those who — so it is said — are guilty, to suffer together with those who are blameless. For after all, during the course of karma all these things are balanced out. You cannot say: Are not the good spirits going to intervene? They do intervene to the extent that we open ourselves to them, if we have the courage to do so. But first of all we must be serious about understanding things; we must be deeply serious about trying to understand.

As a contribution to this understanding it is necessary that a number of people muster the strength to oppose the surging waves of materialism with their deepest personal being. For something else is going to unite with the materialism that works in the industrial, commercial impulse; something coming from other, retarded impulses from the Chinese and Japanese element, particularly the Japanese element, will become increasingly caught up in materialism.

Yesterday somebody asked whether the societies working from the West for a particular group did not take into account that the Japanese might follow suit from the East. Indeed, the people who belong to these societies do not regard this as something terrible, for they see it as a support for materialism. For what follows suit from Asia will simply be a particular form of materialism. What we must be clear about, at all costs, is that we have to oppose the waves of materialism with all our strength. Every human being is capable of doing this. And the fruits of such efforts will be sure to follow. There is no need to give a name to whatever it is that must work against materialism. Don't call it 'Central European', don't call it 'German'; that is not necessary. But do consider how a counteraction of forces can come about and how this can be objectively proved.

You can summarize in two sentences what is needed to work against materialism — which, after all, has some justification. In the fifth post-Atlantean period the world will become even more pervaded by the industrial and commercial element; but the opposite pole must also exist: There must be people who work on the opposite side because of their understanding of the situation. For what is the aim of these secret brotherhoods? They do not work out of any particular British patriotism, but out of the desire to bring the whole world under the yoke of pure materialism. And because, in accordance with the laws of the fifth post-Atlantean period, certain elements of the British people as the bearer of the consciousness soul are most suitable for this, they want, by means of grey magic, to use these elements as promoters of this materialism.

This is the important point. Those who know what impulses are at work in world events can also steer them. No other national element, no other people, has ever before been so usable as material for transforming the whole world into a materialistic realm. Therefore, those who know want to set their foot on the neck of this national element and strip it of all spiritual endeavour — which, of course, lives equally in all human beings. Just because karma has ordained that the consciousness soul should work here particularly strongly, the secret brotherhoods have sought out elements in the British national character. Their aim is to send a wave of materialism over the earth and make the physical plane the only valid one. A spiritual world is only to be recognized in terms of what the physical plane has to offer.

This must be opposed by the endeavours of those who understand the necessity of a spiritual life on earth. Looked at from this point of view, you can express this counter-force in two sentences. One of these is well-known to you, but it does not yet come fully out of the hearts and souls of human beings: 'My kingdom is not of this world.' The sentence 'My kingdom is not of this world' must sound forth against that kingdom which is to be spread over the physical plane, that kingdom which is only of this world, that kingdom of commercial and industrial materialism.

There is not enough time today to explain to you how the words 'My kingdom is not of this world' link up with the cultivation of what belongs to mankind as a whole — not to what is German, but to what belongs to mankind as a whole. In ancient India there were four castes, in ancient Greece four estates. They came into being one after the other during the course of the second, third and fourth post-Atlantean periods. In the fifth post-Atlantean period the fourth estate, social life, that which belongs to mankind as a whole, must come into being. Not everyone can be a priest, but the priestly element can strive to become the powerful, the dominant estate. We see it doing this in the third post-Atlantean period; there we see it coming to life again in the hierarchical, theocratic, Roman force. And we can see the second caste, the kingly estate in ancient Greece and Rome, coming to life again in the second post-Atlantean element, where the diplomatic, political element is particularly active; for the republican element in France is only the opposite pole of this, just as everything generates its own counterpart. The actual character of the French state corresponds solely to the monarchic principle, so that even now France is a Republic in name only. In reality she is ruled by a king, who happens to be a lawyer who used to conduct cases in Romania.[14] It is not a question of terminology but of facts. What is so terrible today is the way people allow themselves to be so easily intoxicated by words. If somebody is called a president it does not necessarily mean that he is a president, for what matters is the actual situation.

The third estate, as we know, is the industrial element, what was commerce in ancient Egypt and Greece. This is striving to come to the fore again in the British Empire and for the moment must still be dominant over the fourth element, which will eventually be the general, human element. It is interesting to observe this in one particular phenomenon. You do have to gain some insight into what is really going on if you want to understand the world. Ask the question: Where has the theory of Socialism been worked out with the greatest discernment? You will receive a curious answer: Among German Socialists. For in accordance with the principle I explained to you, the Germans always have the mission to work concepts out in their purest form. So even for Socialism the Germans have worked out pure concepts, but the German concept of Socialism does not fit in at all with the state of affairs in Germany.

Social conditions in Germany do not correspond in any way to the German theory of Socialism! For instance, it is quite comprehensible that, after teaching in a Socialist school[15] for a while, I should have been banned from teaching there, after I said that it ought to be in keeping with Socialism to develop a theory of freedom. On behalf of the leader of the Social Democrats I was told: It is not freedom that matters, but reasoned persuasion! Socialist theory does not fit in with social conditions. In other words, social theory ought to be developed on the basis of the evolution of mankind. On this basis its three great principles are developed: Firstly the principle of the materialistic view of history, secondly the principle of added value, and thirdly the principle of class war.

The three principles are minutely worked out, but they do not fit in with social conditions in Germany. However, they correspond exactly to social conditions in England. That, after all, is where they were worked out. That is where Marx[16] worked on them first of all, and then also Engels,[17] and Bernstein.[18] This is their source. Here they fit in because — to take the third principle — they are founded on the class war. And this class war is waged, basically, in the British soul. Think of Cromwell.[19] If you study all the impulses that have reigned in the British soul since Cromwell, you will wind up with material for the third principle, the principle of class war. Furthermore, since the invention of the spinning-jenny and the commencement of the social life which came into being as a result, everything that has flowed into the theory of added value has been uppermost in the British Empire. And the materialistic view of history is, when you look at it, nothing but Buckle's[20] view of history translated into a pedantic German way of thinking. Look at Buckle's *History of Civilisation*. It is written in accordance with the way such things are written within the framework of British culture: namely, according to the principle of never entering into consequences. Darwin, too, did not enter into the consequences. He limited himself in a certain way. But in Karl Marx's materialistic view of history the matter is transformed with severity — regardless of consequences — in, if you like, a pedantic, German way.

It is interesting that no theory has been worked out for the general human element, the fourth caste or class. In this element there can be no question of dominance, for there is nothing below it over which dominance might be exercised; it is solely a matter of laying the foundation for human beings to relate with one another. A theory for this will only come about when the general human element given in anthroposophical spiritual science is made the foundation.

This, if it is not misunderstood, will lead to that other, second sentence which is to be added to the first: 'My kingdom is not of this world.' The second sentence is: 'Render unto Caesar what is Caesar's and unto God what is God's.' This means that a proper attitude to life, a real cultivation of life, can only come about when one realizes that the spiritual element must be cultivated, because the spiritual world must penetrate down into the physical world. But there is no point in making any statements at all unless they can be comprehended wholeheartedly in the soul. These statements must be comprehended: 'Render unto Caesar what is Caesar's and unto God what is God's' and 'My kingdom is not of this world.' Then the atmosphere of the spiritual world will come, an atmosphere that has nothing to do with those materialistic things which have especially to develop in the fifth post-Atlantean period. But for this to happen, things must be seen in their true guise. To summarize what we have been considering, let me say: May your hearts strive to see things in their true guise. Only if hearts exist which see things in their true guise and penetrate that terrible fog of untruth which shrouds everything in the world today, can we progress in an appropriate way. As I said: Since the bow-string is stretched to its limit, it will break. In this sense this document[21] that people have had the temerity to present to the world at this late stage, and whatever is said in response to this document, does in the first instance hold out a prospect of improvement. Whatever horrors still lie ahead of us, this document represents a challenge to the Spirit of Truth himself, and he will certainly intervene in these matters in an appropriate manner! You need only remember — let me say this in conclusion — the exemplary, or should I say non-exemplary, manner in which we ourselves have been treated.

We have endeavoured to be as cosmopolitan as possible over the years. We have tried in the most conscientious way to preserve this archetypal German trait of cosmopolitanism. And what is the consequence? Read the slanderous things said about us in Britain; the theosophists there have slanted everything to make it appear that we have some kind of Germanic aspirations. We have no such aspirations; they have been foisted on us by others.

Edouard Schuré,[22] — one on whom we relied so heavily in France, and towards whom we have never been tempted to display any kind of Germanic quality, since he is fundamentally himself the bearer of German cultural life to France — even he has interpreted things containing no trace of nationalism as being 'pan-Germanic'. How curious that only the other day we should have found under 'Edouard Schuré' in an encyclopaedia: 'The mediator of German culture to France.' This is entirely apt, for truly the only French thing about Schuré is the language he speaks. Of course, if language is taken to be paramount, then naturally the whole man can be considered French. So one is a pan-Germanist if one does not speak about the Germans in the manner preferred by the French chauvinist Schuré. And one is a German agent if one does not speak about the Germans in the way required by Mrs Besant. Similar things are beginning to appear in Italy, too, among our former friends.

So it became necessary to defend ourselves. And the present time is proving most opportune for those who want to point fingers at us and say: See what attacks they are making; that shows who is the aggressor! There is the Vollrath method, and there is the Gösch[23] method. We see it everywhere and we know it from within our own circles. First you force the other fellow to defend himself and then you treat him as the aggressor. It is a very effective method and one that plays an enormously strong role in the world today. The attacker hides behind the clamour he raises after he has forced the other to defend himself by labelling him the aggressor.

Yet we have no other purpose than to serve the mission of furthering spiritual life and gaining recognition for spiritual life. This is linked on the one hand with the principle: 'My kingdom is not of this world', and on the other with the principle: 'Render unto Caesar what is Caesar's and unto God what is God's.' Both are also, as you know, good Christianity. But it will be a long time before such things are understood in every detail.

Nowadays strange things are once again being said. Let me just mention this as my very last point. It is said: The Entente has stated its aims with regard to the war; now let the Central Powers state their aims, so that like can be compared with like. Indeed, this clamour for the war aims of the Central Powers has been heard for some time. Well, we have discussed some of the war aims of the Entente. But why should Central Europe name its war aims? It never had any! It has none! So quite naturally it took the stand: We will gladly negotiate, for then it will become clear what it is you want and then we shall have something on which to base our talks; but as far as we are concerned, we have nothing in particular to say; we merely want to live. Of course this does make it possible for the others to say: They are not willing to tell us what their war aims are; that means there must be something suspicious going on. There is nothing suspicious going on. Central Europe wants nothing now that it did not want in 1913 and 1912. It had no war aims then and it has none now.

It is not what is said that is important but whether what is said conforms with reality. On every side we now hear the loud cry that a particularly cunning, wily trick lies at the bottom of the Central Powers' Christmas call for peace. So this Christmas call for peace is supposed to contain some trick, some wish to dupe everybody else. On many sides it is said that the Central Powers never wanted peace but were only seeking for some clever way of carrying on the war.

The answer to that is: If only they had reacted to this call for peace! All they needed to do was accept it and they would soon have known whether it was some kind of trick. Along this path lies genuine thinking rather than an inclination to believe in empty phrases. We must, my dear friends, overcome the empty phrase with all the forces of our soul. This is the most intimate task we have to accomplish in our own soul.

LECTURE TWENTY-ONE
Dornach, 20 January 1917

Impulses connected with the spiritual world, whatever their direction, can only be understood from the viewpoint of spiritual science. As we have seen, playing into today's events there are impulses which we have traced back to human beings, but only to those who know how to handle spiritual impulses in one way or another.

We must ask ourselves: Why do certain people do the kind of things we have been talking about? Which leads to the next question: Why are we living in an age when untruth — untruthfulness — is working as a dominant force in the world, a force which drives human beings with a veritable passion that could, if only it would turn towards the truth instead, bring about infinitely much in the way of healing?

These things are indeed connected with what are, at the moment, the deepest impulses of humanity. We can gain a closer understanding of them, in a manner appropriate for our time, by including in our considerations the most urgent task of that spiritual-scientific view of the world which we have made our own. Remember that our anthroposophical spiritual science seeks to understand certain spiritual aspects which exist in the world, certain forces which are at work in the world of human beings in so far as they develop not only between birth and death but also between death and a new birth. It is difficult for people today to think about these things in the right way, because they have lost certain faculties which were once present in human evolution; for a while these faculties had to go underground, but now they must light up again through spiritual science.

We know well enough that in olden times the human soul was linked with the spiritual world in a way that was more elementary, more natural; such links did not have to be brought about by active spiritual work but existed of themselves. We called them atavistic. We know, too, that in those days it was impossible for human beings to doubt the existence of life after death. The possibility of such doubt only arose for an interim period which is now to be succeeded by an age in which all shall know about life between death and a new birth.

In those olden times something else — a third condition — came as naturally to the human soul as waking and sleeping do today. In today's state of being awake, human beings are restricted

entirely to the physical world which they can perceive with their
senses; they live between birth and death in a world which they can
experience through their senses and through their understanding which
is bounded by the brain. And in sleep they are unconscious. The
entities of ego and astral body in which they live between falling asleep
and waking up are not yet strong enough to supply them with a
comparable consciousness. We know that the astral body has only
been developing since the time of ancient Moon and the ego only since
the beginning of Earth evolution. Both are young measured against
cosmic evolution and they are not yet strong enough to achieve consciousness when left to themselves between going to sleep and waking up.

Dreams, however, with all their manifold pictures, do rise up out
of sleep. These dreams can contain a great deal that belongs to the
spiritual world. There is a great deal in dreams which belongs to the
spiritual world, but the human soul as it is today is not capable of
seeing beyond the dreams in order to discover what it is that lives
in these dreams. Dreams are deceptive pictures woven out of a veil
of maya. When they are rightly interpreted they yield experiences
of earlier times or prophetic indications for the future. They also reveal
the interplay which takes place between the living and the dead during
sleep. Everything can come to us through dreams. But, at the present
stage of their evolution, human beings do not understand the strange
language of dreams. Dream pictures remain incomprehensible, and
this is quite natural. Just as Europeans cannot interpret the sounds
spoken by the Chinese, so people today cannot interpret the picture
language of dreams.

Thus during this interim period the human being is totally restricted
in consciousness to whatever he can discover through those older
instruments, the physical body and also the etheric body, which have
been developing since the time of ancient Sun and ancient Saturn and
are therefore so constituted that they can offer him consciousness as
long as he is in them, that is, between waking up and going to sleep.

Now the spiritual science for which we are striving gives us concepts
of the supersensible world working in and behind the sense-perceptible
world. The concepts and ideas given to us by spiritual science and
which we make our own are related to nothing that can be perceived
by the senses. They relate either to what lies between death and a
new birth, or to the supersensible world which lies beyond the world
of the senses. Comprehension of these is not, or ought not to be, a

mere comprehension of certain theories. We are not concerned with knowing one thing or another but with achieving a certain inner mood of soul when we take in truths relating to the supersensible world.

It is difficult to describe these things in words because our language has been coined for the external, physical plane, so we have to exert ourselves when applying it to supersensible conditions. You could say that everything to which we ordinarily apply our understanding lives coarsely, densely in our soul because our brain is always at our disposal and is trained to deal with ideas and concepts relating to the physical plane. But to explain things which do not relate to the physical plane we have to exert our soul to such an extent that, when we study spiritual science, our brain plays an ever-decreasing part. When we experience difficulties in understanding what spiritual science gives us, this is only because our brain impedes our understanding. Our brain is adjusted and adapted to the coarse concepts of the physical plane and we have to exert ourselves to acquire the subtler concepts — subtler only in so far as human comprehension is concerned — of the spiritual world. This exertion is entirely healthy, it is certainly good, because with spiritual science we then live in our soul in a new way, quite different from that required by physical knowledge and understanding and ideas. We transport ourselves into a world of mobile, subtle pictures and ideas, and that is significant.

It is possible for all of you to be aware of the point at which you are sufficiently within the sphere where the etheric body more or less lives on its own, using the brain only in faint vibrations. It is the point at which you begin to feel that you no longer have to exert yourself to think the thoughts given by spiritual science, in the way in which you have to exert yourself to think everyday thoughts. You know very well that you yourself make the thoughts which you think about everyday matters on the physical plane; you develop the concepts in accordance with the daily requirements and conditions of life, in accordance with sympathies and antipathies and with whatever is prepared by your senses and by your brain-bound understanding. With spiritual science, however, once you really enter into it, you will begin to sense: I have not thought all this myself; it has already been thought before I think it; it is floating there as a thought and merely enters into me. When you begin to feel: This is floating in the objective thinking of the universe and merely enters into me — then you will have won a great deal. You will have experienced a relationship to that delicate etheric, floating and weaving world in which your soul lives. After that it is really only a matter of time, though it might be quite a long time, before you gradually enter that sphere which we share with those among the dead with whom we are karmically linked.

I said that in olden times there was no question of discussing whether immortality existed or not. People then had a third condition apart from sleeping and waking, an in-between condition which was not merely a state of dreaming. It was an elementary and natural condition, in which human beings saw their dead spiritually face to face. They were there and they lived together with them. In those earlier times, when people did something, or when something happened to them which was a little out of the ordinary — and this of course happened and still happens all the time, for we are not only creatures of habit — they then felt beside them one or another of those who had gone through death before them, either long, or not so long, ago. They felt as though the dead person acted with them, or joined in their counsel. So when the soul of a person living on the earth decided to do something, or when something happened to that person, this soul felt that there was one who had died who joined in the action or the suffering. The dead were present. So there was no discussion about immortality or the lack of it. It would have been as pointless as questioning whether someone with whom we are speaking is actually there or not. Whatever we experience is a reality, and in olden times people experienced how the dead shared in all that happened.

We know the reasons why those times had to go into the underground of existence. But they will return, though in a different form. The manner of their return will be brought about by human beings who achieve the mood of soul which can be achieved through spiritual science, through actively living in the pictures of the spiritual world given by spiritual science. This will enable the soul to attain a delicate attuning, and then into this delicate attuning the souls of the so-called dead will enter. Of course they are always present, but what matters now is that we should be aware of how they enter into our soul-sphere. Of course, the dead always surround those of us with whom they were karmically linked during life. But to enable them to enter our consciousness we must go to meet them with the fine attuning I have just described. For you see it is always possible for the dead to gain entry into human souls if these souls lead their life in a mood such as that described just now, where the concepts and ideas formed by these souls live, somehow, in a supersensible sphere. From the bodily, physical aspect of man the dead have to flee, for at the moment they cannot enter there. Neither can they enter those thoughts which only rise up from the brain after the manner of the physical world. And because today human beings mostly entertain only thoughts that rise up from the brain, it is so very difficult for the dead to make contact with the living.

But if the living go to meet the dead by developing the fine attuning that arises when one concerns oneself a great deal with supersensible ideas, then the dead can enter that floating and weaving world which extricates itself from the bodily aspect and takes no account of it. Today everything depends on whether human souls will find it possible, in some measure, to tread the path which leads to the dead. For then the dead will come to meet them. There must be a meeting in a common realm.

I have often stressed that what spiritual science has to say about the supersensible world, the concepts and ideas we develop — all this is there for both the living *and* the dead. That is why I have recommended the practice of reading to the dead: that is, of unfolding thoughts orientated to them which refer to the supersensible world. Doing this is a way of offering them a bridge and it is one which can reach not only those who have died recently, but all those who have died, even a very long time ago.

In this way the living have the possibility of approaching the dead. And similarly the dead have the possibility of working into the thoughts of the living. When you have absorbed the spirit of spiritual science you will be able to form from such arguments a fair conception of the fact that in the materialistic age we human beings have lived through for so long the dead can have less and less influence on the course of events here in the physical world where human beings have turned towards more materialistic ideas relating only to the physical plane, ideas which are of no use to the dead. So events in the physical world now run their course without any, or with only very little, influence from those who have passed on. This will have to change. Active communication must once more be established between the living and the dead. Those who have died must become able to work into the physical world, so that what takes place there no longer goes on solely under the influence of conceptions which arise in this physical world.

So our pursuit of spiritual science is indeed intimately bound up with giving the dead an opportunity to work here in the physical world. It must be said that a grave and lofty aim of our work in spiritual science is the creation of a link between the spiritual world, where the dead have their home, and the physical world. Then the dead will no longer have to say to themselves that they are more or less exiles from the physical world owing to the fact that the living, down here, cannot develop thoughts through which the dead might bring their influence to bear in this physical world.

Many, for sure, will say: I have been striving to open myself to the ideas of spiritual science, but I have seen no sign of any influence emanating from the dead. My dear friends, these things demand a good deal of patience. You must take into account the degree to which for centuries the life of mankind on the physical plane has tended towards materialism and against anything that might make it possible for the dead to work here in a suitable way. Amongst all that has been going on for centuries, certain feelings, certain sensations have developed which human beings now entertain quite unconsciously towards the spiritual world. To these feelings and sensations, what comes today from spiritual science frequently appears as no more than abstract theory. One may well be convinced that what spiritual science has to say about the spiritual world is true. And yet it has not thus far entered so fully into one's whole soul life as to enable one to develop those sensations and feelings which do not disturb the delicate and subtle play of what comes over from the dead.

It is not easy to see these things in their proper light. People today are the children, or the grandchildren, or the great-grandchildren, or even the great-great-grandchildren of those who have lived during recent centuries and who have, under the influence of rising materialism, turned their sensations and feelings in certain directions. These directions are now expressed in every detail of these feelings and sensations. We can have the best will in the world to turn in the right way to someone who has died, to remember someone in the right way. But the whole disposition of our feelings and sensations working, perhaps one could say, through our blood which flows down to us from our ancestors, is not suited to placing before our soul in a proper way the delicate and intimate manifestations and revelations which come from the dead. Instead our feelings are like flickering lights, excitable flickering lights which interpose themselves in front of these subtle impulses which are today still so very delicate and intimate.

But though this may be the case we need not be discouraged, but should always cling to the positive aspect. And the positive aspect is that we genuinely strive for that condition which in certain moments of life, as the fruit of studying spiritual science, can give us a peacefulness of soul. What matters is that peacefulness of soul, the fine attuning in that peacefulness of soul, which makes it possible for us to receive these delicate, intimate manifestations and revelations from the kingdom of the dead.

Something else, too, is necessary, and that is the goodwill to resist all that untruthfulness about which we have been speaking in these lectures. All these untruthfulnesses that buzz about in the world enter into what might be called the spiritual aura and generate there a thick fog which the dead find impossible to penetrate. This thick fog contains all that black rubbish which comes, for instance — to name only one source — from today's journalism, in the form of untruths which are printed and repeated, creating an aura of untruthfulness spanning the earth. It is no exaggeration to say that it is exceedingly difficult for the dead to penetrate this black fog. Therefore, with the help of ideas such as those we have been developing concerning the absolutely concrete untruthfulness buzzing about in the world, it is necessary to endeavour to reach clarity, to really make the effort in this field to recognize the purely external truth of the physical plane in so far as this can become accessible to us, in order not to cover our soul with a dense fog through which the spiritual world simply cannot penetrate. You will understand how very necessary this is.

In conjunction with the concepts we have just been discussing, let us now touch on the question: What is the aim of those secret societies which send impulses of the kind we have been describing into the world, impulses which then live in the life of untruthfulness and which have led, out of this untruthfulness, to the painful events of today? What do these secret societies want? Among others — we cannot go into everything — there is one particular thing they want: They want to materialize materialism even further; they want to create even more materialism in the world than would come about as part of the natural evolution of mankind in the fifth post-Atlantean period. They want even more materialism. This is only one aspect of what they are aiming for, but it is the aspect we want at least to touch on here. With this aspect in mind such societies are founded and with this aspect in mind people are persuaded to join them, people who are approached during their lives because they are deemed suitable.

There are the most varied types of such societies. One type, much in evidence in the West and taking all kinds of forms, includes organizations which practise ceremonial magic. Ceremonial magic can, of course, be good magic, but we are speaking now of those societies which do not practise ceremonial magic for the good of mankind in general, but for the good of certain groups of people, or certain specific aims which are not general human aims.

Let us look first at those societies which practise ceremonial magic from this point of view. As we have said, it can be good, but in these societies it is not good. Certain kinds of ceremonial magic have definite effects on the human physical body. Everything physical is, after all, a manifestation of the spirit. Certain spiritual aspects which come into being under the influence of ceremonial magic can have an effect on the human physical body, specifically on the system of ganglia, as I described it the other day, and also on the spinal system. The cerebral system is the most difficult of all to influence by means of ceremonial magic. All this has to be done via the detour of the spiritual element, but it can be done and it can become effective.

Imagine certain secret societies carrying on a form of ceremonial magic directed towards its grey or black aspects. Imagine they influence their members in a way that affects even their physical body, even the delicate vibrations and weavings of their physical body, so that something spiritual flows into this physical body.

What is the consequence? The consequence is that something now comes about which was suitable in earlier periods of human evolution but is no longer permissible today. Such procedures make it possible for the spiritual world to influence those human beings who participate, even though they do not turn towards it along the path I have described. This means that it becomes possible for the dead, as well as other spirits, to influence the members of a circle created by ceremonial magic. In this way today's materialism can be made hyper-materialistic.

Imagine a human being — and there are countless such in the West — who is entirely materialistic, not only in his view of the world but also in all his feelings and sensations. And then imagine this materialistic disposition increasing to a high degree. Such a person must of necessity develop an urge to exercise an influence on the material world, not only while he lives in his physical body but also after he has died. He is bent on the following: When I die I want to have some abode through which I can affect the people I have left behind on the earth, or who are trained in such a way in relation to me. There are indeed certain people today whose materialistic urge is so great that they strive for means by which they can cultivate connections with the physical world even beyond death. And such means, through which a person secures for himself the possibility of affecting the material world from beyond death, are abodes of certain kinds of ceremonial magical practice.

This is something that can have immense consequences. Imagine a number of people brought together to form a certain brotherhood. These people know: Others have gone before us; their urge to exercise their power was so great that their life on earth was not enough for its gratification, so they want to go on gratifying it even after death. For them we are creating an abode, and through the acts of ceremonial magic we perform, they work into our bodies. Because of this we gain greater power than we have; because of this we are enabled to exercise a certain degree of magical power over other, weaker people who stand outside such brotherhoods. When we speak words, when we give a speech, these dead souls work in us because we have been prepared by sharing in these acts of ceremonial magic.

It is one thing if somebody who simply participates honestly in the cultural processes of our time gives a speech in parliament or writes a newspaper article. But it is something entirely different if a person who belongs to a circle of ceremonial magic, and is thus strengthened by the power urges of some who have died, gives a speech in parliament or writes an article for a newspaper. The latter exercises an immensely greater degree of influence in the direction of his wishes than would be the case if he did not have this backing. This is one side of the matter.

The other side is that those who enter the circle of certain societies practising ceremonial magic are securing for themselves a power that reaches beyond death, a kind of ahrimanic immortality. For these people this is their main concern. For them, the society they enter provides a kind of guarantee that certain forces — which should by rights only live in them until the moment of death — will continue to live, even beyond death. More people than you might think are nowadays filled with this idea of guaranteeing for themselves an ahrimanic immortality, which consists in exercising influence not only as an individual human being, but also through the instrument of a society of this kind. Such societies exist in the most varied forms, and individuals who have attained certain degrees of advancement in these societies know: As a member of this society I shall become to some degree immortal because forces which would otherwise come to an end at my death will continue to work beyond death.

What these people then experience through this ceremonial magic makes them quite oblivious to a thought which would concern someone who takes such things truly seriously and in a genuinely dignified way. This is that the more a person gains by way of materialistic immortality, or rather ahrimanic immortality, the more he loses of the consciousness of true, genuine immortality. Yet materialism has taken such a hold on many souls today that they remain unconcerned about this and are tricked into striving for ahrimanic immortality. It could indeed be said that societies exist today which, from a spiritual or occult point of view, could be called 'insurance companies for ahrimanic immortality'!

It is only a small number of people in each case who understand all these things. For as a rule these societies are organized in such a way that the ceremonial magic they practise influences only those who are unaware of the implications, merely desiring to make contact with the spiritual world by means of symbolic ceremonies. There are many such people. And those who have this desire are by no means necessarily the worst. They are accepted as members of the circle of ceremonial magic among whom there are then a few who simply use the rest of the members as instruments. Therefore one should beware of all secret societes administered by so-called higher grades whose aims are kept hidden from the lower grades. These administrative grades usually comprise those who have been initiated to a stage at which they only have a vague idea of what I have just been explaining to you. They comprise those who are to work positively in connection with certain goals and aims which are then realized by the wider group of those who have been merely inveigled into the circle of ceremonial magic. Everything these people do is done in such a way that it leads in the direction required by the higher grades but is strengthened by the forces which come from ceremonial magic.

Those who know how huge a number of such societies exist in the West can begin to gain an idea of what immensely effective tools such societies of ceremonial magic can be for certan far-reaching plans for the world. As you have seen, the chief aim is to prolong into our time a way of proceeding in which the spiritual world works into the sense-perceptible, physical world in a manner that was right in earlier times. For our times, however, the right procedure is for human beings to go towards the dead and meet them half-way. In the mood we have just been discussing, however, a path is sought which was appropriate in earlier, atavistic times but which today is brought about through the medium of ceremonial magic.

This should give you an idea of the disproportionate lengths to which exaggerated materialism, materialism that is hyper-materialistic, is prepared go in order to cross the border to the spiritual world, a border which today should only be crossed by means of attuning the soul to that mood which can be achieved through contemplating supersensible concepts. An attitude appropriate for today is one that never accepts things which are given out by many secret societies, and which are not understood, for indeed a great deal that has not been understood is today both given out and accepted. Today it is appropriate to treat what these societies give out as something that is at most a failure to give the spoken word its true value, that is, something that uses words as mere concepts.

In much that today buzzes about in the world by way of untruthfulness and by way of egoism, in much that has even led to the canonization of egoism — not by the Pope, of course — in much that has led to the coining of the phrase *sacro egoismo*,[1] which has become a new saint, though not canonized by the Pope, in much that today buzzes about in the world by way of egoisms and untruthfulnesses, influences and impulses are at work which gain extra strength from the world of the dead, in the manner described. And by searching for these impulses you will be led on to link up with other impulses about which you may find information in my book *The Spiritual Guidance of Man*.[2] The lectures on which this book is based were given in 1911 in Copenhagen, for the most varied reasons. You will find there a description of how certain angelic powers remained behind in the third post-Atlantean period, in order today to unfold a force resembling that developed during the ancient Egyptian epoch. In those lectures I said:

'Anything wonderful can become a tempter and seducer of mankind if people follow it one-sidedly; and then if this one-sidedness starts to take a hold, the great danger arises that all kinds of good endeavours begin to manifest as fanaticism. True though it is that mankind progresses by means of its noble impulses, it is equally true that an over-enthusiastic, fanatical pursuit of these most noble impulses can lead to all that would be worst for their right unfolding.'

The lecture then goes on to describe how certain forces which had their proper place in the third post-Atlantean period are now starting to work in our time. One may now add that just as an individual quite rightly finds a connection with his proper angel, so is it also possible for him to find a connection to those retarded spirits of the Egypto-Chaldean period, those retarded angels, if he seeks those forces and impulses which, in fact, are exaggerated ahrimanic forces coming in the manner described from the realm of the dead. These retarded angels play an important role in the secret societies I have been describing to you. There they are important helpers and leading spirits. A great deal that goes on in such secret societies is aimed at bringing Egypto-Chaldean elements in the old way into the present time. When these matters are no mere tomfoolery but stand fully in occult life, this takes place under the influence of retarded beings from the hierarchy of the angels who become leaders there. These are the beings from the hierarchy next above man who are sought by these societies.

This points to something exceedingly important. When we understand how the living testaments of these societies — not written testaments left over for those still alive, but testaments which are forces going beyond death — when we understand how these work and are preserved, which is something that ought not to happen, then we understand something of the magical power wielded by such societies which often enables them to impress the stamp of truthfulness on to something untrue. And indeed, one of their important magical functions is to spread untruth in the world in such a way that it gives the effect of being the truth. For in this working of the 'untruth in what is true' lies one of the mighty strengths of evil. This strength of evil is then put to considerable use in all kinds of quarters.

This I wanted to say today, in order to give you the esoteric background to the more exoteric matters I have been describing. Tomorrow we shall continue with this and endeavour to enter even more deeply into certain aspects.

LECTURE TWENTY-TWO

Dornach, 21 January 1917

Let me start by drawing your attention to a number of things which might be of interest to you, beginning with an article in yesterday's issue of *Schweizerische Bauzeitung*,[1] reporting on the *Johannesbau* in Dornach, near Basel. This is the result of a recent visit of a group of Swiss engineers and architects. The article is most gratifying and fair. Indeed, it is like an oasis in the midst of other things which have recently appeared in print about our efforts which had their source in our very midst. It is most satisfying to find such a fair discussion that gives the building its due, especially since it comes from specialist, objective quarters outside our own circle. Do read it. Herr Englert,[2] who acted as guide for that group of Swiss engineers and architects who showed such genuine interest in our building from the technical and also the aesthetic point of view, has just reported that the article is also due to be published in French in the Geneva journal *Bulletin de technique*.

Further, I should like to draw your attention to a book — you will excuse my inability to tell you the title in the original language — just published by our friend Bugaev under his pen-name of Andrei Belyi.[3] The book is in Russian and gives a very detailed account in great depth of the relationship between spiritual science and Goethe's view of the world. In particular it goes into the connections between Goethe's views and what I said in Berlin in the lecture cycle *Human and Cosmic Thought*[4] about various world views, but it also discusses a good deal that is contained in spiritual science. Its connections to Goethe's views are discussed in depth and in detail and it is much appreciated that our friend Bugaev has published a revelation of our spiritual-scientific view in Russian.

Herr Meebold,[5] too, has just published a book in Munich to which I should also like to draw your attention. The title is *The Path to the Spirit. Biography of a Soul.* You will find it interesting because Herr Meebold describes in it a number of experiences he had in connection with the Theosophical Society.

These are the oases in the desert of attacks. It seems that another has just appeared, written by one of our long-standing older members. It is said to be particularly scandalous, but I have not yet seen it. These attacks from among our members are particularly unwelcome because we realize that it is precisely these long-standing older members who ought to know better.

Yesterday we spoke about aspects of the human being's connections with the supersensible world, particularly with regard to the fact that our dead, and indeed all those who have left their bodies and gone through the gate of death, must be thought of as being in that world. In our present context it is particularly important to understand that in the world through which man passes between death and a new birth an evolution, a development is taking place just as much as is the case here on the physical plane.

Here on the physical plane, taking a shorter span to start with, such as the post-Atlantean time, we speak of the Indian, the Persian, the Egypto-Chaldean, the Greco-Latin, the modern period, and so on. And we consider that during the course of these periods an evolutionary process takes place — in other words, that human souls and the manner in which these souls manifest in the world during this sequence of periods differ in characteristic ways.

Similarly, if only one can find sufficiently graphic concepts, one can speak of an evolution that takes place for these periods of time in the sphere through which the dead pass. There, too, an evolution takes place. On all kinds of occasions, where this has been possible, this evolution has been discussed in different ways.[6] But relatively easy though it is to speak of evolution on the physical plane — and as you know it is not all that easy in this materialistic age — it is naturally less easy to do so with regard to the spiritual world, since for that world we lack sufficiently graphic concepts. Our language was created for the physical plane, and we are forced to use all kinds of paraphrases and graphic substitutes in order to describe the spiritual sphere in which the dead are living, especially with regard to evolution.

Naturally, of particular interest now is the fact that life between death and a new birth in our fifth post-Atlantean period is suitably different from what it was in earlier times. While the materialistic cultural period is running its course here on earth, a great deal is also taking place in the spiritual world. Since the dead have a far more intense experience of everything connected with evolution than is the case for people living on the physical plane, their destiny is most intensely dependent on the manner in which a certain evolution takes place in definite periods. The dead react far more intimately, far more subtly, to what lives in evolution than do the living — if we may use these expressions — and this is perhaps more noticeable in our materialistic age than has ever been the case before.

Now, to assist our understanding of a number of things we shall be discussing, I want to introduce into these lectures something that has emerged in relation to this, as a result of careful observation of the actual situation. To do this I shall have to widen our scope somewhat and speak today about various aspects in preparation for the statements towards which our train of thought is leading.

I have already pointed out that the right way to look at the human being in relation to the universe is to consider the individual parts of his being separately. From the spiritual point of view, what exists here on the physical plane is more a kind of image, a manifestation. Thus we may regard as fourfold the physical human being we see before us.

First we see the head. As you know from earlier discussions, the head as it appears in a particular incarnation is supposed to have reached its final stage in that incarnation. The head is the part most strongly exposed to death. For the way our head is formed is, for the most part, the consequence of our life in our previous incarnation. On the other hand, the formation of our next head in our next incarnation is the consequence of the life of our present body. A while ago I expressed this briefly by saying: Our body, apart from our head, metamorphoses itself into our head in our next incarnation, while our next body is growing towards us; whereas our present head is the metamorphosed body of our previous incarnation, the rest of our body has grown towards us more or less — there are varying degrees — out of what we have inherited.

This is how the metamorphosis takes place. Our head, as it were, falls away in one incarnation, having been the outcome of our body in our previous incarnation. And our body transforms itself, metamorphoses itself — as does leaf to petal in Goethe's theory of metamorphosis — into our head in our next incarnation. Now because our head is formed from the earthly body of our previous incarnation, the spiritual world has a great amount of work to do on this head between death and our new birth, for its archetypal form must be fashioned by the spiritual world in accordance with karma. That is why, even in the embryo, the head appears before anything else in its complete form, for more than any other part it has been influenced by the cosmos. The body, on the other hand, is influenced for the most part by the human organism. So this appears later than the head in the embryo. Apart from its physical substance, which has of course been gathered through heredity, our head, in its form, its archetypal form, is indeed shaped by the cosmos, by the sphere of the cosmos. It is not for nothing that your head is more or less spherical in shape, for it is an image of the sphere of the universe; the whole sphere of the universe works to form your head. Thus we can say that our head is formed from the sphere.

Just as here on earth people busily work to construct machines and build up trade and commerce, so in the spiritual world human beings are busy, though not exclusively, developing all the technical requirements, the spiritual technical requirements for building the head for their next incarnation from out of the sphere of the universe, the whole cosmos, in accordance with the karma of their earlier incarnations. We glimpse here a profound mystery of evolution.

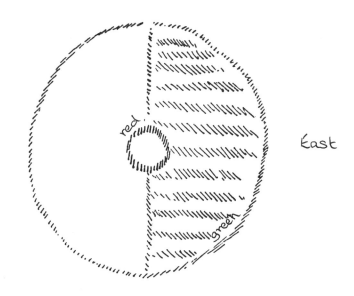

The second aspect we must consider, if we want to view man as a revelation of the whole universe, comprises all the organs of his breast, centred around lung and heart. Let us look at them without the head. The head is an image of the whole spherical cosmos. Not so, the organs of the breast. These are a revelation of all that comes from the East. They are formed out of what might be called the hemisphere. (See diagram).

Imagine the cosmos like this. Then you can see the head as an image of the cosmos. And the organs of the breast can be seen as an image of what streams in from the East — the hemisphere I am shading green. This hemisphere alone works on the organs of the breast. Or, expressed as a paradox: The breast organs are half a head.

This is the basic form. The head is based on the sphere, the breast organs on part of a circle, a kind of semicircle, only it is bent in various ways so that you can no longer recognize it exactly. You would be able to see that your head really is a sphere had luciferic and ahrimanic forces never worked on man. And you would see that the organs of the breast are really a hemisphere, had these forces never exercised their influence. The direction in relation to the centre — one would have to say for ordinary earthly geometry, the infinitely distant centre — is eastwards. An eastward-facing hemisphere.

Now we come to the third part of the human being, excluding head and breast organs: the abdominal organs and the limbs attached to the abdomen. Although this is not an exact term, I shall call all this the abdominal organs. Everything I comprehensively call the abdominal organs can also be related, like the other parts, to forces which work and organize from without. In this realm they work, of course, on man from the outside via embryological development in the way they do because during pregnancy the mother is dependent on the forces which have to be gathered together to form the abdomen, just as forces have to be collected from the sphere to form the head and from the East, the hemisphere, to form the organs of the breast.

The forces that work on the organs of the abdomen must be imagined as coming from the centre of the earth, but differentiated, with all that this entails, according to the region inhabited by the parents or ancestors. The forces all come from the centre of the earth, but with differentiations depending on whether a person is born in North America, Australia, Asia or Europe. The organs of the abdomen are determined by forces from the centre of the earth with differentiations according to region.

Seen from the occult point of view, the complete human being also has a fourth aspect. You will say that we have already dealt with the whole human being, and this is so, but from the occult point of view a fourth aspect must be considered. We have examined three parts, so now all that is left is the total human being. This totality, too, is a part. Head, chest and abdomen all together form the fourth aspect, the totality, and this totality is in turn formed by certain forces. This totality is formed by forces that come from the whole circumference of the earth. They are not differentiated according to region. The total human being is formed by the total circumference of the earth.

Herewith I have described to you the physical human being as an image of the cosmos, an image of the forces of the cosmos working together. Other aspects, too, might be considered in connection with the cosmos. For this we would have to think of the spiritual cosmos in relation to the human being, not only the physical cosmos. We have just been examining the physical human being, so we were able to remain with the physical cosmos. Once we start to consider the discarnate human being between death and a new birth we cannot remain with the elements of space, for the three-dimensional space that we have — though it determines the measure of the physical human being living between birth and death — does not determine the measure of the spiritual human being living between death and a new birth. We have to realize that those who are dead have at their disposal a world that is different from the one which lives in three dimensions.

To turn now to the discarnate human being, the one we call a dead human being, perhaps we need a different kind of consideration. Our method of consideration must remain more mobile. Also there are various points of view from which we could conduct our considerations, for life between death and a new birth is just as complicated as life between birth and death. So let us start with the relationship between the human being here on earth and the human being who has entered the spiritual world through death.

Once again we have the first part, but it is temporal rather than spatial. We could call it the first phase of a development. The dead human being goes, you might say, out into the spiritual world in a certain way; he leaves the physical world but, especially during the first few days, is still very much connected with it. It is very significant that the dead person leaves the physical world in close connection with the constellation arising for his life from the positions of the planets. For as long as the dead person is still connected with his etheric body, the constellation of planetary forces resounds and vibrates in a wonderful way through this etheric body. Just as the territorial forces of the earth vibrate very strongly with the waters of the womb that contains a growing physical human being, so in a most marked way do the forces of the starry constellations vibrate in the dead person who is still in his etheric body at the moment — which is, of course, karmically determined — when he has just left the physical world.

Investigations are often made — unfortunately not always with the necessary respect and dignity, but out of egoistic reasons — into the starry constellation prevailing at birth. Much less selfish and much more beautiful would be a horoscope, a planetary horoscope made for the moment of death. This is most revealing for the whole soul of the human being, for the entry into death at a particular moment is most revealing in connection with karma.

Those who decide to conduct such investigations — the rules are the same as those applied to the birth horoscope — will make all kinds of interesting discoveries, especially if they have known the people for whom they do this fairly well in life. For several days the dead person bears within himself, in the etheric body he has not yet discarded, an echoing vibration of what comes from the planetary constellation. So the first phase is that of the direction in the starry constellation. It is meaningful as long as the human being remains connected with his etheric body.

The second phase in the relationship of the human being to the cosmos is the direction in which he leaves the physical world when he becomes truly spiritual, after discarding his etheric body. This is the last phase to which terms can be applied in their usual, rather than in a pictorial, meaning to describe what the dead person does, terms which are taken from the physical world. After this phase the terms used must be seen more or less as pictures.

So, in the second phase the human being goes in the direction of whatever is the East as seen from his starting point — here, direction is still used in a physical sense, even though it is away from the physical world. Through whatever is for him an easterly direction the dead person journeys at a certain moment into the purely spiritual world. The direction is to the East. It is important to be aware of this. Indeed, an old saying found in various secret brotherhoods, preserved from the better days of mankind's occult knowledge, still points to this. Various brotherhoods speak of one who has died as having 'entered into the eternal East'. Such things, when they are not foolish trappings added later, correspond to ancient truths. Just as we had to say that the organs of the breast are formed out of the

East, so must we imagine the departure of the dead as going through the East. By stepping out of the physical world through the East into the spiritual world, the dead person achieves the possibility of participating in the forces which operate, not centrifugally as here on earth, but centripetally towards the centre of the earth. He enters into the sphere out of which it is possible to work towards the earth.

The third phase may be described as the transition into the spiritual world; and the fourth as working or having an effect out of the spiritual world, working with the forces from the spiritual world.

Such ideas bring us intimately close to what here binds the human being to the spiritual worlds. The table below shows that the conclusion of number 4 meets up with the beginning of number 1, namely working on the head out of the realm of the sphere. This work is done by the human being himself after he has entered into the spiritual world by way of the East.

1	2	3	4
Head:	Breast organs:	Abdominal organs:	The totality:
from the sphere	from the East	from the centre of the earth, differentiated according to territory	by the circumference of the earth
First Phase: Direction in the starry constellation	Second Phase: Towards the East	Third Phase: Transition into the spiritual world	Fourth Phase: Working out of the spiritual world

In our dealings with the dead we can perceive strongly that those who have died have to leave the physical world in an easterly direction. They are to be found in the world which they reach via the door of the East. They are beyond the door of the East. And in this connection the experiences we undergo now, in the fifth post-Atlantean period, in the sphere of development of materialism are very significant.

For you see, in this fifth post-Atlantean period, the dead now lack a great deal because of the materialistic culture prevalent in the world.

Some aspects of this will be clear to you from what we said yester-day. When, by suitable means, we come to know the life of the dead today, we discover that they have a very strong urge to intervene in what human beings do here on earth. But in earlier times, when there was less materialism on the earth than there is today, it was easier for the dead to intervene in what took place on the earth. It was easier for them to influence the sphere of the earth through what those on earth felt and sensed of the after-effects of the dead.

Today it can be experienced very frequently — and this is always surprising in the actual case — that people who have been intensely involved in certain events during their life are unable, in their life after death, to have any interest in the events which take place after their death, because they lack any kind of link. Amongst us, too, there are souls who showed great interest for events on earth while they were here but who now, having gone to the spiritual world, find the events taking place since their death quite foreign to them. This is frequently the case, even with distinguished souls who here on earth were greatly gifted and filled with the liveliest interest.

This has been going on for a long time, indeed it has been on the increase during the whole of the fifth post-Atlantean period, ever since the fifteenth and sixteenth centuries. Expressed in commonplace terms — which are unfortunately all we have in our language — our experience is that, because they are less and less able to intervene in what human beings do, the dead have instead to intervene in the way people manifest as individual personalities. So we see that since the fifteenth and sixteenth centuries the interest and the work of the dead has been concentrated increasingly on individual personalites rather than on the wider contexts concerning mankind. Since I have occupied myself closely with this very aspect, I have reached the con-viction that it is connected with a certain phenomenon of modern times that is very noticeable to those who are interested in such things.

In recent history, unlike former times, we have the remarkable phenomenon of people being born with outstanding capacities. In general they work with tremendous idealism and distinguished endeavour but are incapable of gaining a broader view of life or of widening their horizons. In the whole of literature this has been expressing itself for some time. Individual ideas, concepts, and feel-ings, expressed either in literature or art, or even science, sometimes display strong promise. But an overall view is not achieved. This is also the reason why people find it so difficult to achieve the broader view needed in spiritual science. It happens chiefly because the dead approach individuals and work in them on capacities for which the foundations are laid during childhood and youth. The faculties which enable individuals to gain a broader view when they reach maturity are more or less untouched by the activities of the dead in this materialistic age. Incomplete talents, unfinished torsos — not only in the wide world, but also in individual situations — are therefore very prevalent because the dead can more readily approach individual souls rather than what lives socially in human evolution today. The dead have a strong urge to reach what lives socially in human evolution, but in our fifth post-Atlantean period this is exceedingly difficult for them.

There is another phenomenon today of which it is most important to become aware. There exist today many concepts and ideas which have to be very definite if they are to be of any use. Modern, more mercantile, life demands clearly defined concepts based on calculations. Science has become accustomed to this, but so has art. Think of the development art has undergone in this connection! It is not so long ago that art was concerned with great ideals on a wide scale, when, thank goodness, concepts were insufficient for an easy interpretation of great works which were full of meaning. This is no longer the case to the same extent. Today, art strives for naturalism, and concepts can easily encompass works of art because now they have often arisen merely from concepts instead of from an elemental, all-embracing world of feeling. Mankind is today filled to the brim with commonplace, naturalistic concepts which are determined by the fact that they have been conceived entirely in relation to the physical plane where it is in the nature of things to be sharply defined and individualized.

Now it is significant that the so-called dead do not appreciate such concepts. They do not appreciate sharply-defined concepts which are immobile and lifeless. One can learn some extraordinary things, some very interesting things in this connection — if I may be permitted to use such commonplace and banal expressions for these venerable circumstances. As you know, for we have gone through all this together here, I have recently been endeavouring to discuss, using lantern slides, all kinds of considerations about periods in the history of art.[7] I have been endeavouring to find concepts for all kinds of artistic phenomena. To communicate through speech one has to find concepts. Yet I have constantly felt the need to avoid firm, clearly-defined concepts for artistic matters. Of course, for the lectures I had to attempt to define the concepts as far as possible, for they have to be defined if they are to be put into words. But while I was preparing the lectures and formulating the concepts I must say I had a certain aversion, if I may use this word, to expressing what had to be said in such meagre concepts as have to be used if things are to be expressed in words. Indeed, we shall only understand one another in these realms if you translate what has been expressed in close-textured concepts back into concepts of which the texture is less clearly defined.

If one comes up against this experience at a time when one is also concerned with the world of discarnate souls, the following can happen. One may be attempting to comprehend a phenomenon which gives one the feeling of being far too unintelligent to grasp it in concepts. One looks at the phenomenon but has insufficient understanding with which to bind it properly into concepts. This experience, which is particularly likely when one is contemplating a work of art, can bring one into especially intimate contact with discarnate souls, with the souls of the dead. For these souls prefer concepts which are not sharply defined, concepts which are more mobile and can mingle with the phenomena. Sharply defined concepts, concepts similar to those formed here on the physical plane under the influence of the physical conditions of the sense-perceptible world, give the dead the feeling of being nailed to one particular spot, whereas what they need for their life in the spiritual world is freedom of movement.

Therefore it is important that we occupy ourselves with spiritual science so that we may enter those intimate spheres of experience where, as was said yesterday, the living can encounter the dead; because the concepts of spiritual science cannot be as closely defined as can those of the physical plane. That is why malevolent or narrow-minded people can easily discover contradictions in the concepts of spiritual science. The concepts are alive, and what is alive is mobile, though it does not, in fact, harbour contradictions. We can achieve this by concerning ourselves with spiritual matters, and to do so we have to approach things from various sides. And approaching things from various sides really does bring us close to the spiritual world. That is why the dead feel comfortable when they enter a realm of human concepts which are mobile and not pedantically defined.

Indeed, the dead feel most ill at ease of all when they enter the realm of the most pedantic concepts. These are the ones that have recently come to be defined in relation to the spiritual world for those people who do not want to live in anything spiritual, but who want the concepts for sense-perceptible things to apply to the spiritual world as well. These people conduct spiritualistic experiments in order to imprison spiritual concepts in the world perceptible to the senses. They are, in fact, more materialistic than any others. They seek rigid concepts in order to hold commerce with the dead. Thus they torture the dead most of all, for if they want to approach they force them to enter the very realm most disliked by them. The dead love mobile concepts, not rigid ones.

These are experiences to which the fifth post-Atlantean period seems to be particularly prone, given the two circumstances of materialism here on earth and the peculiar situation of the dead as described. One and the same thing determines materialism here on earth and a certain kind of life in the spiritual world. In the Greco-Latin period the dead most definitely approached the living in a manner which differed from that of today. Nowadays, in the fifth post-Atlantean period, there is what I would like to call a more earthly element — but you must imagine this of course in a more pictorial sense — a more earthly composition in the substantiality of the dead than there used to be. The dead appear in a form that is much more like those of earthly conditions than used to be the case. They are more like human beings, if I may put it this way, than formerly. Because of this they have a somewhat paralysing effect on the living. It is nowadays so difficult to approach the dead because they bring about a numbness in us. Here on earth materialistic thoughts reign supreme. In the spiritual world, as a karmic result, the materialistic consequence reigns supreme, for there the spiritual corporeality of the dead has assumed earthly qualities. It is because the dead are super-strong, if I may put it thus, that they numb us. To overcome this numbness it is necessary to develop the strongest possible feelings for spiritual science. This is the difficulty today, or one of the difficulties, standing in the way of our relationship with the spiritual world.

For the earthly realm seen spiritually — indeed the earthly realm can be seen spiritually — things appear different from what might be assumed when they are not seen spiritually. It is correct to say, as we have done many a time, that we live in the age of materialism. Why? It is because human beings in this materialistic age — human beings in general, rather than those who understand these things — are too spiritual — paradoxical though this may sound. That is why they can be so easily approached by purely spiritual influences such as those of Lucifer and Ahriman. Human beings are too spiritual. Just because of this spirituality they easily become materialistic. It is so, is it not, that what the human being believes and thinks is something quite different from what he is. Those very people who are most spiritual are the ones most open to the whisperings of Ahriman, as a result of which they grow materialistic.

Strongly though one must combat materialistic views and materialistic ways of life, nevertheless one may not maintain that the most unspiritual people belong to the circles of materialists. I have personally met many spiritual people, that is, people who are themselves spiritual, not just in their views, among the monists and suchlike, and equally many coarse materialists especially among the spiritualists. Here, though they may speak of the spirit, are to be found the most coarsely materialistic characters. Haeckel, for instance, is a most spiritual person, regardless of what he often says. He is most spiritual, and just because of this can be approached by an ahrimanic world view. He is a most spiritual person, entirely permeated by the spirit. This once became clearly apparent to me in a café in Weimar. I have told this story before, perhaps more than once. Haeckel was sitting at the other end of the table with his beautiful, spiritual blue eyes and his marvellous head. Nearer to me sat the well-known bookseller Herz, a man who has done great service to the German book trade and who knew quite a bit about Haeckel in general. But he did not know that that was Haeckel sitting at the other end of the table. At one point Haeckel laughed heartily. Herz asked: Who is that man laughing so much down there? When I told him it was Haeckel he said: It can't be, evil people can't laugh like that!

Thus the concepts entertained by present-day materialists are so bare of spirituality that they are unable to discern the revelations of the spirit in the material world. So spiritual and material worlds fall apart and the spiritual world becomes no more than a set of concepts. Anyway, the biggest materialistic blockheads are often found today in societies and associations that call themselves spiritualistic. Here are the materialistic blockheads who on occasion have even succeeded in tracing mankind's descent from the apes, even from a particular ape, to the greater glory of the human race. These people were not satisfied with the descent of man from the apes in general, they even traced the lines back to particular apes. For those of you have not heard about this, let me explain. A few years ago a book appeared[8] in which Mrs Besant and Mr Leadbeater described exactly which apes of ancient days they were descended from. They traced their family trees back to particular apes and you can read all about this. Such things are possible, even in much-read books today.

We need the concepts I have elaborated today in order to penetrate more deeply into certain aspects of the theme we are discussing. For our world is definitely dependent on the spiritual world in which the dead live; it is connected with the spiritual world. That is why I have endeavoured to unfold for you certain concepts which relate directly to observations of the immediate present. Everything that takes place here in the physical world has certain effects in the spiritual world. Conversely, the spiritual world with the deeds of the dead shows itself either in what the dead can do for the physical world or in what they cannot do because of the present materialistic age. I also described this present materialistic age in so far as it has been made excessively materialistic by certain secret brotherhoods, as I showed yesterday. The type of materialism that underlies all world events to a high degree today is what we might call the mercantile type.

I ask you to take good note for tomorrow of the concepts I have put before your souls today, concerning the life of the dead. But also please note how little the present age takes certain things for granted which were taken much more for granted in earlier times. We shall see tomorrow how all these things are linked. However, it is characteristic for our time that certain conceptual views are extended to mercantile life which would escape someone who fails to pay attention to such features of our time. We ought not to let them escape us. Mercantilism is all very well as long as it is put in the right light in the way it stands within social life. For this to happen it is necessary for us to have certain yardsticks for everything. Today, however, much conceptual chaos reigns. Yet within this conceptual chaos, concepts are given quite clear definitions, as is our way in the age of materialism in which concepts are fixed to ideas based on what the senses can experience. And when a chaos of concepts then results, as happens in today's materialism, this really does draw the sharpest possible line between the physical world in which human beings live between birth and death, and the supersensible world in which they live between death and a new birth.

Only consider in this connection the fact that in Central Europe — in contrast to other regions where the inclination to philosophize is less pronounced — there is a tendency to philosophize about the mercantile system even though this is not at home in Central Europe. In

Central Europe there is a tendency to make a philosophy of everything. Thus people also philosophize about what aspects of materialism are typical for our time. An interesting book by Jaroslav[9] was published long before the war: *Ideal and Business*. Certain chapters interested me particularly because of their significance with regard to cultural history. It was not the content that interested me but their relation to cultural history; so, for instance, the chapter entitled 'Plato and Retail Trade'. This deals with everything to do with commerce, with the mercantile system. Another interesting chapter is 'The Astrological System Applied to the Price of Pepper'. Not uninteresting is also 'Wholesale Trade as Described by Cicero'. Another chapter is entitled 'Holbein's and Liebermann's Portraits of Merchants'. Not uninteresting, too, is the chapter 'Jakob Böhme and the Problem of Quality'. Very interesting is 'The Goddess Freya in Germanic Mythology in Relation to Free Competition'. And finally, especially interesting is 'The Spirit of Commerce as Taught by Jesus'.

As you see, everything is thrown in the pot together. But by this very fact things gain that characteristic which makes for materialism. Let us take all this as a preparation for our considerations tomorrow.

LECTURE TWENTY-THREE

Dornach, 22 January 1917[1]

In the cycle of lectures in Vienna on *The Inner Nature of Man and the Life between Death and New Birth*,[2] you will remember that I described concepts — or rather, inner experiences of soul — through which the human being can approach those worlds of which we have spoken and which we share with the disembodied souls of those who have passed the portal of death and are preparing themselves for a new life on earth. On the basis of those lectures, you will be able to imbue with life a concept which is indispensable if we seek to arrive at a true understanding of the spiritual world, and that is that many things — I say many things, not everything — are, from the point of view of the spiritual world, entirely the opposite of what is revealed in the physical world. On this basis, let us consider the way the human being steps over, and also looks over, into the life of the spiritual world.

Here on earth, bound to our physical body as we are between waking up and going to sleep, using this physical body as a tool for our experiences in the world, we feel a lack of ability to comprehend the spiritual world and grasp its revelations. As long as we are enclosed within our physical body, and in order to perceive anything, we have to use the rough and ready instruments of this physical body. We cannot avoid using them. And when we are unable to use them, as is the case between going to sleep and waking up, our astral body and our ego-being — which are recent additions from the time of ancient Moon and the earlier periods of Earth — are too attenuated, too intimate, to detect anything. Of course the spiritual world is ever about us, just as the air surrounds us constantly. And if our astral body and our ego-being were — let me say — sufficiently dense, we should always be able to perceive, to grasp, what is all around us in the spiritual world. We cannot do so because in our astral body and our ego-being we are too attenuated; they are not yet fully-formed instruments, like the physical senses or the brain, which our capacity for forming ideas uses in order to attain waking experiences in the soul.

Having stepped through the portal of death, human beings find themselves on the whole, as you know — at least for the first few decades — endowed with a degree of substance similar to that of our sleeping state while on earth. This substance cannot remain quite so attenuated as that pertaining to the time of our physical incarnation, otherwise all experiences between death and a new birth would remain totally unconscious. They do not, as we know. On the contrary, a certainly different, but much brighter and more powerful consciousness than that which prevails while we are in our physical body comes about between death and a new birth. So we must ask how this form of consciousness emerges while we dwell in our astral body and ego-being.

In physical life here on earth we possess our physical instrument which permeates us — or we could say envelops us — with all the ingredients which make up the physical world: that is, the mineral, the plant and the animal kingdoms. The physical body thus prepared for us is our tool for waking life. In a similar way a tool is prepared for us which serves us between death and a new birth. Because we are human beings, the first thing to be prepared for us after death, as soon as we have laid aside our etheric body, is something that comes from the hierarchy of the angeloi. We are mingled with the substance of the hierarchy of the angeloi. One being from this hierarchy actually belongs to us, is the leading being of our human individuality. As we now grow upwards into the spiritual world this being from the hierarchy of the angeloi who belongs to us is joined by other beings from this hierarchy, and together they mould in us — or rather for us — a kind of angeloi organism, the structure of which differs from that of our physical organism.

To make a diagram of this, we could say: We grow upwards through the portal of death into the spiritual world. This is a sketch of our own individuality (mauve in the diagram overleaf). Linked with it is the one angel being who, we feel, is given to us by the hierarchy of the angeloi (red). But when we lay aside our etheric body, this angel being forms a relationship with other beings of the hierarchy of the angeloi — it links up with them, and we feel the whole of the world of the angeloi within ourselves. We feel it to be within ourselves, it is an inner experience — except, of course, for the external experiences which also result.

This permeation by the world of the angeloi makes it possible for us to relate to other disembodied human beings who have passed through the portal of death before us. Let me put it like this: Just as here our senses link us to the external world, so the condition of being embedded in the world of the angeloi links us to the spiritual

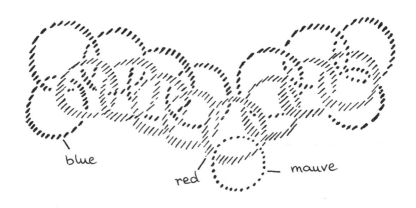

blue

red

mauve

beings, including human beings, whom we find in the spiritual world. Just as here in the physical world, in accordance with the prevailing conditions, we receive an organism which is organized in a certain way, so do we receive an organism of spirit which is brought into being by this network of angeloi substances. How this network of angeloi substances is structured, however, depends very much on the manner in which we work our way up to the spiritual world. If we work our way up in such a way that we have little sensitivity for the spiritual world because we have far too many echoes of physical pleasures, urges and instincts, physical sympathies and antipathies, then the formation of our angeloi organism is difficult. This is why we tarry for a while in the soul world, as we called it, so that we can free ourselves from all that permeates us from the physical world and prevents us from forming our angeloi organism properly. It is gradually developed while we tarry in the soul world. We grow towards this angeloi organism. But concurrently another necessity arises — the necessity to permeate ourselves not only with this angeloi organism but also with another substance, that of an archangeloi organism. Our consciousness in the spiritual world between death and a new birth would remain exceedingly dull if we could not permeate ourselves with the archangeloi organism. If we were to be permeated only with the angeloi organism, we would be dreamers in the spiritual world. We would be woven out of all kinds of Imaginative substances belonging to the spiritual world, but we would dream away our time between death and a new birth. So that we do not dream this time away, so that a strong, clear consciousness can come about, we have to be permeated by the archangeloi organism (blue in the diagram).

This gives our consciousness the right clarity. Only through this do we wake up in the spiritual world. Now the degree to which we wake up in the spiritual world determines the degree to which we can have a free relationship with the physical world. And a free relationship with this physical world is something we must have. Let us ask what is the relationship of the physical world with the excarnated human beings who have passed through the portal of death. You can find the answer to this, too, in the lectures given in Vienna. Here in the physical world it is difficult for human beings, however strong their yearning, to rise up in thought and feeling to a perception of the spiritual, heavenly world. Human beings thirst for ideas about the heavenly world, but they cannot easily unfold the powerful capacity for forming ideas necessary to bring this heavenly world into their reach. In a certain sense the situation is the opposite during life in the spiritual world between death and a new birth. Into this world we are followed by what we experience in the physical world; we are followed by what was important in the physical world, by what we perceived here. We are followed by all this in a very extraordinary way. The examples I give will show you how complicated these things are. In the light of our capacity to form ideas in the physical world, these examples will sometimes appear grotesque — even paradoxical — but it is impossible to enter in a concrete way into the spiritual world without also taking account of precisely these ideas.

Perception of all that exists in the mineral kingdom is lost almost as soon as we step through the portal of death. Here in the physical world, because we have senses, our capacity for perception is greatest with regard to the mineral kingdom. Indeed, we could almost say it is virtually exclusive, for other than the mineral kingdom there is not much that we can perceive as long as we are confined to our senses. You might say that we perceive animals and plants as well. Why do we? A plant is full of minerals, and what we perceive in the plant is everything mineral that streams and pulsates through it. The same goes for the animals. So it is true to say that here on earth human beings perceive with their senses almost exclusively what belongs to the mineral kingdom. When we die this mineral kingdom, so clearly perceived here, disappears. Take an example. Every day you perceive salt on your table, you perceive it as an external mineral product. But someone who has left his body and gone through the portal of death cannot see this salt in the salt-cellar. However, when you sprinkle the salt in your soup, and then swallow it, a process takes place within you, and that process, which is accompanied by the sensation of the salty taste, is perceived by the one who has died. From the moment when your tongue begins to taste the salt, from the moment when a process takes place within you, the one who has died can perceive the salt in the way it works. This is how things are. So those who have gone through the portal of death cannot perceive the mineral kingdom unless it has an influence in some way on a human or animal or plant organism. This shows that what might be called the external environment of the dead is quite different from what we are accustomed to calling our environment here between birth and death.

One thing, however, always remains perceptible to the dead, and it is important to pay attention to this. It is whatever has been filled with human thoughts and feelings; it is the human thoughts which are perceived. Salt in a salt-cellar, as a product of nature, is not perceived by the dead. Nor do they perceive the salt-cellar, whether it is made of glass or any other material. But in so far as human thoughts have come to rest in the salt-cellar during the process of its manufacture, these human thoughts are perceived by the dead. When you consider how everything around us, except what is purely the product of nature, bears the signature of human thoughts, you will have a good idea of what the dead can perceive. They also perceive all relationships between beings, including those between human beings. All this is alive for them.

There are certain things in the physical world, however, of which the dead endeavour to rid themselves; they want to expel them from their ideas and soul experiences — as it were, wipe them out. Their desire to do this is comparable to the longing on the part of human beings here on earth to gain certain insights about the world beyond. Here we long to achieve ideas about the next world. After death, as regards certain human matters here on earth — the world beyond, from the viewpoint of the dead — we long to extinguish them, to wipe them away. But to do this it is necessary to be filled with the substances of the higher hierarchies of angeloi and archangeloi. Once the dead are filled with these substances they can extinguish from their consciousness what must be extinguished.

This, then, gives you an idea of how the dead grow into the spiritual world by filling their individuality through and through with the substances of beings of the higher hierarchy. It is very important to understand that in order to remove from consciousness all the things with which they are more or less personally connected — and that means everything manufactured and consequently bearing within it human thoughts which enable the dead to perceive it — the dead must, above all else, fill themselves with the substance of the angeloi. Other things, too, must be cast aside, must be extinguished, so that the dead can find their way to a proper sojourn in the spiritual world.

Strange though it may sound from our standpoint here on earth, there is an obstacle to growing into what gives us a clear, enlightened consciousness in the spiritual world. This obstacle standing in the way of growing easily into the spiritual world is, strangely enough, human language, the language we use here on earth for the purpose of a physical understanding from one human being to another. The dead have to gradually grow away from language, otherwise they would remain stuck in the affinities which bind them to language and which would prevent them from growing into the kingdom of the archangeloi. Language is definitely only suitable for earthly conditions. And within earthly conditions the human being has, in his soul, become very strongly linked with language. For many people, especially now in this materialistic age, thinking has come to be virtually contained in language. People today think hardly at all in thoughts but very strongly indeed in language, in words. That is why they find it so satisfying to find the right term for something. But such terms, such definitions in words, are only valid here in physical life, and after death our task is to extricate ourselves from definitions in words.

In such matters, too, spiritual science gives us a certain possibility to find our way into the realm of the supersensible. How often do I say to you that to reach a genuine concept we can only approximate; we can only, so to speak, feel our way all around the actual words. How often have I not shown you how we have to endeavour to reach the concept by approaching it from all sides, by experimenting with the use of different expressions in order to free ourselves of the actual words. Spiritual science in a certain sense emancipates us from language. Indeed it does this very fully, thus bringing us into the sphere which we share with the dead.

Emancipation from language is intimately bound up with the way the dead grow into the substance of the archangeloi. By emancipating ourselves from language in spiritual science, by creating concepts in spiritual science which are more or less independent of language, we build a bridge between the physical and the spiritual world. Take a clear look at what I have just said. You will then find that you have understood an important connection between the physical and the spiritual world. And if you think the thought through in a living way you will discover an important means by which to understand all kinds of impulses that emanate from those brotherhoods about which we have spoken on numerous occasions in the past weeks. From various things I have said you will have gathered that these brotherhoods make it their business to fetter human beings to the material world. Just recently we spoke of how these brotherhoods are eager to make materialism super-materialistic or, in a way, to create a kind of ahrimanic immortality for their members. They can do this most strongly by representing group interests, group egoisms, and they certainly do this outstandingly.

One way of representing a group interest is followed by the most influential among these brotherhoods, whose point of departure is something I have already described to you. It is their aim to thoroughly immerse the fifth post-Atlantean cultural period in everything connected with the English language. To these brotherhoods the very definition of the fifth post-Atlantean period is that every English-speaking element belongs to the fifth post-Atlantean period. Thus, even in their primary principle, they restrict things to an egoistic group interest.

This involves something extremely important from the spiritual point of view. It means that their intention is nothing less than the aim of influencing not only human individuals while they are incarnated in physical bodies between birth and death, but indeed all human individuals, including those who are living between death and a new birth. They are striving to let human individualities enter into the spiritual world and become immersed in the hierarchy of the angeloi, but then to prevent them from becoming immersed in turn in the hierarchy of the archangeloi. The aim is, one could say, to depose the hierarchy of the archangeloi from the evolution of mankind!

Perhaps not those of you who have recently joined us, but certainly those who have been with us for some considerable time will discover, if you pay close attention to many things you have been told, that there are clear signs of such things, even in the Theosophical Society. Those of you who shared in the life of the Theosophical Society will surely remember that certain leading members of that society, especially the notorious Mr Leadbeater, said in so many words that in many ways the life between death and a new birth was a kind of dream-life. Those of you who had been members of the Theosophical Society for some time will know that such things were circulated.

It is not extraordinary that such things have been said, for in the case of some souls, who had been successfully influenced in this way and who were found by Leadbeater in the spiritual world, this had actually happened. These souls had indeed been prevented from contact with the world of the archangeloi and they therefore lacked any strong, clear consciousness. So in his way Leadbeater was observing souls who had fallen prey to the machinations of those brotherhoods, only he did not go so far as to observe what became of those souls after a while. Such souls cannot spend their whole time between death and a new birth without the ingredients which would normally be given to them by the world of the archangeloi, so they have to receive something else instead. And they do indeed receive something that is an equivalent; they are indeed permeated by something; but what? They are permeated by something that comes from archai who have remained behind at the stage of the archangeloi. So, instead of being permeated by the substance of the real archangeloi — as would be normal — they are permeated by archai, by time spirits, but by those who have not ascended to the level of the time spirits but have remained behind at the level of the archangeloi. They would have become archai if they had evolved normally, but they have remained behind at the level of the archangeloi. That means that these souls are permeated by ahrimanic influences in the strongest manner.

You need to have a proper idea of the spiritual world in order to comprehend the full significance of a fact such as this. When occult means are used in an endeavour to secure for a single folk spirit the rulership over the whole world, this means that the intention is to influence even the spiritual world. It means that in the place of the legitimate rulership of the dead by the archangeloi, is put the illegitimate rulership by archai who have remained at the stage of the archangeloi and who are, therefore, illegitimate time spirits. With this, ahrimanic immortality is achieved.

You might ask why human beings can be so foolish as to allow themselves to be programmed away from normal evolution and into quite another evolutionary direction. This is a short-sighted judgement, for it fails to take into account that out of certain impulses human beings can indeed come to long for immortality in worlds other than those that would be normal. It is well and good that *you* do not long for any part in some kind of ahrimanic immortality! But just as all kinds of things are incomprehensible, so you will have to admit that it must be allowed to remain incomprehensible, if people in the normal world — including life between death and a new birth — want to escape from this normal world, saying — as it were: We do not want Christ to be our guide, Christ, who is the guide for the normal world; we want a different guide, for we want to oppose this normal world. From the preparations they undergo — I have described these to you — from the preparations brought about by ceremonial magic, they gain the impression that the world of ahrimanic powers is a far more powerful spiritual world and that it will above all enable them to continue what they have achieved in the physical world — making immortal their materialistic experiences in physical life.

The time is ripe for looking into these things, because those who do not know about them, those who do not know that such endeavours exist today, are not in a position to understand what is going on. Behind everything visible in the physical world there lies something that is supernatural, something physically imperceptible. And there are today not a few who work, either for good or for bad, with means, with impulses that are hidden behind what the senses can perceive. It can be said that the world in which we live will follow its proper evolution if human beings place themselves in the service of Christ. But there are many and varied means by which this can be avoided, and some of these are so close to home that it is not easy to speak about them. People have no idea of what can spread through human souls, yet at the same time work as an immeasurably strong occult impulse.

You know — now this is close to home — that at a certain point of time the doctrine of infallibility was declared.[3] This doctrine of infallibility — and this is the important aspect — is accepted by many people. But someone who is a true Christian might wonder about this doctrine of infallibility. He could ask himself what the early fathers of the Church, who were much closer to the original meaning of Christianity, would have said about it. They would have called it a blasphemy! In a truly Christian sense, this would hit the nail on the head. And at the same time it would point to an exceptionally effective occult method of stimulating faith by means of something eminently anti-Christian. This faith represents an important occult impulse in a particular direction, away from normal Christian evolution. As you see, we can touch on something quite close to home, and wherever we do so in the world we find occult impulses.

A similarly powerful occult impulse, which failed, was sought by Mrs Besant when she launched the Alcyone fiasco. If a belief in the incarnation of Jesus in Alcyone had taken hold, this would have become a strong occult impulse. So you see that even the mere spread of certain concepts, certain ideas, can contain strong occult impulses. And since those brotherhoods of whom I have spoken have set themselves the task of making the fifth post-Atlantean period — in the egoistic interest of their group — into the long-term aim of earthly evolution, eliminating what ought to come into this earthly evolution in the sixth and seventh post-Atlantean periods, you will understand why these brotherhoods send out into the world the things that I have described. To achieve their aims they have to create impulses which are meaningful not only for incarnated human beings but also for those who are not incarnated. The time has come when it is necessary that at least a few solitary individuals understand these things so that they can gain an idea of what is actually going on and being accomplished.

For this to be possible, concepts about the life of mankind on earth must come into being which are ever more and more right. It is unthinkable that those concepts can continue which are causing so much harm in our time. For the more human beings there are who have the right concepts, the less will certain occult trends be able to stir up trouble. However, as long as the things which are being said continue to be said in Europe today, things deliberately distorting the truth about the relationships of nations with one another, this is a sign that many occult impulses are at work with the aim of distracting earthly evolution away from the sixth post-Atlantean period. After all, important things are going to be brought about by the sixth post-Atlantean period. I have stressed very strongly that Christ died for the individual human being. We must see this as an essential aspect of the Mystery of Golgotha. He has an important task during the fifth post-Atlantean period which we shall leave aside for the moment. But He also has an important task in the sixth period. This is to help the world to overcome the last vestiges of the principle of nationality. That this should not happen, that steps should be taken in good time to prevent any influence by Christ in the sixth post-Atlantean period — this is the purpose served by the impulses of those brotherhoods who want to preserve the fifth post-Atlantean period in the manner I have shown.

The only counter-measure is to create the right concepts and gradually imbue them ever increasingly with life. These right concepts must live. Nations could dwell so peacefully side by side if only they would endeavour to discover the right concepts and ideas about their relationships. As I have said, no programme, no abstract idea, but solely the right concrete concepts, can lead to what must come about. Difficult though it is in the face of current ideas, by which our friends, too, have of course been not a little infected, nevertheless it is necessary to draw people's attention to various aspects which can lead to the right concepts. You all have at your disposal the necessary materials on which to base these right concepts, but these materials are not illuminated properly. As soon as they are correctly illuminated you will arrive at the correct, concrete ideas.

Let us now take up something we have already discussed from a certain viewpoint. Here on this globe, in the Europe we inhabit, the relationships between nations are spoken about in a way that inflicts utter torture on the dead, for all the ideas and concepts are based on the peculiarities of language. By forming concepts about nationality based on the peculiarities of language, people persistently torture the dead. One way of torturing the dead, one way of failing to show them love, is to participate in spiritualist seances. For this forces them to manifest in a particular language. The dead person is expected to speak a particular language, for even with table-rapping the signs have to refer to a particular language. What is done to the dead by forcing them to express themselves in a particular language might very well be compared with pinching someone living in the flesh with red-hot tongs. So painful for the dead are spiritualist seances which expect them to express themselves in a particular language. For in their normal life the dead are striving to free themselves from the differentiations between languages.

So, simply by speaking about the relationships between the peoples of Europe in concepts based on language, we are doing something about which we are barely able to communicate with the dead. That is why I could say that it is necessary today, or beginning to be necessary, to form concepts of a kind which can be discussed with the dead, or about which we can have communication with the dead. Of course there is no need to inundate the world with Volapuk or some other constructed language, for though it is true that all people wear clothes, they need not all wear the same clothes. On the other hand, though, we cannot be expected to see our clothes as part of ourselves. Similarly something we need for the physical world, namely the differentiation between languages — which serve the purpose of bringing the spiritual realm into the physical world — cannot be seen as belonging to our inmost archetypal being. We must be clear about this.

So how can we arrive at concepts which gradually rise above the ethnic elements which are almost exclusively based on language? In this, too, Anthroposophy must rise above mere anthropology, which has really no other means of answering this question except by referring to the differentiations of language.

As I said, the peoples of Europe could easily live in peace if only they could find suitable concepts, concepts which are alive. We took a step towards this when we discussed Grimm's law of sound-shifts.[4] There I showed you how some languages have remained behind at an earlier stage. We spoke of the sequence of stages: Gothic, Anglo-Saxon — present-day English — and then High German. High German has continued to advance while English has remained at a certain stage. This is not a value judgement but merely a fact which has to be observed as objectively as a law of nature. In English we have *d* where in High German there is *t*, and we saw that this conforms with a certain law, the law of sound-shifts. However, this law of sound-shifts is, in a certain sphere, an expression of more profound conditions prevailing in the whole of European life. In this connection it is worth noting that certain concepts and ideas work with a vengeance, albeit unconsciously, to bring about misunderstandings. These things, too, must be seen entirely objectively.

Taking our departure from what we have said so far, we could state that in Central Europe there existed what we might call the 'primordial soup' for what later streamed out to the periphery, particularly towards the West. Let us take a closer look at this 'primordial soup' (see diag, p.179). For a very long time it has been customary for the nation which represents this 'primordial soup' to call itself 'das deutsche Volk'. The peoples of the West have exercised a kind of revenge on this nation by refusing to call them by the name they have chosen for themselves, a name which signifies a profound instinct. They are called 'Teutons', 'Allemands', 'Germans', all kinds of things, but never, by those who speak a western language, 'Deutsche'. Yet this is the very name that has deep links with the nature of this people which is, in a way, the 'primordial soup'. One stream of this went southwards. We described it as the papal, hierarchical cultic element.

Another stream went towards the West. We described this when we spoke of the diplomatic, political element. And a third stream went towards the North-west. We described it in connection with the mercantile element. At the centre there remained something that has retained a fluidity which allows for further evolution. You need only remember that in the periphery even language has stopped developing, whereas in the German language of Central Europe there still exists, in the sound-shifts, the possibility of growing beyond the sounds and ascending to the next stage of sound-evolution.

What is the basis for this? The 'primordial soup' was still virtually undifferentiated, bearing within it all the elements which then streamed outwards. They really did stream outwards. The migrating peoples moved right down through Italy. Present-day Italians are not the descendants of the Romans; they are the result of all that arose through the mingling of the Germanic tribes as they moved southwards. The whole process began when the Romans used the Germans whom they had absorbed to wage war on other Germans, for these were their best warriors. Things then continued in the manner familiar to us from history. Similarly, the Franks migrated westwards and the Anglo-Saxons north-westwards. How can we gain a proper conception of what it was that migrated outwards in this way?

The undifferentiated 'primordial soup' of humanity was not quite without structure, even though it was undifferentiated. It is right to distinguish between what was at first undifferentiated and what later became differentiated. The 'primordial soup' contains what migrated down towards the south; it is there as one of the parts. This part (red in the diagram) migrated southwards with all its one-sidedness. Drawing an analogy to what people meant by the ancient castes, we could say that a caste migrated southwards, a caste with a capacity for priestly things — a priestly caste. Since then a priestly element has always emanated from that part of the periphery. This has taken many forms and, although in an extraordinary way, even the latest phase has a kind of priestly character. Not only is the impulse called 'holy egoism', *sacro egoismo*, but also, d'Annunzio, for instance, could not have used words of a more priestly nature. Right down to the rephrased 'Beatitudes',[5] everything that came from that quarter was clothed in priestly robes. Whether good or bad, everything was of a priestly nature. What remained in the 'primordial soup' became the opposition to all this, in the way I have described. What appeared in the Reformation was the element which had remained in the 'primordial soup'; it came to be the opponent of the one-sided priestly element. The fact that today nothing more can be detected of this priestly element, or that all that can be detected is what is obviously there, is simply the result of that hollowing-out of which I have spoken.

The second element migrated westwards: the warrior caste, the kingly caste, the element of kingship. We have spoken of this, too. This western part only fell into republicanism because of an anomaly. In actual fact it is inwardly structured through and through in a warlike, kingly manner and it will ever and again fall back into this warlike, kingly element. Again we have something that has streamed out, so that a part of this element which has streamed out towards the West has also remained in the 'primordial soup' and will in turn have to provide the opposition to what takes place in the West (blue).

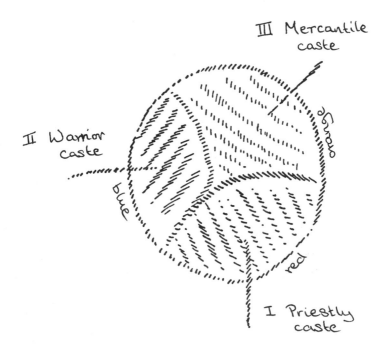

And north-westwards went the mercantile element. It, too, remains as a part (orange) and will have to stand in opposition to what has developed one-sidedly. No moral evaluation is meant by this, for let no one believe that I in any way share the opinion, expressed so frequently, that the mercantile element is something despicable in comparison with the priestly element. All these things must be seen in their dissimilarity, but they must not be labelled and evaluated. Indeed, for the fifth post-Atlantean period, as we have seen, the mercantile element is something utterly essential. But we really must see the realities as they exist. If people cannot see them now, then they will come to see them in the future.

From one quarter many occult impulses have emanated which have used the priestly element in the interests of certain groups, and from another quarter have come occult impulses which have used the warlike element. In the same way, from a third quarter, occult impulses are emanating today which prefer to use the mercantile element as their vehicle. They will be stronger than the others, for numbers I and II are only repetitions of the third and fourth post-Atlantean periods, whereas number III belongs fully to the fifth post-Atlantean period. Therefore, all the impulses that come from the third quarter will be stronger than those coming from the first and second quarters because they coincide with the fundamental character of the fifth post-Atlantean period. They will be as strong as certain impulses were during the Egyptian civilization in the third post-Atlantean period, and others which emanated from the Near East and transplanted themselves through the cultures of Greece and Rome during the fourth post-Atlantean period. The sorcery of the ancient Egyptians and the blood sacrifices — these are the forerunners of what comes from the secret brotherhoods of which we have been speaking, though what comes from them will be something different. Because it makes use of the mercantile element it will have a more common-or-garden character in the ordinary human sense.

We really must be clear about these things. Only if human beings feel themselves to be immersed in a living way in what truly exists can healing come to evolution. Through this alone is it possible, within what happens, to learn to distinguish what is true from what is untrue. We have heard how necessary it is to learn to distinguish between truth and falsehood — that falsehood which is the cause of the huge groundswell of impulses now running through the world. So many false ideas bear within them a powerful occult force if they are believed by human beings.

Just as in earlier times other media served the impulses which were at work, so in our own time, in the fifth post-Atlantean period, the art of printing books and everything that exists in the mercantile element serves these purposes. We have a foretaste of the terrible things to come in people's strong dependence on everything put out in the Press by mercantile groups by means of the medium of printing. The aims of these groups are anything but what they say they are in their newspapers. They want to make profits, or achieve certain things through doing business, and for this they possess the means by which they can disseminate views whose truthfulness is irrelevant but which serve the purpose of entering into certain kinds of business. In the case of much of the printed matter distributed around the world today the right question to ask is not: What does this person mean? but: In whose service does this person stand? Who is paying for this or that opinion? This is often the crucial question these days. The secret brotherhoods about whom we have been speaking are not concerned with suppressing these things, but rather promoting them as an important occult means of which they can make use. An important aim is achieved by them when what is said no longer matters, as long as it exercises influence over people in the interests of certain groups.

The important thing is to see these things as clearly and soberly as possible. And we can only discern the nuances sufficiently if we see them properly in their connections with the spiritual worlds. I am referring to the symptoms, to the symptoms of history,[6] as I have said. Of course you must not expect to find black magic behind every phenomenon. But there are phenomena which are used in the service of grey or black magic. It is also not necessary to pass moral judgements on everything; you must simply see things in the proper light.

For someone who wants to see things in the proper way, certain words spoken by Sir Edward Grey will surely be unforgettable and startling — words appearing among other, less important, things which nevertheless also had to be said in order to make the whole thing credible. These words were part of the great speech[7] he made to introduce England's entry into this European war, and they are saturated with the blood — I mean the soul blood — of the fifth post-Atlantean period. These words are not only true but more than true; their truth is drawn from what lives in a materialistic way in the fifth post-Atlantean period. 'We are going', says Grey, 'to suffer, I am afraid, terribly in this war whether we are in it or whether we stand aside. Foreign trade is going to stop, not because the trade routes are closed, but because there is no trade at the other end. Continental nations engaged in war — all their populations, all their energies, all their wealth, engaged in a desperate struggle — they cannot carry on the trade with us that they are carrying on in times of peace, whether we are parties to the war or whether we are not,' and so on. The whole of western Europe stands today under the dominion of a single question of power. This talk of trade, and that it is for considerations of trade that it is important not to remain detached from the war — this is far more profoundly truthful than all the other things contained in this speech, things which only had to be said in order to make this speech credible. It no longer matters what people say, as long as it is believed. They might even say it unconsciously. Neither am I passing a moral judgement on anyone. What does matter is the ability to recognize — on the basis of the inner truth of human evolution — where the truth is being expressed. And this was a point at which the truth in the truest sense was spoken. The same facts, the same truths are truthfully expressed which, once they have been suitably developed by those brotherhoods of whom we have spoken, lead to the impregnation of the mercantile trend with occult impulses.

This must become known to mankind; it must be experienced by mankind. If human beings were not to experience this, they would not grow sufficiently strong. They must harden themselves by opposing what lies in the impulses we have described. In an earlier age there existed a tyranny which forced people to believe only what was recognized by Rome. A far greater tyranny will come about when neither philosophers nor scientists decide what should be believed but when the tools of those secret brotherhoods alone specify what is to be believed, when they alone make sure that no human soul may harbour any beliefs other than those dictated by them, when nothing new is done in the world except what is stipulated by them alone. This is the goal of these brotherhoods. And though I have nothing against idealists — for idealism is always something good — certain idealists are naive if they believe that these things are only temporary and will disappear again once the war comes to an end. The war is only the beginning of the way things are tending to go. And the only possibility of getting beyond this lies in the clear and proper understanding of what is going on. Nothing else is of any use. Therefore — although certain quarters will not be pleased to hear and see them and will take steps against them — there will always have to be people who clearly point out the full intensity of what is really going on, people who cannot be deterred from pointing out the full intensity of what is happening.

At the beginning of these considerations I said that the Germans called themselves 'Deutsche', but that they met with no understanding on the part of those who call them 'Germans', or whatever else. Seen from their own point of view, 'German' is exactly what they are not, for those who call themselves 'Deutsche' consider that 'Germanic' refers to all those whose languages are at the same stage historically, and this does not include High 'German' or anything that is 'Deutsch'. From their point of view the Scandinavians, the Anglo-Saxons, the Dutch are 'Germans', and they mean by this nothing more than that below the surface their languages are related. So 'Germans' no longer means much to those who call themselves 'Deutsche' because all of this no longer has any reality today. Thus, when outside Germany the phrase 'pan-Germanic' is coined, this is quite meaningless to those who call themselves 'Deutsche' because for them 'Germanic' can no longer have any real substance. Different national structures have formed, and to use the purely theoretical expression 'pan-Germanic' is simply to regress to an earlier age; it expresses nothing that has any connection with the future or even with the present. The designation 'Deutsch', however, is based on a profound instinct.

Differentiated out of what I called the 'primordial soup' came the three castes, the first, the second and the third caste. They developed and migrated. The fourth caste I have already described as those who simply wanted to be human beings, and nothing else. They always remained where they were and, as a result, underwent developments which to the others seemed grotesque — for instance, in relation to the first sacramental stage of alliteration, which went on to develop into the sound-shift. This is most interesting because it is a link among many others.

Let us put it this way: Those who migrated were various differentiations of 'the people'; and those who remained were 'the people' *per se*, the 'volk', the 'diet'. The name Dietrich, for instance, means 'he who is rich in people'. 'Diet' later became 'deutsch', and to be 'Deutsch' means nothing other than to be 'the people'. The people who remained where they were are the fourth caste. The other three migrated, 'the people' remained.

So this is the profound instinct that lies behind the designation 'Deutsch'; it simply denotes the human element. Therefore, what stayed where it was as 'the people' has the capacity to be felt, not as something that has developed organically, but as something that has remained fluid in its development so that it can go beyond all the differentiations. Certainly the priestly element is there, but there is the possibility of going beyond the priestly element. The warlike element is there, but there is the possibility of going beyond the warlike element. The mercantile element is also there, but there is the possibility of going beyond the mercantile element. Similarly in language; the older form was there, but there was the possibility of going beyond it.

Connected with this, though, is a phenomenon which understandably has led to endless misunderstandings. Seen at a deeper level, these are tragic misunderstandings, but they come about because, of course, in the 'primordial soup' there is much which contains the germs of what later reappears in the periphery. Yet whereas in the periphery it is seen as characteristic and fitting, when it is discovered in the 'primordial soup' it is thought to be totally abnormal. Let us take militarism. This does not belong to the nature of the German people at all, it belongs to the French. In France no fault is found with it, because there it has developed organically. But when it is discovered in Germany it is seen as something improper which ought not to be there. Fault is found with it when it comes to the fore as a result of some emergency situation such as the geographical situation we discussed at length earlier. Or take the German 'Junker'; all he represents is what developed in the British Empire into something absolutely acceptable, the aristocratic squire. Simply because it developed in its own way in Central Europe it stands out like a sore thumb and is seen as a provocation. Thus there arise endless misunderstandings; indeed the world is full of things that are misunderstood, it is full of subjective interpretations of reality. Wherever you look, you find all kinds of ideas which crumble on closer inspection. Those who really understand what is going on have no use for these things, those whose thinking is based on reality have no use for them, and yet they work as impulses; in public opinion they act like dynamite. They elbow their way into public opinion. Some would be infinitely funny if they were not so infinitely tragic.

Here is an example. Treitschke is described by the nations of the Entente as a monster, as a person whose views are an abomination for Europe. He is presented as typifying those views about Central Europe which justify inflicting on Central Europe its just deserts. But let us look at some of Treitschke's views. What does he think, for instance, of the Turks? He thinks that they should depart from Europe, that they should not be allowed to live in Europe but should scatter themselves across Asia. What we read today in the note to Wilson exactly expresses Treitschke's view! Fault is found with Treitschke, but in this matter, as in countless others, his opinion is taken up and even acted upon. His views on Turkey might just as well have been copied straight down in the note to Wilson. This is what I mean by an idea which crumbles; as soon as you apply any knowledge or understanding it disintegrates. Other concepts disintegrate, too, as soon as a little knowledge is applied. But most people today make statements without any knowledge, much to the advantage of those who want to spread their ideas in the dark. How often do we hear today that it is perfectly 'humane' to surround and starve out Central Europe. Among the various reasons given for this most humane method of warfare is the justification that in 1870 the Germans did just the same. They found it perfectly 'humane' to surround and starve out Paris; and the relative size of the territories in question is irrelevant. Only someone who knows nothing of history can talk like this — of course I do not mean the history you can read in the newspapers!

But what were the facts? In 1870/71 Bismarck, who was responsible for starving Paris out, was totally against doing any such thing. You can read in his book[8] how distressed he was that the impulse came from England, via the English princess who later became the Empress Friedrich,[9] to conquer Paris by starvation rather than by any other means. He writes that unfortunately they were forced by the Englishwoman to apply 'this humane method' to Paris; he speaks of the humane English method.

That is the real historical context. But, of course, you have to know about it if you want to judge things without using ideas which crumble. Comparing the two situations, they seem so truly alike. But very often things are not at all alike when they are compared against the full background. In this case the 'humane' method of starving Paris out is an English invention of recent history. So the objection now being made should not be made, if reality is to be the basis. To work with reality, to understand things on the basis of reality — this alone can lead to salvation today.

To be able to meet the request of many of our friends to investigate current events, we have had to discuss things we usually discuss in other connections, in order that our souls might experience the deep seriousness with which the reality of events must be seen. If just a few people can be found who are willing to see things as they really are, then the grim times we are about to face will be followed by better times . The seeds take a while to ripen. But if you sow thoughts of reality in your souls today, these are real seeds capable of ripening, and we can add that these are thoughts about which one can be in agreement with the dead. It is so painful to hear on all sides these days that 'we owe this or that to the dead'. This event, which for convenience sake is still termed 'war', though it has long since become something utterly different — how often do those who want to prolong this event proclaim all the things we are supposed to owe to the dead, to those who have fallen! If people only knew how they blaspheme against God when they maintain that we owe it to the dead to prolong these bloody events; if only they knew the position of the dead in this matter, they would quickly distance themselves from this blasphemy!

So, my dear friends, from all these things which come about through human beings, you see how necessary it is to build a bridge between the living and the dead. Spiritual science will build this bridge. Spiritual science will bring about a possibility of reaching an understanding, even with those who have passed through the portal of death. A life of community will embrace all human souls — those embodied on the earth and those living between death and a new birth — when the fundamental nature of the human being is understood, when it is understood that life in the body and life without the body are simply two forms of one and the same all-embracing life. This knowledge, that the human being has two forms of life, one in the body and one without the body — this knowledge, if it is fundamentally understood, bears within it salvation for the future, but only if human beings fill themselves with these ideas in a truly living way.

LECTURE TWENTY-FOUR

Dornach, 28 January 1917

Today I shall speak more generally, perhaps aphoristically, to prepare the way for Tuesday, when I shall discuss our anthroposophical spiritual science and its significance for the present time and for human evolution. I shall then bring to your notice some things which we should certainly take to heart. On the one hand we will look back on our work, and on the other hand I shall present certain matters which are important for the whole way in which we assess our spiritual scientific movement, as well as the manner in which we relate to it. It seems to me to be appropriate, at this time, to take into our hearts a consideration of this kind.

Let me start today with some remarks on what it is that can give us, as human beings, a sense for our situation in the cosmos. Actually, human beings in this materialistic age feel, you might say, deserted and isolated in the cosmos. If you cut off a person's finger or hand, or amputate his leg, he feels you have taken away something that belongs to his physical, bodily nature; he feels that the missing part belongs to the whole of his bodily nature. In earlier periods of human evolution people felt quite differently about this. Not only did they feel their hand, or arm or leg to be a part of their whole being, but they felt that they were, in turn, a part of a totality. In those days it was possible to speak quite differently about a group-ego. Tribes, families, for generations back, felt themselves to be a totality. We have gone into this frequently. As for their external, physical existence, however, people felt something quite different. They felt in a way as though they stood within the cosmos as a whole, as though they had been formed out of the whole cosmos.

Just as today we feel that our finger, our hand, is one member of our total organism, so in olden times people felt: Up there is the sun; it runs its own course but it is not unrelated to us; we are a part of the region traversed by the sun; we are a part of the universe as it is given certain rhythms by the moon. In short, they felt the universe to be one great organism and that they were within it, just as today our finger might feel that it is part of our body. The fact that this feeling, this perception, is virtually lost to us today has not a little to do with the rise of materialism. Today's science, in particular, disdains to have anything to do with an idea that man might be a part of the cosmos. Science regards a human being as an individual body, of which the separate parts are examined and described anatomically and physiologically. It is no longer customary in science to regard the human being as a member of the total organism of the universe in so far as this is physically visible.

But people's view of things, especially their scientific view, will have to return to the concept of man embedded in the whole cosmos. Human beings will have to sense once again that they stand within the cosmic universe. This will not be possible in the way that was the case in olden times. They will have to achieve it by expanding their science, which today is abstract and directed to the individual, to include certain considerations. They will have to apply certain judgements, of which we shall discuss only one today — which we mentioned several weeks ago. This will show us the direction scientific thinking will have to take — having become far more human than current scientific thinking — if human beings are to find once again an awareness of how they stand within the universe as a whole.

You know that the position of the sun on the ecliptic at the spring equinox moves forward in the Zodiac. You know that this point has always been designated, ever since mankind began to think, according to its position in the Zodiac. So from about the eighth century before the Mystery of Golgotha until about the fifteenth century after the Mystery of Golgotha, the sun at the spring equinox rose in the sign of the Ram, though not always at exactly the same spot. During this period the sun traversed the sign of the Ram. Since then, the sun at the spring equinox has been rising in the sign of the Fishes. Note, please, that astronomy takes no account of the constellations, so you will find that calendars still say that the sun rises in the constellation of the Ram at the beginning of spring, which is in fact not the case. Astronomy has stuck to the earlier cycle. It simply divides the Zodiac into twelve equal parts, each of which is named after one of the signs. You know from our calendar what the situation is.

However, this is immaterial as far as we are concerned. What is important for us is the fact that the position of the sun at the spring equinox moves forward, passing through the whole Zodiac little by little. It traverses the whole Zodiac until it finally returns to the original position, taking approximately 25,920 years. These 25,920 years are termed the Platonic Year, the Cosmic Year. The exact figure varies according to the various methods of calculation. However, we are not concerned with exact figures but with the rhythm this precession entails. You can imagine that a cosmic rhythm must lie in this movement which repeats itself every 25,920 years.

We can say that these 25,920 years are very important for the life of the sun, for during this time the life of the sun passes through one unit, a proper unit. The next 25,920 years are then a repetition. We have a rhythm in which one unit measures 25,920 years.

Having looked at this great Cosmic Year, let us now turn our attention to something small, something intimately connected with life between birth and death, that is, with our life in so far as we are inhabitants of the physical universe. It is indisputable that one of the most important things in this life in the physical body is a single breath, an in-breath and an out-breath, for our very life depends on this breathing in and breathing out. If it were to be interrupted, we should cease to be capable of living. One breath is indeed something very important. A breath brings in the air which enlivens us in a particular way. Within our organism we transform this air into the breath of death, for it would kill us if we were to breathe it in again once we have breathed it out.

On average, a human being takes eighteen breaths a minute. Not all breaths are equal, for those in youth differ from those in old age, but the average is eighteen breaths a minute. Eighteen times a minute we rhythmically renew our life. Multiply this by 60 and you have 1,080 times an hour. Now multiply by 24, and the number of breaths in twenty-four hours comes to 25,920!

You see how a remarkable rhythm underlies the course of our life in one day. Let us take one unit of life to be one breath. This is something very important for us, since the rhythmical repetition of our breathing maintains our life. In one day we are given exactly as many units of life as the years it takes the sun to return to its original position on the ecliptic at the spring equinox. This means that if we imagine one breath to correspond to one microcosmic year, then we complete one microcosmic Platonic Year in one day, an image of the macrocosmic Platonic Year. This is most exceptionally significant, for it shows us that the process of our breathing, something which takes place within us, is based on the same rhythm, on a different time-scale, as the great rhythm of the sun's passage.

It is important for us to consider such a thing in our soul. For if we transform what has been said into a feeling, then this feeling will tell us that we are an image of the macrocosm. To say that the human being is an image of the macrocosm is no mere empty phrase, no idle chatter, for it can be proved down to the last detail. From this you can gain a feeling of the solid foundation on which stand all the laws that come from spiritual science. They are all based on similar intimate knowledge of the inner connections of the cosmos, even though it is not always possible to go into every detail.

Now in considering these things, it must above all be clear to us that the human being is, in some way and to some extent, detached from the cosmos. He stands within the rhythm of the cosmos and yet he is to some extent free. He changes things subtly, so that the rhythms do not exactly match, but it is just this fact of not quite matching which gives him the possibility of freedom. In general, however, he stands within the rhythms of the cosmos.

I had to bring forward these considerations so that what I now want to say might not be misunderstood. Having considered the rhythm of breathing, let us now turn to a larger one, the next in size: the alternation of sleeping and waking. A single breath is the smallest element of life. Now let us look at the alternation between sleeping and waking, which is indeed, to some extent, an analogy to the rhythm of breathing.

As you know, I have often described the taking in of the astral body and ego on waking up, and the letting go of the astral body and ego on going to sleep, as a breathing in and a breathing out in the course of a day and a night. But we can look at this in an even more materialistic sense. When we breathe the air, it goes in and it goes out. We inhale, we exhale. Something material swings back and forth like a pendulum; out, in, out, in. The alternation of sleeping and waking occurs as a very similar rhythm. In the morning, when we wake up and take in our ego and our astral body, our etheric body is displaced, is pushed down from the head and more into the other elements of the organism. And when we go to sleep again, pushing out our astral body and our ego, then our etheric body spreads back into our head and is there just as it is in the whole of the rest of our body. Thus there is an incessant rhythm. When the etheric body is pressed down, we wake up, and it stays down while we remain awake. When we go to sleep it is pushed back up into our head. Up and down it goes in the course of twenty-four hours. The etheric body moves rhythmically during the course of twenty-four hours. Of course there are irregularities, and this is in keeping with the human being's capacity for freedom, his degree of freedom. But, overall, what I have described takes place.

We could say that something breathes in us — though it is not an in-and-out but an up-and-down — something breathes in us during the course of a day which resembles our breathing every eighteenth of a minute. Let us see whether what breathes in this up-and-down of the etheric body also represents a kind of circulation, something which returns to its starting-point. We must fathom the meaning of 25,920 days, for 25,920 such up-and-down movements could be seen as a replication of the Platonic Year. Just as a day corresponds to 25,920 breaths, so 25,920 days ought to correspond to something in human life too. How many years does this come to? A year has 365 ¼ days and if we divide 25,920 by 365.25 the answer is: nearly 71. Let us say 71 years, which is the average life-span of the human being. The human being is free, however, and often lives much longer, but you know that the patriarchal life-span is given as 70 years. The span of a human life is 25,920 days, 25,920 great breaths, and so we have another cycle wonderfully depicting the macrocosm in the microcosm. We could say that by living for one day, taking 25,920 breaths, we depict the Platonic Cosmic Year, and by living for 71 years, waking up and going to sleep 25,920 times — a breathing on a larger scale — we once again depict the Platonic Year.

Now let us turn to something which time will not allow us to discuss in detail today, but which I nevertheless want to indicate, something that can be sensed in an occult way. We are surrounded by air. It is the air which gives us the possibility of that closest element of life that takes place in the rhythm of breathing. This rhythm is given to us by the air, which is something belonging to the earth. And what gives us the other rhythm? The earth itself! That rhythm arises because the earth turns on its own axis — speaking in accordance with modern astronomy — and brings about the alternation of day and night. So the air breathes in us when we take a breath. And the earth, by letting us wake up and go to sleep, breathes, pulses in us by turning on its axis and giving us the alternation of day and night. Our life-span can be seen in relation to the earth as one day in the life of an organism which, instead of taking one breath every eighteenth of a minute, takes one breath in one day and night. For such an organism seventy years are one day, and ordinary days and nights are its breaths.

You see how we can feel ourselves to be within a life on a larger scale, a life which takes one breath every twenty-four hours and for which one day takes seventy, seventy-one, years. We can feel ourselves to be within a living being which has much longer rhythms of pulse and breathing. So you see that it is quite correct to speak of the microcosm as being an image of the macrocosm, for every part of the image can be proved mathematically. If we maintain that the air breathes within us, that it breathes itself in us, that the earthly realm breathes in us because we belong to this greater living organism, then we might come to ask: Apart from being related to the air, which is on the earth, and to the whole of the earth with its rhythm of day and night, are we perhaps also related in a certain way to the rising of the sun as a whole, as it progresses during the course of the Platonic Year, returning to the position from which it set out?

These things are of the utmost interest, yet science today takes no more notice of them than of shadows. On one occasion I found myself startlingly confronted by this contrast between today's science and the science which must come in the future. Perhaps I have told you that in the autumn of 1889 I was called by the Goethe and Schiller Archive in Weimar to edit Goethe's natural-scientific works for the extended complete works. I had to examine all the documents left behind by Goethe containing his studies on anatomy, physiology, zoology, botany, mineralogy, geology and also meteorology. He made an enormously thorough study of the weather during the course of a year, recording especially the barometric data, and it is astonishing how many tables he worked out in this connection. Only small parts of this work have been published. A few of the tables are reproduced in my edition, but otherwise little is publicly known. Like temperature charts, he made graphs showing the barometric data at a particular place compared with other places and he recorded his readings every few hours for months on end. In this way he hoped to show how the curves differed in different places.

Graphs showing barometric data are something for which today's science has little use as yet. But Goethe wanted to record these curves which for him represented an analogy with the pulse as we record its fluctuations in temperature charts. He wanted to record a kind of pulse of the earth, the regular, day-to-day earth-pulse. Why? He wanted to prove that the fluctuations in the barometric data during the course of the year are not as irregular as ordinary meteorology supposes but are subject to a certain degree of regularity which is only modified by secondary conditions pertaining at certain times. He wanted to prove that the earth's gravity depicts a breathing out and a breathing in during the course of a year; he wanted to point to the very thing that is expressed in the human being's breathing out and breathing in. He wanted to find the same thing in the barometric data. Science will embark on such projects in the future, when once again the microcosm will be examined in its relationship to the macrocosm.

So you see how Goethe was working towards a form of science which will come about at some time in the future. We also gain an idea of the immense diligence he applied in order to reach the results he achieved. He never simply makes an assertion, as is so often the case with others. When others speak of the pulse of the earth, they often intend this simply as a metaphor, an *aperçu*. But when Goethe says, in three or four lines, for instance, that the earth breathes, he can back this statement with a large pile of tables. Empirical knowledge is behind whatever he says. Yet most people consider empirical knowledge to be stuff and nonsense. We can learn from Goethe that one must have material with which to back one's assertions. In this way we now have material to back our statement that the earth breathes like a great organism.

Let us now see whether we can speak in a similar way about breathing if we place ourselves within the great Platonic Year of the sun, which has a span of 25,920 years. Without more ado let us now regard these 25,920 years as a single year, and let us see how much a single day amounts to. To do this we must divide by 365¼, and the answer will be a single day. We have already done this sum, and the answer was seventy-one years, the span of a human life. This means that a human life takes one day of the whole Platonic Year. So we could look at the whole Platonic Year with regard to the human life-span as follows: As physical beings we are breathed out by the whole process of the Platonic Year, so that if seventy-one years are seen as a single day, this would be one breath of the being who lives in the rhythm of the Platonic Year.

With regard to an eighteenth of a minute we are a limb of the life of the air, and with regard to a day we are a limb of the life of the earth. With regard to our life-span it is as though we were breathed out and breathed in again in one day of that being who lives in the rhythm of 25,920 years. So we could consider our physical body, which lives out its patriarchal span, to be a single breath of that great being which lives so long that 25,920 years are as one year for it. Our patriarchal life-span is then one day. So looking at a being who lives with our earth and experiences day and night in twenty-four hours, this is one breath for our etheric body. And one breath for our astral body is our actual breath of one-eighteenth of a minute. Herein you have an analogy for an ancient assertion, for something that was called the 'days and nights of Brahma'. Think of a spiritual being for whom our seventy-one years are as is a single breath for us. We find we are a single breath for that being. When we enter the world as a tiny baby, that being for whom the Platonic Year is one year breathes us out. It breathes us out into the cosmos, and when we die it breathes us in again; we are breathed out and we are breathed in. Now turn to the earth: It breathes us out and in again in one day. Now turn to the air, which is a part of the earth: It breathes us out and in again in an eighteenth of a minute. Whichever way we look at it, the number 25,920 represents the return to the starting point. This is a regular rhythm; it gives us the feeling of being embedded in the cosmos; it teaches us that the span of a human life, and one day in a human life, are indeed, for greater, more all-embracing beings, the same as is one breath for us. If we can transform this knowledge into feeling, then the expression 'resting in the world-all' assumes immense significance.

Such things really do belong in the orbit of scientific research, and nothing other than the attitude of mind of spiritual science will lead to such research into these figures, which are to be found, after all, in any encyclopaedia. One day such research will be carried out and then ordinary science will be able to find a link with anthroposophical spiritual science.

As we have seen, everything is ordered according to numbers. But it is also ordered according to measure. Human science will lend great depths to the Biblical words: Everything in the universe is ordered in accordance with measure and number.

Let us continue. There is something connected with our breathing, a kind of dependant of our breathing, and that is our speech. Organically, speech is connected with breathing. Not only does it emerge from the same organ but it is also connected with the rhythm of breathing, the rhythm of an eighteenth of a minute. Thus we speak, and thus speak those who are with us on the earth. Just as the air surrounds us on the earth, so are we surrounded by human beings whose speaking bears a relationship to the rhythm of breathing. It should follow that the other breathing, the breathing connected with day and night, also has a kind of speaking linked with it. This would be a speaking by beings who belong to the organism of the earth, just as human beings belong to the air.

In olden times, the wisdom imparted to human beings by higher beings came, not via the breathing rhythm of an eighteenth of a minute, but via the rhythm of breathing which has one day as its unit. In those ancient days they could not learn as quickly as we can today; they had to tarry longer for words which were linked to a breathing rhythm of twenty-four hours. In this way ancient knowledge came to man, knowledge which is at the foundation of everything and which can be discovered in various traditions. It was brought by higher beings who are linked to the earth in the way man is linked to the air, and who approach man. Those who today work towards an initiation still notice something of this. For knowledge which comes from the spiritual world comes to us far, far more slowly than does that which is imparted to us on the wings of our ordinary air processes.

That is why it is so important for one striving for initiation to learn to sense within himself the great significance of the transitions of going to sleep and waking up. In going to sleep and in waking up, in this transition, we are most likely to sense how spiritual beings mysteriously speak with us. Later we can then gain some control over this. If you seek entry into the world inhabited by the dead, it is good to be aware that the dead are most likely to speak at the moment of going to sleep and the moment of waking up. The moment of going to sleep is more difficult, because here we usually become immediately unconscious and fail to perceive what the dead have said. But in waking up, if we succeed in becoming fully aware of the moment of waking up, that is when the dead are most likely to communicate with us. But we must seek to gain a firm hold of the moment of waking up. This means that we must endeavour to wake up without immediately entering into the light of day. You know that there is a — shall we say — superstitious rule, that if we want to hold on to a dream we must not look at the window or the light because if we do, we will forget easily. This applies just as much to the delicate observations which flow to us from the spiritual world. We must endeavour to wake up in the dark, in darkness which we wilfully create by not listening to noises, by not opening our eyes, by waking up consciously while not yet going out to meet the day. That is when we best notice the approach of communications from the spiritual world.

You could say that if this is the case we shall receive precious few communications during the course of our lifetime! For just think how difficult it would be if this situation meant that in the course of our

196 THE KARMA OF UNTRUTHFULNESS — VOLUME TWO

lifetime we could only receive as many communications as could come to us during the course of one day. This would be sufficient, no doubt, but we should have no chance of making use of any of them, for think of the time taken up by our childhood, and so on. However, the earth takes part in all this — please bear this in mind — the earth receives these communications into its etheric body. And because they are inscribed on the earth's etheric body, the communications remain available for study. We can also study, in the sun-ether which fills the whole world, the more comprehensive communications given to us by the being whose life element is the Platonic Year. This is described in *Knowledge of the Higher Worlds*[1] and other books.

You see how a thread can be spun to link ordinary science with spiritual science, although those who are strangers to spiritual science will hardly find themselves in a position to evaluate what ordinary science gives them in a suitable way. But those who have the attitude of mind of spiritual science will not doubt, when they approach these matters, that a time will come one day when external science and spiritual science will join forces fully.

As I said, I have only spoken to you about a part of all this, namely, the rhythmical process which is built into breathing. There are many other things which, if studied in relation to numbers, show how the microcosm is in harmony with the macrocosm, and human beings can gain a comprehensive sense for this harmony. Such a comprehensive sense for this harmony was given to the pupils of the ancient Mysteries, right up to the fifteenth century. Before any knowledge was imparted to them, their teachers endeavoured to imbue them with a feeling for the way man stands within the cosmos. It is another sign of these materialistic times that knowledge today can be absorbed without any preparation in the feeling life. I pointed this out in the opening words of the first chapter in *Christianity as Mystical Fact*.[2]

A feeling for the correspondence between microcosm and macrocosm will be especially important when the endeavour is made to reach concrete concepts for what at the moment only exists in abstractions. For instance what is 'a people, a nation' in today's abstract materialism? Nothing but so and so many people who speak the same language! For our materialistic age has, of course, no conception of a folk being as a separate individuality, such as we have often described. We speak of a folk being as a separate individuality, a real single individuality. But in the materialists' view a folk being is merely a collection of people who speak the same language. This is an abstraction, for the concept does not refer to a concrete being. So what does it mean to you when discussing a people or a nation to speak, not of an abstraction but of a concrete being?

Well, in Anthroposophy we have the possibility of studying the human being, who is also a concrete being, and who possesses a physical body, an etheric body, an astral body and an ego. So can we assume that a folk being is also a concrete being with differentiated parts?

Indeed we can. In addition to man, true occultism studies all the beings who exist, and who are as concrete as man. However, in the case of a folk soul we have to look for different elements, for if they were the same as in man, then a folk soul would be a human being, but it is not; it is a different kind of being. In fact, in the case of folk beings we have to study each folk soul individually in order to arrive at concepts which are real. Generalization would lead us back to abstraction, so each has to be considered individually.

Let us do so. Take the folk soul which today rules the Italian people to the extent that the individual members of a people can be ruled by a folk soul. What can we say about it? In the case of a human being we say that he has a physical body consisting of various salts, various other minerals, five per-cent solids, so much that is liquid, so much that is gaseous, and so on. That is his physical body. A folk soul such as that of the Italian people does not possess a human body, but it does possess something which can be seen as analogous to the physical body. The Italian folk soul does not have a physical body made up of salts or solids or liquids, though this does not mean that other folk souls have no liquid components. However, the Italian folk soul has none; it begins with components which are aeriform. There are no liquid or other components, for the most densely material part of the Italian folk soul is woven out of air. All its other components are even less dense. The human being has earthly substance, whereas the Italian folk soul has, to start with, aeriform substance. And where the human being has liquid substance, the Italian folk soul has warmth. The human being has aeriform substance which he breathes in and out, and the Italian folk soul has light which corresponds to air in the human being. The human being has warmth, and the Italian folk soul has sounds instead, the sounds of the spheres.

This is approximately what corresponds to the physical body, but the ingredients are different. Instead of solid, liquid, gaseous and warmth elements, as in the human being, the Italian folk soul has something similar — though not a physical body in the same sense — consisting of air, warmth, light, sound. From this you can see that if the Italian folk soul wants to ensoul the human beings who belong to it, this can take place via their breathing, since its lowest, densest component is air. And indeed it is so that the communication between the individuals and the Italian folk soul takes place through the breathing process. In the breathing the folk soul spreads down into the human beings. This is an actual, real process. Of course breathing is done through something quite different, but in the actual breathing process the folk soul steals in and influences its people.

In a similar way we could consider what corresponds to our etheric body. This would start with the life ether, and then in place of the light ether there would be what I called in my *Theosophy*[3] 'burning desire'; then, corresponding to the sound ether, would be what is there described as 'mobile sensitivity', and so on. You can find all the ingredients in *Theosophy*, but you have to know how to apply them. If you were to take further this study of the correspondence, the communication, between the folk soul and the individual human being; if you were to continue on the basis of what we have said so far, you would find that all the qualities in the character of the Italian people are connected with these things. This can be studied concretely in every detail.

Only examples can be given here. Suppose we wanted to study the Russian folk soul. We would find that the lowest component has nothing material in it, nothing solid, liquid, gaseous, aeriform, not even warmth. The lowest component, what in the Russian folk soul corresponds to the salt, the solid element in the human being, would be found to be the light ether. The sound ether would be what corresponds to the liquid element in the human being; the life ether would correspond to the air in the human being; the 'burning desire' to warmth in the human being. Then we could ask how the Russian folk soul communicates with the individual Russian human being. This takes place in that light, streaming down, is reflected in a certain way by the earth. Light exercises certain influences on the earth. It is reflected not only physically, but also out of the vegetation, out of whatever is in the soil. The light does not work directly on the individual Russian. First it works into the earth, not the coarse, physical earth, but the plants and everything that grows and flourishes on the earth. And this light is reflected. In what is reflected back lies the medium through which the Russian folk soul communicates with the individual Russian. That is why the Russians' relationship to their soil, to everything brought forth by the earth, is so much stronger than is the case with other nations. It is because of this extraordinary bearing of the folk soul. And 'mobile sensitivity' — this is immensely significant — is the first etheric ingredient of the Russian folk soul, corresponding to light in the human being.

Thus we come to the concrete folk being; thus we can study how one spirit speaks to another, when one is a human being and the other a folk soul. This takes place in the subconscious realm. When an Italian breathes, when he maintains his life by breathing — when what he consciously wants is to maintain his life by breathing — then, in his unconscious, the folk soul speaks and whispers to him. He does not hear it, but his astral body perceives it and lives in the exchange that goes on beneath the threshold of consciousness between the folk soul and the individual human being.

And in what streams back out of the Russian soil, fructified by sunlight, are contained the mysterious runes, the whispering runes by which the Russian folk soul speaks to the individual Russian while he paces across the face of his land or senses the life which rays forth from the light. Do not imagine that these things must be taken in a material way. Of course a Russian might live in Switzerland, but in Switzerland, too, there is light which is reflected by the earth. If you are an Italian you will hear your folk soul whispering in your breathing when you are in Switzerland. If you are a Russian you will feel rising up from the soil of Switzerland whatever it is you can hear as a Russian. You must not take these things in a material way. Such things are not tied to locations — though, of course, because the human being is to some extent material, one's own location yields more. The air of Italy, together with the whole climate there, naturally facilitates and promotes the kind of speaking I have described. And the soil of Russia facilitates and promotes that other kind of speaking. But you must not take these things materialistically, for of course a Russian can be a Russian not only in Russia — although it is Russian soil which especially promotes Russian-ness. You see, on the one hand materialism is given its due, but on the other hand we have here something relative, not absolute. For light above the soil of Russia is not only part of the body of the Russian folk soul, but it is also light, as elsewhere. On the other hand the Russian folk soul — I have described all this before — has the rank of an archangel. And archangels are not fettered to one location, they are supra-spatial.

Concrete concepts such as these are what ought to underlie any talk of the relationship of the individual to his people. Yet consider how far mankind is today from even the faintest notion of what is contained in the name of a people. Notwithstanding such considerations, world programmes are scattered abroad and the names of nations cast in every direction. When you take proper account of the fact that a folk-being is a concrete being and that every folk-being differs from every other, you will be able to realize fully just how much of what is flying around in the world today is nothing but empty phrases. What is air for the Italian folk-being is light for the Russian folk-being, and these things lead to quite different kinds of communication between the folk-being and the individual human being. Anthropology is the materialistic, external view; Anthroposophy will have to reveal the true conditions, the actual realities. Since, in their materialism, people today are such a long way from any reality, it is no wonder that things which are included in world programmes are spoken about in such an arbitrary and mendacious manner.

On Tuesday we shall continue to speak about the nature of our anthroposophical spiritual science. In connection with this I also want to refer to a number of things at the present time which can really only be properly understood from the standpoint of spiritual science. The suffering mankind is having to bear today is connected in large measure with the fact that people do not want to find clarity with reference to the things they discuss. Instead they send into the world furious messages which bear no relation to reality. This is once again brought home to us when we come across something like the pamphlet which has been published in Switzerland, *Conditions de Paix de l'Allemagne* by someone who calls himself 'Hungaricus'.[4] For those of us whose attitude of mind is that of spiritual science, we need only read this through in order to discover every single defect in present-day materialistic thinking with all its awkward complications. So on Tuesday I shall say a few words about this pamphlet and its method and the kind of thinking it reveals, for it really is so very characteristic of today's awkward and complicated materialistic thinking.

LECTURE TWENTY-FIVE
Dornach, 30 January 1917

Today it seems appropriate to mention certain thoughts on the meaning and nature of our spiritual Movement — anthroposophical spiritual science, as we call it. To do so will necessitate references to some events which have occurred over a period of time and which have contributed to the preparation and unfolding of this Movement. If, in the course of these remarks, one or another of them should seem somewhat more personal — it would, at any rate, only seem to be so — this will not be for personal reasons but because what is more personal can be a starting point for something more objective. The need for a spiritual movement which makes known to people the deeper sources of existence, especially human existence, can be easily recognized by the way in which today's civilization has developed along lines which are becoming increasingly absurd. No one, after serious thought, will describe today's events as anything other than an absurd exaggeration of what has been living in more recent evolution.

From what you have come to know in spiritual science, you will have gained the feeling that everything, even what is apparently only external, has its foundation in the thoughts of human beings. Deeds which are done, events which take place in material life — all these are the consequence of what human beings think and imagine. And the view of the external world, which is gaining ground among human beings today, gives us an indication of some very inadequate thought forces. I have already put into words the fact that events have grown beyond human beings, have got out of hand, because their thinking has become attenuated and is no longer strong enough to govern reality. Concepts such as that of maya, the external semblance which governs the things of the physical plane, ought to be taken far more seriously by those familiar with them than they, in fact, often are. They ought to be profoundly imprinted on current consciousness as a whole. This alone might lead to the healing of the damage which — with a certain amount of justification — has come upon mankind. Those who strive to understand the functioning of man's deeds — that is, the way the reflections of man's thoughts function — will recognize the inner need for a comprehension of the human soul which can be brought about by stronger, more realistic thoughts.

In fact, our whole Movement is founded on the task of giving human souls thoughts more appropriate to reality, thoughts more immersed in reality, than are the abstract concept patterns of today. It cannot be pointed out often enough how very much mankind today is in love with the abstract, having no desire to realize that shadowy concepts cannot, in reality, make any impact on the fabric of existence. This has been most clearly expressed in the fourteen-, fifteen-year history of our Anthroposophical Movement. Now it is becoming all the more important for our friends to take into themselves what specifically belongs to this Anthroposophical Movement. You know how often people stressed that they would so much like to give the beautiful word 'theosophy' the honour it deserves, and how much they resisted having to give it up as the key word of the Movement. But you also know the situation which made this necessary.

It is good to be thoroughly aware in one's soul about this. You know — indeed, many of you shared — the goodwill with which we linked our work with that of the Theosophical Movement in the way it had been founded by Blavatsky,[1] and how this then continued with Besant's and Sinnett's[2] efforts, and so on. It is indeed not unnecessary for our members, in face of all the ill-meant misrepresentations heaped upon us from outside, to persist in pointing out that our Anthroposophical Movement had an independent starting-point and that what now exists has grown out of the seeds of those lectures I gave in Berlin which were later published in the book on the mysticism of the Middle Ages.[3] We must stress ever and again that in connection with this book it was the Theosophical Movement who approached us, not vice versa. This Theosophical Movement, in whose wake it was our destiny to ride during those early years, was not without its connections to other occult streams of the nineteenth century, and in lectures given here[4] I have pointed to these connections. But we should look at what is characteristic for that Movement.

If I were asked to point factually to one rather characteristic feature, I would choose one I have mentioned a number of times, which is connected with the period when I was writing in the journal *Lucifer-Gnosis* what was later given the title *Cosmic Memory*. A representative of the Theosophical Society, who read this, asked me by what method these things were garnered from the spiritual world. Further conversation made it obvious that he wanted to know what more-or-less mediumistic methods were used for this. Members of those circles find it impossible to imagine any method other than that of people with mediumistic gifts, who lower their consciousness and write down what comes from the subconscious.

What underlies this attitude? Even though he is a very competent and exceptionally cultured representative of the Theosophical Movement, the man who spoke to me on this was incapable of imagining that it is possible to investigate such things in full consciousness. Many members of that Movement had the same problem because they shared something which is present to the highest degree in today's spiritual life, namely, a certain mistrust in the individual's capacity for knowledge. People do not trust the inherent capacity for knowledge, they do not believe that the individual can have the strength to penetrate truly to the essential core of things. They consider that the human capacity for knowledge is limited; they find that intellectual understanding gets in the way if one wants to penetrate to the core of things and that it is therefore better to damp it down and push forward to the core of things without bringing it into play. This is indeed what mediums do; for them, to mistrust human understanding is a basic impulse. They endeavour, purely experimentally, to let the spirit speak while excluding active understanding.

It can be said that this mood was particularly prevalent in the Theosophical Movement as it existed at the beginning of the century. It could be felt when one tried to penetrate certain things, certain opinions and views, which had come to live in the Theosophical Movement. You know that in the nineties of the nineteenth century and subsequently in the twentieth century, Mrs Besant played an important part in the Theosophical Movement. Her opinion counted. Her lectures formed the centrepiece of theosophical work both in London and in India. And yet it was strange to hear what people around Mrs Besant said about her. I noticed this strongly as early as 1902. In many ways, especially among the scholarly men around her, she was regarded as a quite unacademic woman. Yet, while on the one hand people stressed how unacademic she was, on the other hand they regarded the partly mediumistic method she was famous for, untrammelled as it was by scientific ideas, as a channel for achieving knowledge. I could say that these people did not themselves have the courage to aim for knowledge. Neither had they any confidence in Mrs Besant's waking consciousness. But because she had not been made fully awake as a result of any scientific training, they saw her to some extent as a means by which knowledge from the spiritual world could be brought into the physical world. This attitude was extraordinarily prevalent among those immediately surrounding her. People spoke about her at the beginning of the twentieth century as if she were some kind of modern sibyl. Those closest to her formed derogatory opinions about her academic aptitude and maintained that she had no critical ability to judge her inner experiences. This was certainly the mood around her, though it was carefully hidden — I will not say kept secret — from the wider circle of theosophical leaders.

In addition to what came to light in a sibylline way through Mrs Besant, and through Blavatsky's *The Secret Doctrine*, the Theosophical Movement at the end of the nineteenth century also had Sinnett's book or, rather, books. The manner in which people spoke about these in private was, equally, hardly an appeal to man's own power of knowledge. Much was made in private about the fact that in what Sinnett had published there was nothing which he had contributed out of his own experience. The value of a book such as his *Esoteric Buddhism* was seen to lie particularly in the fact that the whole of the content had come to him in the form of 'magical letters', precipitated — no one knew whence — into the physical plane — one could almost say, thrown down to the physical plane — which he then worked into the book *Esoteric Buddhism*.

All these things led to a mood among the wider circles of the theosophical leaders which was sentimental and devotional in the highest degree. They looked up, in a way, to a wisdom which had fallen from heaven, and — humanly, quite understandable — this devotion was transferred to individual personalities. However, this became the incentive for a high level of insincerity which was easy to discern in a number of phenomena

Thus, for instance, even in 1902 I heard in the more private gatherings in London that Sinnett was, in fact, an inferior spirit. One of the leading personalities said to me at that time: Sinnett could be compared with a journalist — say, of the *Frankfurter Zeitung* — who has been dispatched to India; he is a journalistic spirit who simply had the good fortune to receive the 'Master's letters' and make use of them in his book in a journalistic way which is in keeping with modern mankind!

You know, though, that all this is only one aspect of a wide spectrum of literature. For in the final decades of the nineteenth century and the first decades of the twentieth, there appeared — if not a Biblical deluge, then certainly a flood of — written material which was intended to lead mankind in one way or another to the spiritual world.

Some of this material harked back directly to ancient traditions which have been preserved by all kinds of secret brotherhoods. It is most interesting to follow the development of this tradition.

I have often pointed out how, in the second half of the eighteenth century, old traditions could be found in the circle led by Saint-Martin,[5] the *philosophe inconnu*. In Saint-Martin's writings, especially *Des erreurs et de la vérité*, there is a very great deal of what came from ancient traditions, clothed in a more recent form. If we follow these traditions further back, we do indeed come to ideas which can conquer concrete situations, which can influence reality. By the time they had come down to Saint-Martin, these concepts had already become exceedingly shadowy, but they were nevertheless shadows of concepts which had once been very much alive; ancient traditions were living one last time in a shadowy form. So in Saint-Martin's work we find the healthiest concepts clothed in a form which is a final glimmer. It is particularly interesting to see how Saint-Martin fights against the concept of matter, which had already come to the fore. What did this concept of matter gradually become? It became a view in which the world is seen as a fog made up of atoms moving about and bumping into one another and forming configurations which are at the root of all things taking shape around us. In theory materialism reached its zenith at the point when the existence of everything except the atom was denied. Saint-Martin still maintained the view that the whole science of atoms, and indeed the whole belief that matter was something real, was nonsense; which indeed it is. If we delve into all that is around us, chemically, physically, we come in the final analysis not to atoms, not to anything material, but to spiritual beings. The concept of matter is an aid; but it corresponds to nothing that is real. Wherever — to use a phrase coined by Du Bois-Reymond[6] — 'matter floats about in space like a ghost': there may be found the spirit. The only way to speak of an atom is to speak of a little thrust of spirit, albeit ahrimanic spirit. It was a healthy idea of Saint-Martin to do battle against the concept of matter.

Another immensely healthy idea of Saint-Martin was the living way in which he pointed to the fact that all separate, concrete human languages are founded on a single universal language. This was easier to do in his day than it is now, because in his time there was still a more living relationship to the Hebrew language which, among all modern languages, is the one closest to the archetypal universal language. It was still possible to feel at that time the way in which spirit flowed through the Hebrew language, giving the very words something genuinely ideal and spiritual. So we find in Saint-Martin's work an indication, concrete and spiritual, of the meaning of the word 'the Hebrew'. In the whole way he conceived of this we find a living consciousness of a relationship of the human being with the spiritual world. This word 'the Hebrew' is connected with 'to journey'. A Hebrew is one who makes a journey through life, one who gathers experiences as on a journey. Standing in the world in a living way — this is the foundation of this word and of all other words in the Hebrew language if they are sensed in their reality.

However, in his own time Saint-Martin was no longer able to find ideas which could point more precisely, more strongly, to what belonged to the archetypal language. These will have to be rediscovered by spiritual science. But he had before his soul a profound notion of what the archetypal language had been. Because of this his concept of the unity of the human race was more concrete and less abstract than that which the nineteenth century made for itself. This concrete concept of the unity of the human race made it possible for him, at least within his own circle, to bring fully to life certain spiritual truths, for instance, the truth that the human being, if only he so desires, really can enter into a relationship with spiritual beings of higher hierarchies. It is one of his cardinal principles, which states that every human being is capable of entering into a relationship with spiritual beings of higher hierarchies. Because of this there still lived in him something of that ancient, genuine mystic mood which knew that knowledge, if it is to be true knowledge, cannot be absorbed in a conceptual form only, but must be absorbed in a particular mood of soul — that is after a certain preparation of the soul. Then it becomes part of the soul's spiritual life.

Hand in hand with this, however, went a certain sum of expectations, of evolutionary expectations directed to those human souls who desired to claim a right to participate in some way in evolution. From this point of view it is most interesting to see how Saint-Martin makes the transition from what he has won through knowledge, through science — which is spiritual in his case — to politics, how he arrives at political concepts. For here he states a precise requirement, saying that every ruler ought to be a kind of Melchizedek, a kind of priest-king.

Just imagine if this requirement, put forward in a relatively small circle before the outbreak of the French Revolution, had been a dawn instead of a dusk; just imagine if this idea — that those whose concepts and forces were to influence human destiny must fundamentally have the characteristics of a Melchizedek — had been absorbed, even partially, into the consciousness of the time, how much would have been different in the nineteenth century! For the nineteenth century was, in truth, as distant as it could possibly be from this concept. The demand that politicians should first undertake to study at the school of Melchizedek would, of course, have been dismissed with a shrug.

Saint-Martin has to be pointed out because he bears within him something which is a last glimmer of the wisdom that has come down from ancient times. It has had to die away because mankind in the future must ascend to spiritual life in a new way. Mankind must ascend in a new way because a merely traditional continuation of old ideas never has been in keeping with the germinating forces of the human soul. These underdeveloped forces of the human soul will tend, during the course of the twentieth century, in a considerable number of individuals — this has been said often enough — to lead to true insight into etheric processes. The first third of the twentieth century can be seen as a critical period during which a goodly number of human beings ought to be made aware of the fact that events must be observed in the etheric world which lives all around us, just as much as does the air. We have pointed emphatically to one particular event which must be seen in the etheric world if mankind is not to fall into decadence, and that is the appearance of the Etheric Christ. This is a necessity. Mankind must definitely prepare not to let wither those forces which are already sprouting.

These forces must not be allowed to wither for, if they did, what would happen? In the forties and fifties of the twentieth century the human soul would assume exceedingly odd characteristics in the widest circles. Concepts would arise in the human soul which would have an oppressive effect. If materialism were the only thing to continue, concepts which exist in the human soul would arise, but they would rise up out of the unconscious in a way which people would not understand. A waking nightmare, a kind of general state of neurasthenia, would afflict a huge number of people. They would find themselves having to think things without understanding why they were thinking them.

The only antidote to this is to plant, in human souls, concepts which stem from spiritual science. Without these, the forces of insight into those concepts which will rise up, into those ideas which will make their appearance, will be paralysed. Then, not the Christ alone, but also other phenomena in the etheric world, which human beings ought to see, will withdraw from man, will go past unnoticed. Not only will this be a great loss, but human beings will also have to develop pathological substitute forces for those which ought to have developed in a healthy way.

It was out of an instinctive need in wide circles of mankind that the endeavours arose which expressed themselves in that flood of literature and written material mentioned earlier. Now, because of a peculiar phenomenon, the Anthroposophical Movement of Central Europe was in a peculiar position relative to the Theosophical Movement — particularly to the Theosophical Society — as well as to that other flood of written material about spiritual matters. Because of the evolutionary situation in the nineteenth century and at the beginning of the twentieth century, it was possible for a great number of people to find spiritual nourishment in all this literature; and it was also possible for a great number of people to be utterly astounded by what came to light through Sinnett and Blavatsky. However, all this was not quite in harmony with Central European consciousness. Those who are familiar with Central European literature are in no doubt that it is not necessarily possible to live in the element of this Central European literature while at the same time taking up the attitude of so many others to that flood. This is because Central European literature encompasses immeasurably much of what the seeker for the spirit longs for — only it is hidden behind the peculiar language which so many people would rather have nothing to do with.

We have often spoken about one of those spirits who prove that spiritual life works and weaves in artistic literature, in belletristic literature: Novalis. For more prosaic moods we might equally well have mentioned Friedrich Schlegel,[7] who wrote about the wisdom of ancient India in a way which did not merely reproduce that wisdom but brought it to a fresh birth out of the western cultural spirit. There is much we could have pointed to that has nothing to do with that flood of written material, but which I have sketched historically in my book *Vom Menschenrätsel*. People like Steffens,[8], like Schubert,[9], like Troxler,[10] wrote about all these things far more precisely and at a much more modern level than anything found in that flood of literature which welled up during the last decades of the nineteenth century and the beginning of the twentieth century. You have to admit that, compared with the profundity of Goethe, Schlegel,

Schelling, those things which are held to be so marvellously wise are nothing more than trivia, utter trivia. Someone who has absorbed the spirit of Goethe can regard even a work like such as *Light on the Path*[11] as no more than commonplace. This ought not to be forgotten. To those who have absorbed the inspiration of Novalis or Friedrich Schlegel, or enjoyed Schelling's *Bruno*, all this theosophical literature can seem no more than vulgar and ordinary. Hence the peculiar phenomenon that there were many people who had the earnest, honest desire to reach a spiritual life but who, because of their mental make-up were, in the end, to some degree satisfied with the superficial literature described.

On the other hand, the nineteenth century had developed in such a way that those who were scientifically educated had become — for reasons I have often discussed — materialistic thinkers about whom nothing could be done. However, in order to work one's way competently through what came to light at the turn of the eighteenth to the nineteenth century through Schelling, Schlegel, Fichte, one does need at least some scientific concepts. There is no way of proceeding without them. The consequence was this peculiar phenomenon: It was not possible to bring about a situation — which would have been desirable — in which a number of scientifically educated people, however small, could have worked out their scientific concepts in such a way that they could have made a bridge to spiritual science. No such people were to be found. This is a difficulty that still exists and of which we must be very much aware.

Supposing we were to approach those who have undergone a scientific education, with the intention of introducing them to Anthroposophy: lawyers, doctors, philologists — not to mention theologians — when they have finished their academic education and reached a certain stage in life at which it is necessary for them, in accordance with life's demands, to make use of what they have absorbed, not to say, have learnt. They then no longer have either the inclination or the mobility to extricate themselves from their concepts and to seek for others. That is why scientifically-educated people are the most inclined to reject Anthroposophy, although it would only be a small step for a modern scientist to build a bridge. But he does not want to do so. It confuses him. What does he need it for? He has learnt what life demands of him and, so he believes, he does not want things which only serve to confuse him and undermine his confidence. It is going to take some considerable time before these people who have gone through the education of their day start to build bridges in any great numbers. We shall have to be patient. It will not come about easily, especially in certain fields. And when the building of bridges is seriously tackled in a particular field, great obstacles and hindrances will be encountered. It will be necessary above all to build bridges in the fields encompassed by the various faculties, with the exception of theology.

In the field of law the concepts being worked out are becoming more and more stereotyped and quite unsuitable for the regulation of real life. But they do regulate it because life on the physical plane is maya; if it were not maya, they would be incapable of regulating it. As it is, their application is bringing more and more confusion into the world. The application of today's jurisprudence, especially in civil law, does nothing but bring confusion into the situation. But this is not clearly seen. Indeed, how should it be seen? No one follows up the consequences of applying stereotyped concepts to reality. People study law, they become solicitors or judges, they absorb the concepts and apply them. What happens as a consequence of their application is of no interest. Or life is seen as it is — despite the existence of the law, which is a very difficult subject to study for many reasons, not least because law students tend to waste the first few terms — life is seen as it is; we see that everything is in a muddle and do no more than complain.

In the field of medicine the situation is more serious. If medicine continues to develop in the wake of materialism as it has been doing since the second third of the nineteenth century, it will eventually reach an utterly nonsensical situation, for it will end up in absurd medical specializations. The situation is more serious here because this tendency was, in fact, necessary and a good thing. But now it is time for it to be overcome. The materialistic tendency in medicine meant that surgery has reached a high degree of specialization, which was only possible because of this one-sided tendency. But medicine as such has suffered as a result. So now it needs to turn around completely and look towards a real spirituality — but the resistance to this is enormous.

Education is the field which, more than any other, needs to be permeated with spirituality, as we have said often enough. Bridges need to be built everywhere.

In technology — although it may appear to be furthest away from the spirit — it is above all necessary that bridges should be built to the life of the spirit, out of direct practical life. The fifth post-Atlantean period is the one which is concerned with the development of the material world, and if the human being is not to degenerate totally into a mere accomplice of machines — which would make him into nothing more than an animal — then a path must be found which leads from these very machines to the life of the spirit. The priority for those working practically with machines is that they take spiritual impulses into their own soul. This will come about the moment students of technology are taught to think just a little more than is the case at present; the moment they are taught to think in such a way that they see the connections between the different things they learn. As yet they are unable to do this. They attend lectures on mathematics, on descriptive geometry, even on topology sometimes; on pure mechanics, analytical mechanics, industrial mechanics, and also all the various more practical subjects. But it does not even occur to them to look for a connection between all these different things. As soon as people are obliged to apply their own common sense to things, they will be forced — simply on account of the stage of development these various subjects have reached — to push forward into the nature of these things and then on into the spiritual realm. From machines, in particular, a path will truly have to be found into the spiritual world.

I am saying all this in order to point out what difficulties today face the spiritual-scientific Movement, because so far there are no individuals to be found who might be capable of generating an atmosphere of taking things seriously. This Movement suffers most of all from a lack of being taken seriously. It is remarkable how this comes to the fore in all kinds of details. Much of what we have published would have been taken seriously, would have been seen in quite a different light, if it had not been made known that it stemmed from someone belonging to the Theosophical Movement. Simply because the person concerned was in the Theosophical Movement, his work was stamped as something not to be taken seriously. It is most important to realize this, and it is just these trifling details which make it plain. Not out of any foolish vanity but just so that you know what I mean, let me give you an example of one of these trifles which I came across only the other day.

In my book *Vom Menschenrätsel* I wrote about Karl Christian Planck[12] as one of those spirits who, out of certain inner foundations, worked towards the spiritual realm, even though only in an abstract

way. I have not only written about him in this book, but also — over
the past few winters — spoken about him in some detail in a number
of cities, showing how he went unrecognized, or was misunderstood,
and referring especially to one particular circumstance. This was the
fact that, in the eighties, seventies, sixties, fifties, this man had ideas
and thoughts in connection with industrial and social life which ought
to have been put into practice. If only there had been someone at that
time with the capacity of employing in social life the great ideas this
man had, ideas truly compatible with reality, then — and I am not
exaggerating — mankind would probably not now be suffering all
that is going on today which, for the greater part, is a consequence
of the totally wrong social structure in which we are living.

I have told you that it is a real duty not to let human beings come
to a pass such as that reached by Karl Christian Planck, who finally
came to be utterly devoid of any love for the world of external physical
reality. He was a Swabian living in Stuttgart. He was refused a place
in the philosophy department of Tübingen University, where he would
have had the opportunity to put forward some of his ideas. I entirely
intentionally mentioned the fact that, when he wrote the foreword to
his book *Testament of a German*, he felt moved to say, 'Not even
my bones shall rest in the soil of my ungrateful fatherland'. Hard
words. Words such as people today can be driven to utter when faced
with the stupidity of their fellow human beings, who refuse to see
the point about what is really compatible with reality. In Stuttgart
I purposely quoted these words about his bones, for Stuttgart is
Planck's fatherland in the narrower sense. There was little reaction,
despite the fact that events had already reached a stage when there
would have been every reason to understand the things he had said.

Now, however, a year-and-a-half later, the following notice may
be found in the Swabian newspapers:

'Karl Christian Planck. More than one far-seeing spirit foretold
the present World War. But none anticipated its scale nor
understood its causes and effects as clearly as did our Swabian
countryman Planck.'

I said in my lecture that Karl Christian Planck had foreseen the present
World War, and that he even expressly stated that Italy would not
be on the side of the Central Powers, even though he was speaking
at the time when the alliance had not yet been concluded, but was
only in the making.

'To him this war seemed to be the unavoidable goal toward which political and economic developments had been inexorably moving for the last fifty years.'

This is indeed the case!

'Just as he revealed the damage being done in his day, so he also pointed the way which can lead us to other situations.'

This is the important point. But nobody listened!

'By him we are told the deeper reasons underlying war profiteering and other black marks which mar so many good and pleasing aspects of the life of the nation today. He knows where the deeper, more inward forces of the nation lie and can tell us how to release them so that the moral and social renewal longed for by the best amongst us can come about. Despite all the painful disappointments meted out to him by his contemporaries, he continued to believe in these forces and their triumphant emergence.'

Nevertheless, he was driven to utter the words I have quoted!

'The news will therefore be widely welcomed that the philosopher's daughter is about to give an introduction to Planck's social and political thinking in a number of public lectures.'

It is interesting that a year-and-a-half later his daughter should be putting in an appearance. This notice appeared in a Stuttgart newspaper. But a year-and-a-half ago, when I drew attention as plainly as possible in Stuttgart to the the philosopher Karl Christian Planck, no one took the slightest notice, and no one felt moved to make known what I had said. Now his daughter puts in an appearance. Her father died in 1880, and presumably she had been born by then. Yet she has waited all this time before standing up for him by giving public lectures.

This example could be multiplied not tenfold, but a hundredfold. It shows once again how difficult it is to bring together the all-embracing aspect of spiritual science with everyday practical details, despite the fact that it is absolutely essential that this should be done.

Only through the all-embracing nature of spiritual science — this must be understood — can healing come about for what lives in the culture of today.

That is why it has been essential to keep steering what we call anthroposophical spiritual science, in whatever way possible, along the more serious channels which have been increasingly deserted by the Theosophical Movement. The spirit that was even known to the ancient Greek philosophers had to be allowed to come through, although this has led to the opinion that what is written in consequence is difficult to read. It has often not been easy. Especially within the Movement it met with the greatest difficulties. And one of the greatest difficulties has been the fact that it really has taken well over a decade to overcome one fundamental abstraction. Laborious and patient work has been necessary to overcome this fundamental abstraction which has been one of the most damaging things for our Movement. This basic abstraction consisted simply in the insistence on clinging to the word 'theosophy', regardless of whether whatever was said to be 'theosophical' referred to something filled with the spirituality of modern life, or to no more than some rubbish published by Rohm[13] or anyone else. Anything 'theosophical' had equal justification, for this prompted 'theosophical tolerance'.

Only very gradually has it been possible to work against these things. They could not be pointed out directly at the beginning, because that would have seemed arrogant. Only gradually has it been possible to awaken a feeling for the fact that differences do exist, and that tolerance used in this connection is nothing more than an expression of a total lack of character on which to base judgements. What matters now is to work towards knowledge of a kind which can cope with reality, which can tackle the demands of reality. Only a spiritual science that works with the concepts of our time can tackle the demands of reality. Not living in comfortable theosophical ideas but wrestling for spiritual reality — this must be the direction of our endeavour.

Some people still have no idea what is meant by wrestling for reality, for they are fighting shy of understanding clearly how threadbare are the concepts with which they work today. Let me give you a small example, from a seemingly unrelated subject, of what it means to wrestle for reality in concepts. I shall be brief, so please be patient while I explain something that might seem rather far-fetched.

There were always isolated individuals in the nineteenth century who were prepared to take up the question of reality. For reality was then supposed to burst in on mankind with entirely fresh ideas about life, not only the unimportant aspects but especially the basic practical aspects of life. Thus at a certain point in the nineteenth century Euclid's postulate of parallels was challenged. When are two lines parallel? Who could have failed to agree that two lines are parallel if they never meet, however long they are! For that is the definition: That two straight lines are parallel if they never meet, whatever the distance to which they are extended. In the nineteenth century there were individuals who devoted their whole life to achieving clarity about this concept, for it does not stand up to exact thinking. In order to show you what it means to wrestle for concepts, let me read you a letter written by Wolfgang Bolyai.[14] The mathematician Gauss[15] had begun to realize that the definition of two straight lines being parallel if they meet at infinity, or not at all, was no more than empty words and meant nothing. The older Bolyai, the father, was a friend and pupil of Gauss, who also stimulated the younger Bolyai, the son. And the father wrote to the son:[16]

'Do not look for the parallels in that direction. I have trodden that path to its end; I have traversed bottomless night in which every light, every joy of my life has been extinguished. By God I implore you to leave the postulate of the parallels alone! Shun it as you would a dissolute association, for it can rob you of all your leisure, your health, your peace of mind and every pleasure in life. It will never grow light on earth and the unfortunate human race will never gain anything perfectly pure, not even geometry itself. In my soul there is a deep and eternal wound. May God save you from being eaten away by another such. It robs me of my delight in geometry, and indeed of life on earth. I had resolved to sacrifice myself for the truth. I would have been prepared for martyrdom if only I could have handed geometry back to mankind purified of this blemish. I have accomplished awful, gigantic works, have achieved far more than ever before, but never found total satisfaction. *Si paullum a summo discessit, vergit ad imum.* When I saw that the foundation of this night cannot be reached from the earth I returned, comfortless, sorrowing for my self and the human race. Learn from my example. Desiring to know the parallels, I have remained without knowledge. And they have robbed me of all

the flowers of my life and time. They have become the root
of all my subsequent failures, and much rain has fallen on them
from our lowering domestic clouds. If I could have discovered
the parallels I would have become an angel, even if none had
ever known of my discovery.

. . . Do not attempt it . . . It is a labyrinth that forever blocks
your path. If you enter you will grow poor, like a treasure
hunter, and your ignorance will not cease. Should you arrive
at whatever absurd discovery, it will be for naught, untenable
as an axiom . . .

. . . The pillars of Hercules are situated in this region. Go
not a step further, or you will be lost.'

Nevertheless, the younger Bolyai did go further, even more so than
his father, and devoted his whole life to the search for a concrete concept in a field where such a concept seemed to exist, but which was,
however, empty words. He wanted to discover whether there really
was such a thing as two straight lines which did not meet, even in
infinity. No one has ever paced out this infinite distance, for that would
take an infinite time, but this time has not yet run its course. It is
nothing more than words. Such empty words, such conceptual
shadows, are to be found behind all kinds of concepts. I simply wanted
to point out to you how even the most thorough spirits of the nineteenth
century suffered because of the abstractness of these concepts! It is
interesting to see that while children are taught in every school that
parallel lines are those which never meet, however long they are, there
have been individual spirits for whom working with such concepts
became a hell, because they were seeking to push through to a real
concept instead of a stereotyped concept.

Wrestling with reality — this is what matters, yet this is the very
thing our contemporaries shun, more or less, because they 'realize',
or imagine they realize, that they have 'high ideals'! It is not ideals
that matter, but impulses which work with reality. Imagine someone
were to make a beautiful statement such as: At long last a time must
come when those who are most capable are accorded the consideration
due to them. What a lovely programme! Whole societies could be
established in accordance with this programme. Even political sciences
could be founded on this basis. But it is not the statement that counts.
What counts is the degree to which it is permeated by reality. For
what is the use — however valid the statement, and however many

societies choose it for the prime point in their programmes — if those in power happen to see only their nephews as being the most capable? It is not a matter of establishing the validity of the statement that the most capable should be given their due. The important thing is to have the capacity to find those who are the most capable, whether they are one's nephews or not! We must learn to understand that abstract concepts always fall through the cracks of life, and that they never mean anything, and that all our time is wasted on all these beautiful concepts. I have no objection to their beauty, but what matters is our grasp and knowledge of reality.

Suppose the lion were to found a social order for the animals, dividing up the kingdom of the earth in a just way. What would he do? I do not believe it would occur to him to push for a situation in which the small animals of the desert, usually eaten by the lion, would have the possibility of not being eaten by the lion! He would consider it his lion's right to eat the small animals he meets in the desert. It is conceivable, though, that for the ocean he would find it just and proper to forbid the sharks to eat the little fishes. This might very well happen. The lion might establish a tremendously just social order in the oceans, at the North Pole or wherever else he himself is not at home, giving all the animals their freedom. But whether he would be pleased to establish such an order in his own region is a question indeed. He knows very well what justice is in the social order, and he will put it into practice efficiently in the kingdom of the sharks.

Let us now turn from lions to Hungaricus.[17] I told you two days ago about his small pamphlet *Conditions de Paix de l'Allemagne*. This pamphlet swims entirely with the stream of that map of Europe which was first mentioned in the famous note from the Entente to Wilson about the partition of Austria. We have spoken about it. With the exception of Switzerland, Hungaricus is quite satisfied with this map. He begins by talking very wisely — just as most people today talk very wisely — about the rights of nations, even the rights of small nations, and about the right of the state to be coincident with the power of the nation, and so on. This is all very nice, in the same way that the statement, about the most capable being given his due, is nice. As long as the concepts remain shadowy we can, if we are idealists, be delighted when we read Hungaricus. For the Swiss, the pamphlet is even nicer than the map, for rather than wiping Switzerland off the map, Hungaricus adds the Vorarlberg and the Tyrol. So I recommend the Swiss to read the pamphlet rather than look at the map.

But now Hungaricus proceeds to divide up the rest of the world. In his own way he accords to every nation, even the smallest, the absolute right to develop freely — as long as he considers he is not causing offence to the Entente. He trims his words a little, of course, saying 'independence' when referring to Bohemia, and obviously 'autonomy' with regard to Ireland. Well, this is the done thing, is it not! It is quite acceptable to dress things up a little. He divides up the world of Europe quite nicely, so that apart from the things I have mentioned — which are to avoid causing offence — he really endeavours to apportion the smallest nations to those states to which the representatives of the Entente believe they belong. It is not so much a question of whether these small territories are really inhabited by those nationalities, but of whether the Entente actually believes this to be the case. He makes every effort to divide up the world nicely, with the exception of the desert — oh, pardon me — with the exception of Hungary, which is where he practises his lion's right! Perfect freedom is laid down for the kingdom of the sharks. But the Magyar nation is his nation, and this is to comprise not only what it comprises today — though without it only a minority of the population would be Magyar, the majority being others — but other territories as well. Here he well and truly acts the part of the lion.

Here we see how concepts are formulated nowadays and how people think nowadays. It gives us an opportunity to study how urgent it is to find the transition to a thinking which is permeated with reality. For this, concepts such as those I have been giving you are necessary. I want to show you — indeed, I must show you — how spiritual thinking leads to ideas which are compatible with reality. One must always combine the correct thought with the object; then one can recognize whether that object corresponds to reality or not.

Take Wilson's note to the Senate. As a sample it could even have certain effects in some respects. But this is not what matters. What matters is that it contains 'shadowy concepts'. If it nevertheless has an effect, this is due to the vexatious nature of our time which can be influenced by vexatious means. Look at this matter objectively and try to form a concept against which you can measure the reality, the real content with which this shadowy concept could be linked. You need only ask one question: Could this note not just as well have been written in 1913? The idealistic nothings it contains could just as easily have been expressed in 1913! You see, a thinking which believes in the absolute is not based on reality. It is unrealistic to think that something 'absolute' will result every time. The present age has no talent for seeing through the lack of reality in thinking because it is always out for what is 'right' rather than for what is in keeping with reality.

That is why in my book *Vom Menschenrätsel* I emphasized so heavily the importance not only of what is logical but also of what is in keeping with reality. A *single* decision that took account of the facts as they are at this precise moment would be worth more than all the empty phrases put together. Historical documents are perhaps the best means of showing that what I am saying has to do with reality, for as time has gone on the only people to come to the surface are those who want to rule the world with abstractions, and this is what has led to the plight of the world today. Proper thinking, which takes account of things as they are, will discover the realities wherever they are. Indeed, they are so close at hand! Take the real concept which I introduced from another point of view the other day: Out of what later became Italy in the South there arose the priestly cultic element which created as its opposition the Protestantism of Central Europe; from the West was formed the diplomatic, political element which also created an opposition for itself; and from the North-west was formed the mercantile element which again created for itself an opposition; and in Central Europe an opposition coming out of the general, human element will of necessity arise. Let us look once more at the way these things stream outwards. (See p.220.)

Even for the fourth post-Atlantean period — proceeding on from the old fourfold classification in which one spoke of castes — we can begin to describe this structure in a somewhat different way. Plato spoke of 'guardian-rulers'; this is the realm for which Rome — priestly, papal Rome — seized the monopoly, achieving a situation in which she alone was allowed to establish doctrinal truths. She was to be the only source of all doctrine, even the highest.

In a different realm, the political, diplomatic element is nothing other than Plato's 'guardian-auxiliaries'. I have shown you that, regardless of what people call Prussian militarism, the real military element was formed with France as its starting point, after the first foundations had been laid in Switzerland. That is where the military element began, but of course it created an opposition for itself by withholding from others what it considered to be its own prerogative. It wants to dominate the world in a soldierly way, so that when something soldierly comes to meet it from elsewhere it finds this quite unjustified, just as Rome finds it unjustified if something comes towards her which is to do with the great truths of the universe.

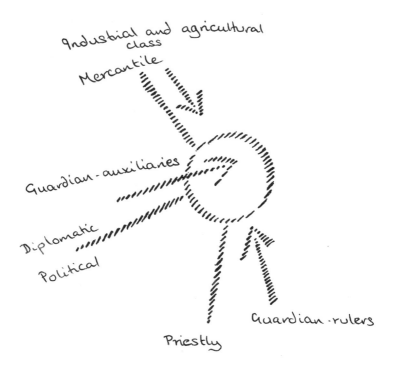

And here, instead of mercantilism, we might just as well write 'the industrial and agricultural class'. Think on this, meditate on it, and you will come to understand that this third factor corresponds to the provision of material needs. So what is being withheld? Foodstuffs, of course!

If you apply Plato's concepts appropriately, in accordance with reality, then you will find reality everywhere, for with these concepts you will be able fully to enter into reality. Starting from the concept, you must find the way to reality, and the concept will be able to plunge down into the most concrete parts of reality. Shadowy concepts, on the other hand, never find reality, but they do lend themselves exceptionally well to idealistic chatter. With real concepts, though, you can work you way through to an understanding of reality in every detail. Here lies the task of spiritual science. Spiritual science leads to concepts through which you can really discover life, which of course is created by the spirit, and through which you will be able to join in a constructive way at working on the formation of this life.

One concept, in particular, requires realistic thinking, owing to the terrible destiny at present weighing down on mankind, for the corresponding unreal concept is especially persistent in this connection. Those who speak in the most unrealistic way of all, these days, are the clergymen. What they express about Christianity or the awareness of God, apropos of the war, is enough to send anyone up the wall, as they say. They distort things so frightfully. Of course things in other connections are distorted too, but in this realm the degree of absurdity is even greater.

Look at the sermons or tracts at present stemming from that source; apply your good common sense to them. Of course it is understandable that they should ask: Does mankind have to be subjected to this terrible, painful destiny? Could not the divine forces of God intervene on behalf of mankind to bring about salvation? The justification for speaking in this way does indeed seem absolute. But there is no real concept behind it. It does not apply to the reality of the situation. Let me use a comparison to show you what I mean.

Human beings have a certain physical constitution. They take in food which is of a kind which enables them to go on living. If they were to refuse food, they would grow thin, become ill, and finally starve to death. Now is it natural to complain that if human beings refuse to eat it is a weakness or malevolence on the part of God to let them starve? Indeed it is not a weakness on the part of God. He created the food; human beings only need to eat it. The wisdom of God is revealed in the way the food maintains the human beings. If they refuse to eat it, they cannot turn round and accuse God of letting them starve.

Now apply this to what I was saying. Mankind must regard spiritual life as a food. It is given by the gods, but it has to be taken in by man. To say that the gods ought to intervene directly is tantamount to saying that if I refuse to eat God ought to satisfy my hunger in some other way. The wisdom-filled order of the universe ensures that what is needed for salvation is always available, but it is up to human beings to make a relationship with it. So the spiritual life necessary for the twentieth century will not enter human beings of itself. They must strive for it and take it into themselves. If they fail to take it in, times will grow more and more dismal. What takes place on the surface is only maya. What is happening inwardly, is that an older age is wrestling with a new one. The general, human element is rising up everywhere in opposition to the specialized elements. It is maya to believe that nation is fighting against nation — and I have spoken about this maya in other connections too. The battle of nation with nation only comes about because things group themselves in certain ways but, in reality, the inward forces opposing one another are something quite different. The opposition is between the old and the new. The laws now fighting to come into play are quite different from those which have traditionally ruled over the world.

And again it was maya — that is, something appearing under a false guise — to say that those other laws were rising up on behalf of socialism. Socialism is not something connected with truth; above all it is not connected with spiritual life, for what it wants is to connect itself with materialism. What really wants to wrestle its way into existence is the many-sided, harmonious element of mankind, in opposition to the one-sided priestly, political or mercantile elements. This battle will rage for a long time, but it can be conducted in all kinds of different ways. If a healthy way of leading life, such as that described by Planck in the nineteenth century, had been adopted, then the bloody conduct of the first third of the twentieth century would, at least, have been ameliorated. Idealisms do not lead to amelioration, but realistic thinking does, and realistic thinking also always means spiritual thinking.

Equally, we can say that whatever has to happen will happen. Whatever it is that is wrestling its way out, must needs go through all these experiences in order to reach a stage at which spirituality can be united with the soul, so that man can grow up spiritually. Today's tragic destiny of mankind is that in striving upwards today, human beings are endeavouring to do so not under the sign of spirituality but under the sign of materialism. This in the first instance is what brought them into conflict with those brotherhoods who want to develop the impulses of the mercantile element, commerce and industry, in a materialistic way on a grand scale. This is today's main conflict. All other things are side issues, often terrible side issues. This shows us how terrible maya can be. But it is possible to strive for things in different ways. If others had been in power instead of the agents of those brotherhoods, then we would, today, be busy with peace negotiations, and the Christmas call for peace would not have been shouted down!

It is going to be immensely difficult to find clear and realistic concepts and ideas in respect of certain things; but we must all seek to find them in our own areas. Those who enter a little into the meaning of spiritual science, and compare this spiritual science with other things making an appearance just now, will see that this spiritual science is the only path that can lead to concepts which are filled with reality.

I wanted to say this very seriously to you at this time. Despite the fact that the task of spiritual science can only be comprehended out of the spirit itself, out of knowledge, and not out of what we have been discussing today, I wanted to show you the significance, the essential nature, of spiritual science for the present time. I wanted to show you how urgent it is for everything possible to be done to make spiritual science more widely known. It is so necessary in these difficult times for us to take spiritual science not only into our heads but really into our warm hearts. Only if we take it into the warmth of our hearts will we be capable of generating the strength needed by the present time.

None of us should allow ourselves to think that we are perhaps not in a suitable position, or not strong enough, to do what it is essential for us to do. Karma is sure to give every one of us, whatever our position, the opportunity to put the right questions to destiny at the right moment. Even if this right moment is neither today nor tomorrow, it is sure to come eventually. So once we have understood the impulses of this spiritual Movement we must stand firmly and steadfastly behind them. Today it is particularly necessary to set ourselves the aim of firmness and steadfastness. For either something important must come from one side or another — although this cannot be counted upon — in the very near future, or all conditions of life will become increasingly difficult. It would be utterly thoughtless to refuse to be clear about this. For two-and-a-half years it has been possible for what we now call war to carry on, while conditions remained as bearable as they now are. But this cannot go on for another year. Movements such as ours will be put to a severe test. There will be no question of asking when we shall next meet, or why do we not meet, or why this or that is not being published. No, indeed. It will be a question of bearing in our hearts, even through long periods of danger, a steadfast sense of belonging.

I wanted to say this to you today because it could be possible in the not too distant future that there will be no means of transport which will enable us to come together again; I am not speaking only of travel permits but of actual means of transport. In the long run, it will not be possible to keep the things going which constitute our modern civilization, if something breaks in on this civilization which, although it has arisen out of it, is nevertheless in absolute opposition to it. This is how absurd the situation is: Life itself is bringing forth things which are absolutely opposed to it.

So we must accept that difficult times may be in store for our Movement too. But we shall not be led astray if we have taken into ourselves the inner steadfastness, clarity and right feeling for the importance and nature of our Movement, and if in these serious times we can see beyond our petty differences. This, our Movement ought to be able to achieve; we ought to be able to look beyond our petty differences to the greater affairs of mankind, which are now at stake. The greatest of these is to reach an understanding of what it means to base thinking on reality. Wherever we look we are confronted with the impossibility of finding a thinking which accords with reality. We shall have to enter heart and soul into this search in order not to be led astray by all kinds of egoistic distractions.

This is what I wanted to say to you as my farewell today, since we are about to take leave of one another for some time. Make yourselves so strong — even if it should turn out to be unnecessary — that, even in loneliness of soul, your hearts will carry the pulse of spiritual science with which we are here concerned. Even the thought that we shall be steadfast will help a very great deal; for thoughts are realities. Many potential difficulties can still be swept away if we maintain an honest, serious quest in the direction we have here discussed so often.

Now that we have to depart for a while we shall not allow ourselves to flag, but shall make sure that we return if it is possible. But even if it should take a long time as a result of circumstances outside our control, we shall never lose the thought from our hearts and souls that this is the place — where our Movement has even brought forth a visible building — where the most intense requirement exists to bear this Movement so positively, so concretely, so energetically, that together we can carry it through, come what may. So wherever we are, let us stand together in thought, faithfully, energetically, cordially, and let us hear one another, even though this will not be possible with our physical ears. But we shall only hear one another if we listen with strong thoughts and without sentimentality, for the times are now unsuitable for sentimentality.

In this sense, I say farewell to you. My words are also a greeting, for in the days to come we shall meet again, though more in the spirit than on the physical plane. Let us hope that the latter, too, will be possible once more in the not too distant future.

226

NOTES

With regard to the special nature of these lectures and the circumstances in which they were given, see the Foreword in Volume One.

LECTURE FOURTEEN

1 *What was said yesterday:* See Rudolf Steiner *The Karma of Untruthfulness.* Volume One, Rudolf Steiner Press, London 1988.

2 *lectures given here:* See Rudolf Steiner *Goethe and the Crisis of the Nineteenth Century.* (English text available in typescript only.)

3 *poetry . . . fabrication:* In German, 'poetry' is 'Dichtung', 'fabrication' 'Erdichtung'.

4 *Gap in report:* The quotation is unfortunately lacking in the shorthand report.

5 *There is no religion higher then Truth:* The motto of the Theosophical Society.

6 *public lecture in Munich:* 29 March 1914. This lecture is not in print, but see Rudolf Steiner *On Evil.* (English text available in typescript only.)

7 *J'accuse affair:* Richard Grelling, *J'accuse, von einem Deutschen* (J'accuse, by a German), Lausanne 1915. On the speech by the member of the Reichstag, David, see also Rudolf Steiner *Impulses of the Past and the Future in Social Occurrences.* (English text available in typescript only.) In Rudolf Steiner's library there is a book by Kurt Eisner *Unterdrücktes aus dem Weltkrieg* (Suppressed Information on the World War), Munich 1919, which deals among other things with David's speech.

8 *lecture cycle on the folk spirits:* Rudolf Steiner *The Mission of the Individual Folk Souls,* Rudolf Steiner Press, London 1970.

9 *a famous novel:* Romain Rolland *John Christopher,* trans. Gilbert Cannan, London 1910. (4 volumes). Quotations 1-3 are from Volume One (pp. 39, 79, 149), quotations 4-12 from Volume Two (pp. 15, 375, 375, 375, 375, 29, 170, 376, 376).

10 *esteemed Austrian critic:* Stefan Zweig, 'Letter to Romain Rolland' in the *Berliner Tageblatt* No. 651 of 22 December 1912. See also Rudolf Steiner's lecture in Berlin of 25 February 1915 in *Aus Schicksaltragender Zeit* GA 64, Dornach 1959.

11 *Heinrich von Treitschke,* 1834-1896. German historian and political writer.

12 *Nietzsche's publisher:* Fritz Koegel, 1860-1904.

13 *man who translated Nietzsche:* Henri Lichtenberger, 1864-1941. Professor of German philology at the Sorbonne.

LECTURE FIFTEEN

1 Rudolf Steiner *Vom Menschenrätsel. Ausgesprochenes und Unausgesprochenes im Denken, Schauen, Sinnen einer Reihe deutscher und österreichischer Persönlichkeiten* (The Riddle of the Human Being.

Spoken and Unspoken Aspects of the Thinking, Vision and Reflections of a Number of German and Austrian Personalities), GA 20, Dornach 1984.

2 *Schelling's 'theosophy': Philosophie der Mythologie* 1842, and *Philosophie der Offenbarung* 1854.

3 *Annie Besant*, 1847-1933. See Volume One, Note 30, Lecture One. Lecture 'Theosophy and Imperialism', Theosophical Publishing Society, London 1902.

4 *Herbert Henry Asquith*, 1852-1928, Earl of Oxford and Asquith. Minister from 1892, British Prime Minister 1908-1916.

5 *Sir Edward Grey*, 1862-1933. British Foreign Minister 1905-1916.

6 *very popular British writer*: This is an article entitled 'The Kaleidoscope' by the Military Correspondent of *The Times* published in *The London Magazine*, Volume XXXVII, No. 73, November 1916, p.327.

7 *so-called answering note from the Entente*: Joint note of 30 December 1916 from the ten Allies (both large and small) to President Wilson (in reply to his appeal for peace on 18 December 1916).

8 *history of the Opium Wars*: See Volume One, Lecture Twelve.

LECTURE SIXTEEN

1 *discussed some time ago*: See Rudolf Steiner *The Gospel of St John and its Relation to the Other Gospels*, Anthroposophic Press, New York 1982.

2 *caustic remark . . . by Hebbel*: Friedrich Hebbel (1813-1863), German poet and dramatist. 'According to the transmigration of souls it is possible that Plato might be beaten in school today because he cannot understand Plato.' Hebbel's diaries, Vol 1, No 1745, p.392, Berlin 1901).

3 *Franz Grillparzer*, (1791-1872). The greatest Austrian dramatist.

4 *John Robert Seeley*, 1834-1895. In 1869 Regius Professor for modern history at Cambridge. English historian, apologist of the British Empire. *The Expansion of England*, London 1883.

5 *maps*: See Rudolf Steiner *The Karma of Untruthfulness* Volume One, Lecture One.

6 *Almanach de Madame de Thèbes*: See Rudolf Steiner *The Karma of Untruthfulness* Volume One, Lecture Seven.

7 *three editors of The Times*: P. Colomb, J. F. Maurice, F. N. Maude, A. Forbes, C. Lowe, D. Christie Murray and F. Skudamore *The Great War of 189-. A forecast*, London 1893.

8 *earlier lectures here*: See Note 2, Lecture Fourteen.

9 *Friedrich von Bernhardi*, 1849-1930. Prussian General. Author of military and political writings.

10 *sometimes Nietzsche is included*: For example E. MacClure *Germany's War-Inspirers Nietzsche and Treitschke*, London 1914.

11 *history of the German people*: Heinrich von Treitschke's *magnum opus* is considered to be *Treitschke's History of Germany in the Nineteenth Century*, London 1915-19, 7 volumes.

12 *J. A. Cramb*: Professor of Modern History, Queen's College, London, *Germany and England*, London 1914; Lecture 'Treitschke and Young

228 THE KARMA OF UNTRUTHFULNESS — VOLUME TWO

Germany', 5 March 1913. The book by General von Bernhardi, whom Cramb calls 'a distinguished cavalry officer' is, *Germany and the Next War.*

13 *General Kuropatkin*, 1848-1925. 1898 Russian Minister for War. On the outbreak of the Russo-Japanese War he was supreme commander of the Russian forces in East Asia but was replaced after the defeat of Mukden. In 1916 he was supreme commander on the northern front. After the Bolshevik revolution he became a teacher in a village school.

14 *'If Russia does not bring to an end'*: The German version of this text is quoted from S. Zurlinden *Der Weltkrieg. Vorläufige Orientierung von einem schweizerischen Standpunkt aus* (The World War. Preliminary Assessment from the Swiss Point of View), Zurich 1917.

LECTURE SEVENTEEN

1 *from the Vollrath camp*: Hugo Vollrath, proprietor of a theosophical publishing house in Leipzig. An opponent of Rudolf Steiner.

2 *British Empire to include Egypt*: From 1882. France in Morocco from 1908. Italy in Tripoli from 1912.

3 *Algeciras Conference*: 16 January to 7 April 1906.

4 *German defence bill*: The first Balkan War took place from October 1912 to May 1913. The German defence bill was passed on 30 June 1913.

5 *William Archer's pamphlet*: *Colour Blind Neutrality*, London 1916. See Volume One, Lecture One.

6 *Vom Menschenrätsel*: See Note 1, Lecture Fifteen.

7 *Robert Fludd*: Robertus de Fluctibus (1574-1637). English physician and mystical philosopher.

8 *Theophrastus Paracelsus von Hohenheim*: 1493-1541. Swiss physician and alchemist.

9 *Sir Oliver Lodge*, 1851-1940. English physicist. *Raymond; or, Life and Death. With examples of the evidence for survival of memory and affection after death*, London 1916.

10 *Gotthilf Heinrich von Schubert*, 1780-1860. See also Rudolf Steiner *Faust's World Pilgrimage and His Rebirth out of the Spirit of German Life.* (English text available in typescript only).

11 *New Year's Eve note*: See Volume One, Lecture Thirteen.

12 *Johann Gottlieb Fichte* (1762-1814). German philosopher and patriot. In 1807-08 in Berlin he delivered his noble addresses to the German nation, *Reden an die deutsche Nation*, full of practical views on the only true foundation for national recovery and glory.

13 *Ludwig von Polzer*: Ludwig von Polzer-Hoditz (1869-1945). *Betrachtungen während der Zeit des Krieges* (Thoughts during Wartime), Linz 1917.

14 *deutsch*: See Lecture Twenty-Three, towards the end, where Rudolf Steiner speaks about the reasons why the Germans call themselves 'Deutsche' while others insist on calling them 'Germans' or 'Allemands', etc.

15 *Is not the whole of eternity mine?*: From Gotthold Ephraim Lessing's *Erziehung des Menschengeschlechts.*

16 *Alexander von Bernus*, 1880-1965. Writer. Publisher of the periodical *Das Reich* in Munich.

17 *new national anthem*: Source unknown.

LECTURE EIGHTEEN

1 *His 'German History'*: See Note 11, Lecture Sixteen.

2 *Wilhelm von Humboldt*, 1767-1835. German philologist, diplomat and man of letters. *The Sphere and Duties of Government*, London 1854. The German title of this work, *Ideen zu einem Versuch, die Grenzen der Wirksamkeit des Staates zu bestimmen*, Breslau 1851, translates literally as 'Ideas towards an Attempt to Determine the Limitations of State Power'.

3 *Schiller's 'Letters on the Aesthetic Education of Man'*, first published in 1795 in the periodical *Die Horen*.

4 *Edouard Laboulaye*, 1811-1883. *L'État et ses limites*, Paris 1863.

5 *John Stuart Mill*, 1806-1873. British philosopher and economist. *On Liberty*, London 1859.

6 *wrote about freedom*: Heinrich von Treitschke *Die Freiheit* (Freedom), Leipzig 1912.

7 *name his fatherland*: These were independent principalities until the creation of the state of Thuringia in 1918.

8 *Romain Rolland*: See Lecture Fourteen.

9 *In his lectures on politics*: Heinrich von Treitschke *Politik*, Leipzig 1899.

10 *Note from the Entente*: Dated 10 January 1917 in answer to Wilson's enquiry as to the conditions for peace.

11 *Karel Kramar*, 1860-1937. Czech statesman, exponent of neo-Slavism. Arrested for high treason in May 1915.

12 *Tomas Garrigue Masaryk*, 1850-1937. Philosopher, Czech patriot and first President of Czechoslovakia.

13 *Czecho-Slovaks*: From *Handbuch der Geschichte der Böhmischen Länder*, Stuttgart, 1967: 'Benes succeeded in having the "Czecho-Slovaks" included in the note of 10.1.1917 in which the Allies replied to Wilson's query as to the conditions for peace ... The note says "Liberation of Italians, Slavs and Romanians from foreign domination". Benes succeeded in having the list extended to include the Czechoslovaks.'

14 Having closed the lecture, Rudolf Steiner continued with the following words: 'What shall we do? Some of our friends have expressed the wish to begin earlier tomorrow, as they do not want to miss the performance of Reinhardt's non-art. I don't mind, so when would you like to start? Perhaps somebody could make a suggestion. When shall we meet? It will be quite a good thing to change our arrangements for tomorrow for the sake of those who are interested in this abuse of art and want to witness personally this event of cultural history, the demise of the art of acting.'

The Deutsche Theater of Berlin under Max Reinhardt were performing at the Stadttheater in Basel.

LECTURE NINETEEN

1 *system of ganglia*: The current anatomical terminology for the systems Rudolf Steiner describes in this lecture, and which he mentions again in Lecture Twenty-One, is: system of ganglia = nerves and plexus of the autonomic system; spinal system = spinal cord and spinal nerves; cerebral system = brain and cranial nerves.

2 Rudolf Steiner *Occult Science. An Outline*, Rudolf Steiner Press, London 1979.

3 *well-known physician*: Quoted in George Moore M.D. *The Power of the Soul over the Body considered in Relation to Health and Morals*, London 1845.

4 *Austrian poet*: Hermann Rollet, 1819-1904.

5 *on the basis of maps*: See Volume One, Lecture One.

LECTURE TWENTY

1 *Spencer and even his predecessor*: John Stuart Mill, 1806-1873. See Volume One, Notes 17 and 18, Lecture Seven.

2 *Cesare Lombroso*, 1836-1909. Italian psychiatrist, founder of criminal anthropology. Author of *Genio e Follia*, Turin 1882.

3 *Oliver Lodge*: See Note 9, Lecture Seventeen.

4 *Mikhail Vasilevich Lomonosov*, 1711-1765, called the father of Russian grammar and literature. See Rudolf Steiner, lecture of 21 January 1909 in *An Aspect of the Spiritual Guidance of Man*, Anthroposophic Press, New York, and Rudolf Steiner Press, London 1986.

5 *Maximilian I of Austria*, 1459-1519.

6 *Johannes Elias Schlegel*, 1719-1749, German poet and writer.

7 *August Wilhelm von Schlegel*, 1767-1645. German translator and critic. Translated Shakespeare's works into German in collaboration with the writer and critic Johann Ludwig Tieck (1773-1853).

8 *Karl Julius Schröer*, 1825-1900. Professor of German literature at the Technical University in Vienna; poet, student of dialects and literary historian.

9 *us and the followers of Mrs Besant*: This refers to the events which led to the separation from the German Section of the Theosophical Society and the formation of an independent Anthroposophical Society in 1913.

10 *Alcyone*: In the Theosophical Society, the name for Jiddu Krishnamurti, born 1895.

11 *Vom Menschenrätsel*: See Note 1, Lecture Fifteen.

12 *Jakobus Baldus*, 1604-1668.

13 *James I of England*, 1566-1625. Son of Mary Stuart. King James VI of Scotland from 1577, and King James I of England and Ireland from 1603. See Volume One, Note 8, Lecture Eleven.

14 *lawyer who used to conduct cases in Romania*: See Volume One, Note 27, Lecture One.

15 *in a Socialist school*: The workers educational establishment founded by Wilhelm Liebknecht in Berlin, where Rudolf Steiner lectured from 1899 to 1904.

16 *Karl Marx*, 1818-1883. Lived in London from 1849.
17 *Friedrich Engels*, 1820-1895. In 1845 wrote *The Condition of the Working Class in England in 1844*, New York 1887. Lived in England permanently from 1850.
18 *Eduard Bernstein*, 1850-1932. Lived in England from 1888 to 1901.
19 *Oliver Cromwell*, 1599-1658. Lord Protector of the Commonwealth from 1653.
20 *Henry Thomas Buckle*, 1821-1862. *History of Civilization in England*, London 1857.
21 *this document*: The note from the Entente to Wilson. See Note 10, Lecture Eighteen.
22 *Edouard Schuré*, 1841-1929. Follower of Rudolf Steiner. Turned against him during the First World War.
23 *Heinrich Gösch*: Member of the Anthroposophical Society. Later an opponent.

LECTURE TWENTY-ONE

1 *Sacro egoismo (per l'Italia)*: A phrase coined by the Italian Prime Minister Antonio Salandra.
2 *The Spiritual Guidance of Man*, Anthroposophic Press, New York, 1970.

LECTURE TWENTY-TWO

1 *Schweizerische Bauzeitung*, Volume 39, No 3. 20 January 1917. *Johannesbau* was the name initially chosen for the Goetheanum.
2 *Joseph Englert*, civil engineer, up to 1918 building manager at the Goetheanum.
3 *Andrei Belyi*, pen name of Boris Nikolayevich Bugaev (1880-1933), Russian poet and writer. His book on Goethe *Rudolf Steiner und Goethe in der Weltanschauung der Gegenwart* (Rudolf Steiner and Goethe in the Thought of Today.) Moscow 1917.
4 Rudolf Steiner *Human and Cosmic Thought*, Rudolf Steiner Press, London 1967.
5 *Alfred Meebold*, 1863-1952. Writer. *Der Weg zum Geist* (The Path to the Spirit), Munich 1917.
6 *evolution has been discussed*: *The Inner Realities of Evolution* Rudolf Steiner Publishing Company, London 1953.
7 *periods in the history of art*: *Kunstgeschichte als Abbild innerer geistiger Impulse* (The History of Art as an Image of Inner Spiritual Impulses), Dornach 1981, GA 292.
8 *a book appeared*: Besant and Leadbeater, *Man: Whence, How and Whither*, London 1913.
9 *Ideal und Geschäft* (Ideal and Business) by Benno Jaroslav, Jena 1912.

LECTURE TWENTY-THREE

1 This lecture was preceded by a recitation by Marie Steiner from the *Nibelungenlied* by Wilhelm Jordan.

2 Rudolf Steiner *The Inner Nature of Man and the Life between Death and a New Birth*, Anthroposophical Publishing Company, London 1959.
3 *doctrine of infallibility*: 18 July 1870 at the First Vatican Council.
4 *law of sound-shifts*: See Volume One, Lecture Six.
5 *rephrased 'Beatitudes'*: See Volume One, Lecture Nine.
6 *symptoms of history*: See Rudolf Steiner *From Symptom to Reality in Modern History*, Rudolf Steiner Press, London 1976.
7 *the great speech*: *European War*. Report of a Speech by the Rt. Hon. Sir Edward Grey (British Secretary of State for Foreign Affairs) in the House of Commons on 3 August 1914.
8 *Bismarck's book*: *Gedanken und Erinnerungen* (Thoughts and Memoires), Stuttgart 1915, Chapter 23, Section III.
9 *Empress Friedrich*, 1840-1901, born Princess Victoria of England, wife of Friedrich III, who reigned for only 99 days.

LECTURE TWENTY-FOUR

1 Rudolf Steiner *Knowledge of the Higher Worlds. How is it achieved?*, Rudolf Steiner Press, London 1969.
2 Rudolf Steiner *Christianity as Mystical Fact*, Rudolf Steiner Press, London 1972.
3 *Theosophy. An Introduction to the Supersensible Knowledge of the World and the Destination of Man*, Anthroposophic Press, New York 1986.
4 *Hungaricus*: (pseudonym) *Conditions de Paix de l'Allemagne*, Zurich 1917.

LECTURE TWENTY-FIVE

1 *Helena Petrovna Blavatsky*, 1831-1891.
2 *Alfred Percy Sinnett*, 1840-1921. Author of *Esoteric Buddhism*.
3 *book on mysticism of the Middle Ages*: Rudolf Steiner *Eleven European Mystics*, Rudolf Steiner Press, London 1971.
4 *lectures given here*: Rudolf Steiner *The Occult Movement in the Nineteenth Century*, Rudolf Steiner Press, London 1973.
5 *Louis Claude, Marquis de Saint-Martin*, 1743-1803. *Des erreurs et de la vérité*, 1775. See Volume One, Note 24, Lecture Seven.
6 *Emil Du Bois-Reymond*, 1818-1866. German physiologist and philosopher.
7 *Friedrich von Schlegel*, 1772-1829. German writer and critic, brother of August Wilhelm von Schlegel. *Von der Sprache und Weisheit der Inder* (On the Language and Wisdom of the Indians), 1808.
8 *Henrik Steffens*, 1773-1845. Norwegian writer.
9 *Gotthilf Heinrich von Schubert*, 1780-1860. See Note 10, Lecture Seventeen.
10 *Ignaz Paul Vital Troxler*, 1780-1866.
11 Mabel Collins (1851-1927), *Light on the Path. A treatise written for the personal use of those who are ignorant of the Eastern Wisdom, and who desire to enter within its influence*, London 1885.

12 *Karl Christian Planck,* 1819-1880. *Testament eines Deutschen* (Testament of a German), Tübingen 1881. See also the lecture of 25 February 1916 in Rudolf Steiner *Aus dem mitteleuropäischen Geistesleben,* GA 65, Dornach 1962.

13 *published by Rohm:* Karl Rohm, publisher of occult books. Opponent of Rudolf Steiner.

14 *Farkas (Wolfgang) Bolyai,* 1775-1856, mathematician.

15 *Carl Friedrich Gauss,* 1777-1855, mathematician.

16 *Johann Bolyai,* 1802-1860. The quotation is from *Urkunden zur Geschichte der nicht-euklidischen Geometrie* (On the History of non-Euclidean Geometry) by Wolfgang and Johann Bolyai.

17 *Hungaricus:* See Note 4, Lecture Twenty-Four.

INDEX OF NAMES
Volumes One and Two